I0902285

DEBT, LAW, REALISM

Chinua Achebe

Debt, Law, Realism

Nigerian Writers Imagine the State at Independence

Neil ten Kortenaar

McGill-Queen's University Press
Montreal & Kingston • London • Chicago

© McGill-Queen's University Press 2021

ISBN 978-0-2280-0628-2 (cloth)
ISBN 978-0-2280-0669-5 (paper)
ISBN 978-0-2280-0780-7 (ePDF)
ISBN 978-0-2280-0781-4 (ePUB)

Legal deposit second quarter 2021
Bibliothèque nationale du Québec

Printed in Canada on acid-free paper that is 100% ancient forest free (100% post-consumer recycled), processed chlorine free

This book has been published with the help of a grant from the Canadian Federation for the Humanities and Social Sciences, through the Awards to Scholarly Publications Program, using funds provided by the Social Sciences and Humanities Research Council of Canada.

Funded by the Government of Canada | Financé par le gouvernement du Canada | Canada

Canada Council for the Arts | Conseil des arts du Canada

We acknowledge the support of the Canada Council for the Arts.
Nous remercions le Conseil des arts du Canada de son soutien.

Library and Archives Canada Cataloguing in Publication

Title: Debt, law, realism : Nigerian writers imagine the state at independence / Neil ten Kortenaar.
Names: Kortenaar, Neil ten, author.
Description: Includes bibliographical references and index.
Identifiers: Canadiana (print) 20210120592 | Canadiana (ebook) 20210120932 | ISBN 9780228006282 (cloth) | ISBN 9780228006695 (paper) | ISBN 9780228007807 (ePDF) | ISBN 9780228007814 (ePUB)
Subjects: LCSH: Nigerian fiction (English)—History and criticism. | LCSH: Realism in literature. | LCSH: Nigeria—In literature. | LCSH: State, The, in literature. | LCSH: Sovereignty in literature. | LCSH: Debt in literature. | LCSH: Politics and literature—Nigeria—History—20th century.
Classification: LCC PR9387.4 .K67 2021 | DDC 823/.08309358669030904—dc23

This book was typeset in 10.5/13 Sabon.

For Arthur

Contents

Acknowledgments

I would like to thank my colleagues who read the manuscript and gave me feedback: Uzoma Esonwanne, Ato Quayson, and especially Cheryl Suzack. Adwoa Opoku-Agyemang provided invaluable research support. Many people have given me useful suggestions and advice, and I would like to single out Tunji Osinubi. This book was written with the generous support of the Social Sciences and Humanities Research Council of Canada. This book has been published with the help of a grant from the Federation for the Humanities and Social Sciences, through the Awards to Scholarly Publications Program, using funds provided by the Social Sciences and Humanities Research Council of Canada.

I began this manuscript while on sabbatical at the Department of Literature at the University of Makerere, and I would like to thank my colleagues there, especially the chair, Susan Kiguli, for hosting me. My students in African Literature at the University of Toronto Scarborough challenged me to refine some of my ideas, as did my students in a graduate course on State Formation in Postcolonial Literature.

I am grateful to my editor, Mark Abley at McGill-Queen's University Press, for his warm support, and to the reviewers, for their attention to the manuscript and its ideas.

Some of the ideas here were originally presented in "Rule, Law, and the Rule of Law in Achebe's Novels of Colonization," part of a special issue on "Law and Literature in the Postcolony" in the *Cambridge Journal of Postcolonial Literary Inquiry* (2.1: 33–51). Small sections have also appeared as part of different arguments in "Fictive States and the State of Fiction in Africa" in *Comparative Literature* (52.3: 228–45) and "The Half Lives of African Fictive States" in the *Cambridge Journal of Postcolonial Literary Inquiry* (6.2: 163–78).

I am grateful for invitations to present part of the material from this research at the University of Utrecht, the University of Waterloo, Pokhara University, the University of London, and the Nouvelle Sorbonne. I have also presented some of this material at the American Comparative Literature Association, the African Literature Association, and the Association for Commonwealth Literature and Language Studies.

I am grateful to Getty Images for permission to reprint the photograph of Chinua Achebe.

DEBT, LAW, REALISM

Introduction

West African fiction in English as we know it today was largely the invention of young men and women who came of age and embarked upon writing careers in the late 1950s and early 1960s, at the very moment that they became citizens of newly independent states.[1] Decolonization was not incidental for Chinua Achebe, Wole Soyinka, and their peers, the first generation to go to university in Nigeria (Achebe and Soyinka attended the newly opened University College Ibadan). They assumed that for a state to be a nation, integrated into the psyches of citizens, it needed a literature no less than laws and institutions, and that it fell to them to fill that need for Nigeria. Writing literature was a complex project that included displacing the colonizer *and* the older generation, earning status in the world republic of letters, setting the record straight about Africa's past, and teaching one's countrymen how to think about their new condition as citizens. Just as, throughout the English- and French-speaking worlds in the mid-twentieth century, the state appeared to be the inevitable locus of all modern politics, something that colonized people should want for themselves, so, too, the novel appeared to be the epitome of literature, what writers should be writing.

The founders of Nigerian or West African literature in English (the slippage here is related to the slippage involved in the notion of *African* nationalism), concerned with the states they were to inherit, reinvented the realist novel in order to teach readers how to be citizens and to explore what citizenship *meant*. Kwame Anthony Appiah describes the novels of "the generation of Achebe's *Things Fall Apart* and Laye's *L'Enfant noir*" as "realist legitimations of nationalism"[2] and writes that the next generation of African writers turned away from that model within the first decade of independence, once the failure of African states had become evident. Appiah's characterization of Achebe and his peers as realist and nationalist is accurate, and he is right about the break made by the following generation, but the cosmopolitan critic nevertheless underestimates the staying power and thus the significance of both realism and the state. Achebe's realism, like realism elsewhere, arose with the modern state. It was later supplanted by other literary modes that defined themselves against it, but realism has never disappeared and rises ever anew, much as the modern state as an ideal does.

Appiah's condescension to the "realist legitimations" of the first generation of African novelists is misplaced. Elsewhere he dismisses the nation and its identity as "morally arbitrary," even while regarding citizenship in a state as an essential foundation for morality: "Since human beings live in political orders narrower than the species, and since it is within those political orders that questions of public right and wrong are largely argued out and decided, the fact of being a fellow-citizen – someone who is a member of the same order – is not morally arbitrary at all."[3] The novels of Achebe and his contemporaries, however nationalist, were also creative inquiries into the nature of the modern state and the duties of the citizen, as well as wagers on the state's significance. Their realism can tell us a great deal about the ideal of the state not just as it was at independence but also as it survives among people who want to "take Nigeria seriously," Odia Ofeimun's formulation for reimagining the political constitution of the Nigerian state.[4]

What is the connection between fictional realism and the state? Realism has two related but distinct aspects that are relevant here: one particularizing and identified with the nation, the other relativizing and associated with the state. On the one hand, realism names and describes and thus proffers the dignity of literature to the particular and ordinary world shared by a collective: the houses and streets, but also the food, the clothes, and the habits of speech and gesture that characterize *this* people and make *this* place distinct. Igbos in particular and Nigerian readers in general will recognize in Achebe's early novels elements of their own experience alchemically transformed into literature and so bestowed with significance. The naming of particular locales and experiences, what distinguishes *this* nation and makes *this* moment distinct from earlier ones, is, however, but one side of realism. Realism also assumes that people and events everywhere and at all times are readable because they follow rules that make them typical, not in the sense of average but in the sense of adhering to a line that can be traced through a series of like items, for instance, the series of educated young men moving to the capital or of young people choosing whom to marry. This readability is the product of a uniformitarian principle: realist fictional characters, even those from the past or from non-bourgeois societies, adhere to general laws about what humans are like.[5] Kwaku Larbi Korang writes that realism such as Achebe's "tasks readers to plausibly see beyond this or that particular setting, and the particular person(s) who inhabit it, the human(ist) likeness or (re)semblance of other settings and other persons. The proposition that a society and culture being represented, for all the concrete particularity of its realization, is 'typical' – and hence 'representative' of a humanity greater than its particularity or individuality – is a typical facet of realism."[6] Readers of novels, who, wherever they are, can be presumed to be citizens of states, are able to make sense of the fate of Obi Okonkwo, who in Achebe's *No Longer at Ease* is on trial for taking bribes, and even, remarkably, that of his grandfather in *Things Fall Apart* at the moment of colonial encounter six decades earlier. This book will argue that the rules of verisimilitude, based on assumptions about psychology and sociology, bear a relation to the rule of law and the would-be rational administration of the ideal state.

Realism is *not*, I hasten to emphasize, the mimetic impulse in narrative. After all, the magic realism of Ben Okri's novel *The Famished Road*, which is filled with spirits moving between adjacent worlds, is arguably as mimetic as *No Longer at Ease*; it just imitates different things.[7] And realism such as Achebe's always harbours something unreal and non-mimetic: the dream of objectivity and knowability. The mimesis to which fictional realism pretends is based on obvious artifice: in a realist novel the thoughts of characters may be fully readable in a way that those of people one knows never are.[8] The combination of verisimilitude (conventions about the plausible) and a preternatural access to interiority renders characters knowable in a way particular to realism. Knowability is a property of realism, one that makes characters credible, even though, paradoxically, it is not a property of real people. Yiyun Li expresses the paradox thus: "When characters forgo realness – their unreadability – they become real and known to a reader."[9] Indeed, if a realist character remained unknowable, inconsistent, and inexplicable, we might suspect that he or she was based on a real person and had not been sufficiently fictionalized. Realism thus involves a magic trick, one that, when realized most fully, might even feel like genuine magic. Realism involves world-making no less than other modes do, but it also emphasizes the readability and the recognizability of the world it narrates and the relation of that world to the world of history books and newspapers. Realism invites readers to imagine that strangers sharing the same world as themselves can be explained and judged.[10]

I do not mean that Achebe was writing with the primary intention of making Africans intelligible to non-African readers. The "extroversion" of the African novel in general[11] and of *Things Fall Apart* in particular is often asserted; Stephanie Newell and Graham Huggan point to the level of ethnographic detail as evidence that Achebe's novel is addressed to metropolitan markets instead of to local readers.[12] I argue in this book, however, that Achebe was writing in the first instance for his fellow citizens and that *Things Fall Apart* was intended to shape readers into citizens of a modern state. As Jonathan Culler explains, novelistic realism is always stereoscopic: "Balzac purveys ethnological information about Parisian habits and types, as if for readers who view them from a distance, but at the same time evokes a community of readers through the presupposition of shared knowledge."[13] The ethnographic focus in *Things Fall Apart*, like the historical detail provided by Balzac, tells readers how things were among people of a certain class in a particular location at a precise historical moment. In explaining the Igbo lifeworld *as if* for an outsider, Achebe is training his fellow citizens to regard their own world as part of a larger history and part of a modern world rendered readable.

The term "realism," based as it is on an unrealizable *ideal* of knowability and objectivity, is ironic. It has this idealized quality in common with Weber's *ideal* of the state, which is not to be identified with any *actual* state, a mistake often made when one compares African states to European ones. Realism's emphasis on characters who are explicable and knowable corresponds to the "representation of a rule," that is, the modern state's promise to its citizens that its operations will be transparent and impartial. If all nations are distinct from one another – as nationalism insists – then all modern states, *insofar as they are states*, are similar to one another in that they share certain ideals, in particular the universal application of the rule of law. Underpinning the international state system since 1945 has been the central presupposition "that all states in principle are, or will become, similar, or at least mutually intelligible, in their structures and in the rationalities governing their actions."[14] Thomas Blom Hansen and Finn Stepputat write that

> the entire idea of political legitimacy, of the difference between naked power and authority, the idea that "the Law" is something that stands above the contingencies of everyday life and incarnates a certain collective justice, the crucial discourse of rights as something that once defined and authorized become unassailable and inalienable: all hinge on the perpetuated myth of the state's coherence and ability to stand "above society," as it were.[15]

The political virtues attached to the rule of law, transparency, impartiality, and objectivity rely on the same notions of the translatability of experience as realism does.

Nothing can seem more ordinary to readers of novels than realism, and nothing can be more taken for granted than the state, but the state and its rule of law always have something ideal about them. Marc Abélès quotes Max Weber: "The State is always an ideal of the State: we cannot treat it as a thing, an institution." To which he adds:

> The State, defined as a complex of mutually supporting activities, is maintained in this ideal relation which is nothing other than a belief in legality, that is the legitimacy of a system of norms. In its contemporary form the State becomes purely and simply synonymous with an abstract "what must be." Unlike traditional and charismatic types, where belief is in a concrete object, an extraordinary person, the transmission of a memory, in our societies it is the representation of a rule, the should-be that floats in our heads, that makes politics function.[16]

The ideal of the state underwrote decolonization and independence in Africa, just as it underwrote, almost two hundred years earlier, the revolutions that created France and the United States. That ideal continues to hold sway even where and when bitter experience suggests that state institutions are merely a source of power for rapacious exploitation, and statist ideology that exploitation's disguise. The state ideal is what allows citizens to measure and to express their disillusionment with the expropriative state as they experience it.

The ideal of the state constitutes a promise that its citizens will not require a personal relationship with those in power and, when engaging with state institutions, will be met with impartial and objective procedures that treat all alike. Members of a modern state need to feel confident that they know what strangers encountered behind the wheel of a public transport vehicle, behind the counter in a government office, or sitting in judgment in court, will think and do. This confidence is a function not of relationships that need to be repeatedly forged anew but of codes of behaviour that can be relied upon to apply generally in a mass society filled with strangers. Liberal governmentality and the market economy require some degree of this trust. If I cooperate with government by paying taxes and performing military service, can I expect that others are doing the same? If I buy insurance, can I trust that the insurance company will not shut its doors at the next violent takeover of state power? This trust is a matter of epistemology. Who does one trust with one's health? Does one trust pills, injections, or sacrifices? Who is telling the truth about HIV? The state, the church, the rumour mill, the traditional healer, or the NGOs? Does one put one's faith in the newspapers? in faith healers? in the schoolmaster? The first generation of Nigerian novelists, I am arguing, turned to the novel because they sensed the connection between that genre and political formation, between readers and citizens, and they were concerned with creating citizens.

The state remains an ideal yet retains an unreality. Philip Abrams writes that the state is but "the mask which prevents our seeing political practice as it is," that there is at best a state-idea "projected, purveyed and variously believed in in different societies at different times."[17] The power of the state is not something separate from its invocation by agents of the state. Pierre Bourdieu warns that he who would *think* the state is always at risk of *being thought* by a state[18] – in other words, the forms of knowledge and discourse with which we question the state have themselves been instituted by the state. This does not, however, make the state-idea negligible: the state's various components invoke it for their legitimacy, and political actors invoke it to challenge their opponents' legitimacy. The ideal does real work.

The trust that other people are knowable to an objective impartial gaze, the trust that I am locating at the heart of both the ideal of the modern state and the realist novel, is itself thematized by the genre of the novel in terms of credit. Credit loomed large in the first English novels in the eighteenth century, which, as Ian Baucom writes, equipped readers "both to *read* the character of the individuals whose promises and money they increasingly had to take on credit and to *evaluate* the credibility of that general system of value that had encircled society and collateralized the fates of each of its members in the desire and credulity of all the others."[19] If anything, debtors and creditors figure even more prominently in the first West African novels than they did in eighteenth-century British ones: R.E. Obeng's *Eighteenpence* (1943) is named for a loan; *Things Fall Apart* (1958) opens with one loan being called in and a request for another; and Flora Nwapa's *Efuru* (1966) is centred on a trader's need to extend credit and collect debts. Credit was very much on the minds of the first West African novelists, because they sensed that the reader's confidence in the world depicted in a novel is of a piece with the credit that underwrites the state.

Here, of course, we have an irony: Achebe was writing about a precolonial society and Obeng and Nwapa about a colonial society: the characters they depicted were *not* citizens of a modern state. While all societies rely on credit, there is a tremendous difference between debtor/

creditor relations in small-scale stateless societies, such as the precolonial Igbo lived in, where everyone knows everyone else, on the one hand, and those in large, mass state societies such as Nigeria or Ghana, filled as they are with strangers, on the other. In village society, debts, like gifts, establish ties of reciprocity between individuals and between families: I lend to my neighbour because tomorrow I may need to borrow. People's relations to local gods and ancestors are similarly reciprocal: devotees sacrifice to spirits in return for protection or other boons. In a mass society, by contrast, debts are to institutions, and as a consequence, as we shall see, they take on a new, transcendental meaning. For mass society to function one must count on strangers to acknowledge the same duty to the law as oneself. The impersonal debt owed to the state and its law parallels what is due to the Christian God, with whom one cannot have a reciprocal relationship and whom one can never hope to repay. To write, as Achebe does, about precolonial village society in realist terms that emphasize that people are knowable because they share an institutional framework with readers is deeply paradoxical. That paradox, however, is precisely the measure of Achebe's project: to teach his fellow Nigerians how to read a novel and think of themselves as citizens, even as he expresses his own ambivalences about the state and the law, and in particular about the colonial violence that had first imposed them.

A historical novel like Achebe's *Things Fall Apart* self-consciously contrasts the rule of law brought by the colonizers with precolonial understandings of debt as interpersonal and reciprocal relations. Achebe and others of the first generation focused on the nature of authority, legitimacy, and the law and on how power was channelled through state institutions, but they also highlighted alternative, precolonial ways of political being in order to gauge the implications of possessing a state of one's own. Their realism did not take the state for granted but was a way of taking the state's measure. They also, not incidentally, asked what a novel is for.

Appiah is not wrong about the break in African literature after Achebe's generation, even if he underestimates the continuities. From the start, the patrilineal obsession of *Things Fall Apart* was challenged by women writers, who, as Susan Andrade shows, deliberately recast the allegorical relation between the micro and macro levels on which nationalism such as Achebe's relies (and which in Chapter 3 I will characterize as the difference between interpersonal debt and transcendental debt).[20] Nwapa's rewriting of Achebe in *Efuru* eschews the recentring on the state and its rule of law performed by realism and insists on the viability of a world that remains centred on the village group, where relations remain interpersonal and ever in need of negotiation.

After 1966, the year of the coups that overthrew both Kwame Nkrumah in Ghana and the First Republic in Nigeria, West African novels everywhere became more pessimistic, more fractured and allegorical. Writers were compelled to question the meaning and even the continued existence of Nigeria. The ideal of a Weberian state held by the independence generation thus came to seem absurd. Satirical allegorists such as the Malian Yambo Ouologuem (Appiah's example of the second generation) instead emphasized the state's calamitous tyrannical power. The skepticism of later generations does not, however, *pace* Appiah, render the "nationalist legitimation" of Achebe and his peers outmoded; rather, it changes how we are to understand it. The next generation's skepticism retrospectively reveals how much the novels written just before and just after independence had already cast doubt on Nigeria's viability and questioned what a state *is*. Achebe was never nationalist in the sense of celebrating a heroic narrative of Nigeria. As Jago Morrison observes, "if Achebe's narrative does present a 'Nigerian master narrative, the organizing story of a nation,' as critics have been wont to claim, then it is certainly not a story told by a believer."[21]

The bulk of African literary criticism has emphasized the anti-colonial and nationalist nature of the first generation of African literature. Almost all criticism of Achebe's oeuvre, for instance, has rightly characterized it as affirming African ways of being in the face of racist European misconceptions and as imagining and narrating the nation. The first chapter of Gikandi's monograph on Achebe[22] is called, appropriately, "Nation Formation and the Novel." Andrade's *The Nation Writ Small* agrees that nationalism was the major impulse of male African writers and shows how women writers responded by qualifying or critiquing the nation men had imagined. It is time, however, to take a fresh look at the first generation of Nigerian novelists. Given the unqualified success of the early African novel's anti-colonial project – there can be no doubting that African literature now exists; it is read and studied around the world – it is possible to build on that anti-colonial foundational work and to ask new questions. This book strives to be faithful to African literature by focusing not on the nation but on the state, on the institutions for ruling inherited from the colonizer, including laws, bureaucracy, currency, courts, and police, and on the statist ideal all of these imply.

African novels of all generations have been obsessed with the state. As such they are closer to political philosophy and to the parables of Rousseau or Nietzsche than to such subgenres of the European novel as the marriage plot, the adventure romance, or the bildungsroman. *Debts,*

Laws, Realism is accordingly concerned with the foundations of the law, the sources of sovereignty, and the monopoly on violence. The interest is in Hobbes, Locke, and Rousseau rather than, say, Renan; in Mahmoud Mamdani and Achille Mbembe rather than Benedict Anderson. *Debts, Laws, Realism* is written with the confidence that a genuine comparative literature should be able to study Achebe and his peers in order to reveal not just the nature of Africa and of colonialism but also the nature of the modern state everywhere and of fictional realism.

COLONY AND STATE

First, a brief account of the modern African state is in order. The following relies heavily on the work of historians of Africa and political philosophers. It risks broaching too vast a subject in too small a space and therefore being too sweepingly abstract to do justice to the particular historical moment of Nigerian decolonization or to the novels written at that time, which are the subject of this book. But the moment of independence was a narrow aperture through which funnelled the entire prior experience of colonialism and all the hopes for an alternative future, so the summary history of colonialism and decolonization that follows is necessary. I trust that what is said here will be filled in and clarified in the close reading of the novels that constitutes the rest of this book.

Decolonization was often proclaimed to be the restoration of a lost African autonomy after a period of foreign domination. The irony here is that it was only ever the colony that achieved independence, never the precolonial polity or the ethnic nation defined by language or religion. All modern African states were once colonies imposed by Europeans in the nineteenth century through the exercise of overwhelming military might.[23] Their borders, capitals, laws, and administrations had been determined from outside when the colonizers imposed their rule. And up until the eve of decolonization, the colonizing powers were prepared to deploy their seemingly limitless capacity for violence to ruthlessly suppress all resistance to imperialism by non-state actors: whether by those dispossessed of their lands, like the Shona in Rhodesia and the Gikuyu in Kenya; by those loyal to a precolonial ruler, as in Ashanti or Buganda; or those loyal to religious leaders like Amadou Bamba in Senegal or Simon Kimbangu in the Congo.

Where Africans who sought liberation *from* the colonial state failed, those who sought freedom *for* the colonial state from the metropolis succeeded. Anti-colonial nationalists, commonly young men educated in Britain or France, adopted the language of human rights, democracy, and national self-determination that the colonial powers themselves had deployed since the world war against fascism in order to demand independence for the colony. Though repeatedly subject to arrest and imprisonment, these nationalists were eventually allowed to contest elections and to claim sovereignty for their colonies. In Nigeria in 1960, as in Ghana in 1957 and Kenya in 1964, sovereignty passed from a colonial regime to an independent state that occupied the same territory and was governed by the same basic law.[24]

As in the Americas a century and a half earlier, during the first great wave of global decolonization between 1776 and 1821,[25] independence was only ever accorded to territories upon which the colonizer had bestowed an administration and laws.[26] The continuity between the colonial and the postcolonial is made clear by a glance at the map: African borders did not change at independence, and most of the new states bore the same name as the colonies. Even where the new leaders adopted the names of ancient empires and kingdoms, as in Ghana, Mali, and Zimbabwe, "the primary purpose of independence was accurately perceived by the nationalists to be the conquest of the colonial state."[27] Frederick Cooper and Gary Wilder have reminded us that anti-colonial nationalists, especially in Francophone Africa, often held political ideals other than self-determination for their colonies, variously calling for democratic multicultural empires, pan-African or pan-Arab federations, or transnational caliphates.[28] Those ideals were not, however, realized. The only decolonizing option that succeeded was independence for the colonial states.

We cannot escape the seemingly paradoxical conclusion that people were judged worthy of self-determination only insofar as they had been subject to colonial law. The UN General Assembly Resolution of 1960 that declared that *all* colonies were entitled to self-determination also assumed that *only* colonies, not ethnic groups or traditional chieftaincies, kingdoms, or empires, merited self-determination: "Only constituted colonial territories with a distinct administrative personality [i.e., states] were entitled to succeed to internationally recognized sovereign status."[29] It was by acknowledging their subjection to the state and its laws that colonial subjects proved in the eyes of the international community that they deserved to be citizens and that their states deserved to be independent. Decolonization was thus retrospectively framed by the colonizers as having been the goal of colonization all along.

To achieve decolonization and expel the colonizer, anti-colonial nationalists had to adopt the idea of the state encrypted in the colony, the Weberian ideal characterized by written laws upholding impartial justice, a bureaucratic administration, and a monopoly on violence. In effect, the new citizens of Ghana, Nigeria, and Kenya were being asked to pretend that the rule of law, originally imposed through colonial conquest, governed the transition of sovereignty from a foreign power to a local one and to forget the law's own origins in violence. The violence that had founded the colony and therefore had also founded the laws governing the successor state was the more easily elided where, as in Nigeria and the rest of West and Central Africa, self-determination was accorded without an armed struggle.[30]

In 1958 the Nigerian nationalist leader Nnamdi Azikiwe wrote in his poem "The Past Is Gone" about the dilemma of the law in the postcolony:

> We were compelled to live under the law,
> This deal, itself, we cannot say was raw,
> But, then, it was imposed against our will,
> And, we were not a party to the deal.[31]

Azikiwe welcomes the law but regrets that it was imposed by coercion. Given the choice, however, those fighting to be citizens would choose the law. In 1964, in his speech from the prisoner's dock at his trial for treason, Nelson Mandela defended the African National Congress's plans for sabotage and guerrilla activity as warranted given the manifest evil of the apartheid state, but also declared that he admired "the British Parliament as the most democratic institution in the world" and "the independence and impartiality of its judiciary." The man who opposed his sentence *and* the law according to which he was sentenced as wrongful did not oppose the institution of the law. The nationalists who led the struggle for decolonization, from Nkrumah to Kenyatta, genuinely believed in the ideal of the law and the rational state even while recognizing as their enemy the imperial colony that had defined the actual state.

Weber's ideal of the state bears a relation to the "idea" that Marlow, the narrator of Conrad's *Heart of Darkness*, finds redeems the injustice of colonial violence:

> The conquest of the earth, which mostly means the taking it away from those who have a different complexion or slightly flatter noses than ourselves, is not a pretty thing when you look into it too much. What redeems it is the idea only. An idea at the back of it; not a sentimental pretense but an idea; and an unselfish belief in the idea – something you can set up, and bow down before, and offer a sacrifice to.[32]

Marlow's "idea," worthy of worship and sacrifice, presumably includes such "unselfish" and rational principles as respect for the law and citizens' rights. This is the abstract law that the ethnologist Sir Henry Maine considered was "free of time and circumstance and so could truly be the basis of a universal, civilizing mission."[33] James Fitzjames Stephens declared that "our law is in fact the sum and substance of what we have to teach [colonial subjects]. It is, so to speak, the gospel of the English, and it is a compulsory gospel which admits of no dissent and no disobedience."[34]

Where Marlow considers that the "idea" merits worship and even sacrifice, a writer like the Nigerian Amos Tutuola registers the state's demand for sacrifice as a tyrant's capricious and unreasoning extortion from his subjects. In his 1981 novel *The Witch-Herbalist of the Remote Town*, the people of Rocky Town have a new god. In addition to the gods of iron and of thunder (corresponding to the Yoruba gods Ogun and Shango outside the novel), they worship "the god of the state," who is as high as "a sternly looking giant" and "too terrible and fearful for the eyes of human beings to see."[35] The god of the state wields the power of life and death and can demand the lives of its subjects as tribute. Every year Rocky Town sacrifices a young man and woman to this indigenized version of Hobbes's Leviathan. A modern political institution is thus incorporated as a spirit force in Tutuola's Yoruba cosmogony, but the god of the state remains explicitly new and different from other gods: it bears more of a resemblance to the fierce God of monotheism who demands of Abraham the sacrifice of his son than it does to a local deity. Juxtaposing Conrad and Tutuola in this way suggests a sinister continuity between the colony and the postcolonial state, but also a bifurcation in the state as established by the colonizer and seized by nationalists: it is at once despotic *and* unselfish; it is imposed by violence and it is an ideal one may bow before. That duality is the subject of this book.

The states that emerged at decolonization inherited both the tyrannical sovereignty and the potentially redemptive idea of the law from the colonies they succeeded. That the very law that guarantees the peaceful transition from one regime to the next rests on foundations of violent conquest is a paradox not peculiar to Africa or to colonies; it is the basis of the political philosophies of Carl Schmitt and Giorgio Agamben, who argue that the sovereignty of the state everywhere precedes and exceeds the law that it established and continues to manifest itself in the right to declare exceptions to the law. Citizens everywhere are first of all subjects: their vaunted freedom depends on their prior subjection to the state and its law. They must believe in and sacrifice to the "idea" that Marlow says can redeem the violence that imposed it.

My argument is that, rather than being an exception, the African state tells us something about the modern state everywhere: the rule of law that guarantees citizens' rights and freedoms is dependent on the original and still present violence with which it was first imposed on subjects. As Schmitt and Agamben signal, modern European states were themselves first established by force by absolute monarchs, who later had sovereignty wrested from them in revolutions. Franz Oppenheimer goes so far as to characterize the state everywhere as "a social institution, forced by a victorious group of men on a defeated group, with the sole purpose of regulating the dominion of the victorious group over the vanquished."[36] According to Michel Foucault, invasion and conquest were at the origins of the sovereign state, including England, where the law was inaugurated by the Norman Conquest, and France, where the state was created by the invasion of Gaul by the Franks and, before that, by the Romans.[37] In terms redolent of modern African history, Nietzsche attributes the state *in Europe* to conquest by

> a herd of blonde beasts of prey, a master race, a race of conquerors which, aggressive, powerful and organized, pounces with its most horrid claws on an unsuspecting population, one which in numbers may be tremendously superior, but is still undisciplined and nomadic. Such is the origin of the "state" (I think we have disposed of that notion, one held enthusiastically by many, according to which the "state" originates with a sort of contract).[38]

Europeans, no less than Africans, had originally had the state imposed upon them and could say with Azikiwe that they "were not a party to the deal."

Western European citizens, however, forget the state's origins in conquest and absolute monarchy and remember instead the long process whereby citizens successfully wrested concessions from or imposed limits on the sovereign and won rights for themselves. In the case of France and Britain, the state's origins in conquest were replaced in national mythology either by the violence of revolution or by the idea of a social contract fought for over centuries. The state, the product of conquest, became the vehicle for representative democracy, the rights of man and citizen, and the rule of law. Democracy became the state's accepted teleology.

The European empires that conquered the Americas and established trading posts on the west coast of Africa in the sixteenth and seventeenth centuries were ruled by absolute monarchs. Those mercantile empires forged trading partnerships with West and Central African states, whose primary export soon became slaves as labour for New World plantations.[39] The transatlantic slave trade, with its growing and seemingly inexhaustible demand, inspired the creation of large predatory African states like Dahomey and Ashante, which waged war on their less organized neighbours in order to take captives to sell into slavery. This was all part of *How Europe Underdeveloped Africa*, the title of Walter Rodney's book. Patrick Manning describes how these "monarchies who succeeded in profiting and expanding at the expense of their neighbors" developed values "centered on hierarchy, centralization, and the glorification of wealth."[40] The slave trade, it has been argued, acted to replicate in Africa the conditions that had given birth to the absolute state in Europe.

Precolonial African history displays a full panoply of empires, kingdoms, and city-states. A focus on the history of such polities, however, obscures the viability of what Robin Horton calls "stateless societies" in which the "wielding of authority as a specialized, full-time occupation is virtually unknown."[41] Africa also knew societies that did without chiefs or kings, where all free men (though not all people) could participate in communal decisions such as whether to go to war, and where relations among individuals, families, and clans were governed by reciprocity rather than by central authority. At the beginning of the colonial period, perhaps one quarter of the population of West Africa lived in such societies.[42] Stateless societies, such as those depicted in Achebe's village novels, flourished in the spaces between predatory states, where the power of two rivals was equally weak or their power overlapped. Such stateless communities have been treated as by-products of the violence and chaos wrought by wars for captives, but that is to regard these societies from the perspective of the history made by states, a history whose teleology is precisely the state. It is not the case that Igbo village groups had somehow failed to create states and were thus doomed to be the source of slaves. Some Igbos, such as the Aro, themselves participated in the slave trade, and others formed healthy societies able "to pay more attention to the demands of efficient agriculture than to those of efficient defence, and so lived in evenly scattered homesteads rather than in large, compact villages."[43] As Susan McIntosh argues, statelessness was not a step on an inevitable evolutionary path toward greater complexity and the state, but a viable alternative historical destination, every bit as complex as the state. These groups were "societies in which central authority, often of a ritual nature, is paired with a power structure that is diffuse, segmentary, and heterarchical, as well as societies in which considerable complexity is achieved through horizontal differentiation and consensus-based decision-making."[44] In contrast to the predatory states, among stateless societies "a contrasting ideology developed in which the values of self-sufficiency, an egalitarian opposition to authority, and a willingness to live without great accumulations of wealth were dominant."[45] John Lonsdale has gone so far as to claim that "the most distinctively African contribution to human history could be said to have been precisely the civilized art of living fairly peaceably together *not* in states."[46] We need to keep the political alternative of statelessness in mind when considering how Nigerian novelists understood the modern state.

Even to speak of "stateless" societies is to imply that centralized states are the norm, as indeed they are for historians.[47] To avoid that implication or its corollary, that Igbo society was not organized, some prefer the terms "decentralized" or "acephalous." Both those terms, however, also imply a negative, a symptom of how ingrained an evolutionary perspective is in everyone who writes about history. I keep the term "stateless" in order to underscore the contrast between the village group and the colonial and postcolonial state. The democratic ethos of stateless societies must be contrasted with the ideal of democracy embodied in the rule of law later introduced by the colonizers.

As noted earlier, the European empires that conquered the Americas in the sixteenth and seventeenth centuries and established trading posts on the west coast of Africa were ruled by absolute monarchs.[48] The vast bulk of those empires, however, were lost over the course of fifty years in the late eighteenth and early nineteenth centuries in a series of great revolutions, the American, the Haitian, and the Spanish American, all of them transatlantic counterparts to the French Revolution. These revolutions on either side of the Atlantic rudely did away with kings, though kings had a habit of reappearing, as they did in Haiti and France. Paul Downes has traced how the figure of the king continued to haunt the new United States.[49] The same period that did away, however incompletely, with kingly power also saw the ideological triumph of abolition. The British declared the slave trade illegal in 1807 and abolished slavery throughout the Empire in 1838. France, having aborted a first attempt to abolish slavery during the Revolution, followed through in 1848. Slavery was abhorred as incompatible with free wage labour and with democracy.[50] Yet in the wake of the democratic revolutions and the abolition of slavery, Britain and France went on to establish new, larger empires in Asia and Africa to replace the ones that the *anciens régimes* had lost in the Americas.[51] The British established their first colony in Africa, Sierra Leone, at the end of the eighteenth century in order to resettle former slaves rescued from slave ships or freed in the Americas.

The notion of *democratic empires* or *imperialist democracies* is paradoxical on the surface: as Hannah Arendt notes, "of all forms of government and organizations of people, the nation-state is least suited for unlimited growth because the genuine consent at its base cannot be stretched indefinitely, and is only rarely, and with difficulty, won from conquered people."[52] Arendt concludes, however, that while "in theory, there is an abyss between nationalism and imperialism; in practice, it can be and has been bridged by tribal nationalism and outright racism."[53] The European nation-state implied both "the notion of a power that is confined to a limited territory and a restricted community" *and* "the notion of a power that has the vocation for universal domination."[54] Arendt finds the apparent contradiction between the democratic nation-state and its vocation for empire implicit in the constitution of the European state:

> When the French Revolution combined the declaration of the Rights of Man with the demand for national sovereignty … [t]he same essential rights were at once claimed as the inalienable heritage of all human beings *and* as the specific heritage of specific nations, the same nation was at once declared to be subject to laws, which supposedly would flow from the Rights of Man, *and* sovereign, that is, bound by no universal law and acknowledging nothing superior to itself.[55]

Eric Santner explains that in the French Revolution, the transfer of sovereignty from the monarch to the People relied on the "sovereign's double nature," modelled on Christ's incarnation. Just as Christ was at once God and man, so the figure of the Renaissance king had been imagined as having two natures: a mortal body and a sublime one.[56] When a king died, the monarchy persisted, hence the cry "the king is dead, long live the king." In the French Revolution, after the king was executed, the sublime sovereign also lived on, but now as the mystic embodiment called the People. As François Furet writes, however, "the 'people' was not a datum or a concept that reflected existing society. Rather, it was the Revolution's claim to legitimacy, its very definition as it were; for henceforth all power, all political endeavour revolved around that founding principle, *which it was nonetheless impossible to embody*."[57] The Revolution claimed to be the action of the People, when actually, it brought the People into being. Michael Warner says of the American Revolution that "the trick was to see how law could be given to the people transcendently and received from it immanently at the same time."[58]

Having wrested sovereign power from the monarch, his former subjects, now constituted by the Revolution as the People, continued to identify with the state ... and with the expansionist aims of sovereignty. The European states that conquered vast empires in Africa and Asia in the nineteenth and early twentieth centuries were democratic at home and imperialist abroad. The seeming contradiction reflects a duality in the nature of state sovereignty that we have already seen in Marlow's "idea" that could redeem conquest. Britain and France justified their rapid and vast conquests in the late nineteenth century by declaring that they were eliminating indigenous slavery in West Africa and fighting the Arab slave trade in East Africa, that is, by claiming to be representatives of a transcendent morality, Marlow's "idea" again, conveniently forgetting how much they themselves had been responsible for fostering the slavery they now opposed. The leading bourgeois states claimed a right to conquer and rule other peoples because, *as democracies*, they judged themselves superior to what they regarded as primitive despotisms. Peoples whose character required tyrannical authority to rule them needed democratic conquerors, or so those conquerors argued.

Ernst Fraenkel has used the term Dual State to describe the legal status of Nazi Germany: a combination of the Normative State, "an administrative body endowed with elaborate powers for safeguarding the legal order as expressed in statutes," and the Prerogative State, "which exercises unlimited arbitrariness and violence unchecked by any legal guarantees."[59] The Normative State is characterized by "rule-*of*-law," where the law is above the officers of the state and they must serve it. The Prerogative State, by contrast, can be defined as "rule-*by*-law," the absolute and arbitrary power expressed in legal fiat that Achille Mbembe calls the *commandement*. An example Fraenkel gives of the Dual State is the case of a prisoner in a German concentration camp who received an assessment for income tax: "In this instance, the prerogative state demanded the man's unlawful detention, while the normative state processed his taxes. The latter treated the man as citizen, the former as subject."[60] An African example would be the case of Nelson Mandela, who as a black African was denied the rights of a citizen by the South African state but put on trial for treason as if he *were* a citizen.

Arendt in *The Origins of Totalitarianism* and Aimé Césaire in *The Discourse of Colonialism* have argued that Nazism, arising as it did after Germany's loss of its African colonies in 1919, represented the transposition to Europe of German genocidal practices in South West Africa and Tanganyika. My argument is rather that Nazi Germany and African colonies reveal a truth about states everywhere. In British law, as in law everywhere, there is an understanding that, in cases of emergency, when the safety of the state requires it, the rule of law may be set aside for martial law, which is not a law at all but the direct agency of the Prerogative State. The law that can imagine its own abrogation has been the focus of political philosophers like Hobbes, Schmitt, and Agamben, who argue that the sovereignty of the state precedes and exceeds the law that it establishes and continues to manifest itself in the right to declare exceptions to the law. "In this sovereign interpellation," Warner writes of the United States, "the people are always coming across themselves in the act of consenting to their own coercion."[61]

Adam Sitze writes of the "antinomy created in and by the English Revolution, between the *sovereignty of law* (the revolutionary principle that nobody is above the law) and the *law of sovereignty*," which uses the health of the state or public order to justify the abrogation of the law.[62] In Britain, however, indemnity for agents of the state who have exceeded the law in the interests of public order, the hallmark of the Prerogative State, has not been granted since 1776 *except* in the colonies, where such indemnity was repeatedly invoked to exculpate colonial officers who responded to rebellion with military force. Sitze writes that "the *innermost inside* of the British Empire," the illegality that defines the law itself, "is constituted by a legal practice that exists almost exclusively at its *outermost limits*."[63] Partha Chatterjee defines "imperial power" in Schmittian terms "as the prerogative to declare the colonial exception."[64] In other words, the Normative State ruled at home, the Prerogative State abroad. It is as though the colonies expressed the violent truth of the state, hidden from people in the metropole but obvious to the colonized.

The colonial condition was a manifest division of the population into citizen and subject, as Mahmood Mamdani has argued. The colonized were subjects supposedly in training to be citizens, and as part of that training, they were forced to pay taxes to cover the costs of the colonial administration that denied them participation in government. In the colony, of course, the duality had everything to do with racial difference. As Sitze explains, the colonial subject was always considered at once "a potential citizen (whose latent capacities could be developed through tutelage and trusteeship) and a potential enemy (whose manifest obedience to law concealed deeper hostilities and proclivities to violence)."[65] The potential citizen had to be brought to appreciate the rule of law embodied in the Normative State; the Prerogative State kept the potential enemy subdued. The justification of colonies was that they would inculcate rational and enlightened government in colonial subjects and make them citizens, but race was invoked to explain why those same subjects were not yet ready for democracy and needed to be ruled by others. Mbembe argues that the postcolonial states inherited the *commandement* of the European colony, "the *principe autoritaire*: the arbitrary discipline of the subject by the state that 'aspires to the exercise of a symbolic hegemony over indigenous societies signified by its claim to a monopoly of legitimate vision' and that incorporates into that exercise of power 'a vocation of modernizing the nation and civilizing the society.'"[66]

The Prerogative State is a truth of the state everywhere. According to Foucault in *Discipline and Punish*, when kings ruled supreme in Europe, they used graphic violence to punish offenders and render their power visible. When, after the great democratic revolutions, sovereignty passed to the abstraction of the People, violence was hidden behind prison walls and citizens integrated within their psyches a sense of their subjection to an abstract, sovereign, all-seeing power. Foucauldian discipline is the form the Prerogative State takes in Europe. Althusser would call it the Ideological State Apparatus, and Freud simply civilization. Everywhere people are subject to the violence of the law, even if, in Europe and North America, such has been the majority's identification as citizens that they often do not register their subjection.

I do not mean, however, that the Prerogative State was the truth of the state or even of the colony, merely masked by the ruse of the Normative State. Many who discuss the colonial "state of exception" as it appears in literature assume both that the Prerogative State is the state gone wrong and, paradoxically, that it is the only truth about the state. The rule of law is then regarded either as what should be but is not, the ideal that the colony contravenes, or as merely a lie, the facade the colony adopts to mask the truth that is the state of exception. The state, however, is genuinely dual: there is no prying apart the Prerogative and the Normative States. The Normative state everywhere, and not just in the colony, required violence in order to be established, a violence that may be reasserted in a state of exception, which is more likely to be found in the colony. But the Prerogative State is also inextricably tied to the Normative State for its legitimacy. E.P. Thompson writes about eighteenth-century England that the ruling class were, "whether willingly or unwillingly, the prisoners of their own rhetoric; they played the games of power according to rules which suited them, but they could not break those rules or the whole game would be thrown away."[67] Something similar might be said of the British and French empires in Africa. If rule of law were no more than the mask the colonizer adopted, it might yet have the value of what

David Dyzenhaus calls "the civilizing power of hypocrisy."[68] Dyzenhaus goes further, however, arguing that hypocrisy's civilizing power "can, somewhat paradoxically, only do its work if the stance of rulers cannot be wholly hypocritical. For, in claiming to rule in law's name, they cannot avoid entirely the discipline of the internal morality of law."[69] According to Dyzenhaus, the rule of law fosters principles of impartiality and respect for rights, even in contexts such as apartheid South Africa, where the Prerogative State devised "wicked" laws and trampled on judicial institutions that might constrain those laws. Dyzenhaus follows Lon Fuller in arguing "that a tyrant who chooses to govern through law rather than through some other medium will find his tyranny disciplined in such a way that his rule becomes less tyrannical, i.e. his rule will perforce serve the interests of legal subjects."[70] Hobbes's sovereign, "while he will have the first and last word about the content of the positive law, has still to speak in the language of the law, that is, in ways that respect what we might think of as the normative grammar of legality."[71] That is why, as we have seen, anti-colonial nationalists like Azikiwe and Mandela valued the law.

If the state is everywhere dual, we need to ask why decolonization in Africa did *not* forge sovereign peoples in the way that the European and American revolutions that deposed or displaced kings are imagined to have done. In Africa at decolonization, with only one large-scale, long-term exception, the "herd of blonde beasts" described by Nietzsche withdrew, bequeathing to their former subjects the state and its law that they had originally imposed by violence. And at the heady moment of independence it may have seemed to many that a successful revolution had occurred. Why then did African independence not feel like the revolutions in Europe or the Americas, an occasion for citizens to inherit the sovereignty of the monarch?

One reason is the recentness of colonialism: in most of West Africa the coming of the law, the establishment of the state administration, and the setting of borders all occurred in the decade and a half before and after the turn of the twentieth century. Typical in this regard is the Igbo setting of *Things Fall Apart*, conquered by the British in a series of military expeditions between 1900 and 1914. The recentness of colonization is so difficult for Achebe himself to credit that he pushes the events of his novel back to the reign of Victoria, who died in 1901. Where European philosophers such as Hobbes and Rousseau could imagine a moment in the misty past when the social contract that founded the state came into existence, almost everywhere in West Africa there were people alive at the time of independence who remembered the establishment of the colony by force. The origins of African states through violent conquest could therefore not be as easily forgotten as similar origins have been in Europe. Because the violence with which state institutions were imposed was still so fresh in memory, decolonization was insufficient to inspire identification with state institutions. Many Africans who resisted the colonizers were not concerned with making the state their own; rather, they wanted to get rid of the state itself as the product of conquest.

Another, seemingly opposite problem faced by the new African states is the weakness of the state inherited from the colonizer. Charles Tilly points out that European states were originally forged in war, their borders written in the blood of people on both sides.[72] The border marked the point where a state either could not overcome another state's resistance or had successfully defended itself against another's attacks. Over time the military competition for territory "acted as a filter whereby weak states were eliminated and political arrangements that were not viable either were reformed or disappeared."[73] The constant presence of war also "caused the state to become more efficient in revenue collection by forcing leaders to dramatically improve administrative capabilities (thereby allowing states to fund nationwide administrative and economic systems)."[74] Richard Bean writes that "once the power to tax had been successfully appropriated by any one sovereign, once he had used that power to bribe or coerce his nobility into acquiescence, that state could face all neighboring states with the choice of being conquered or of centralizing authority and raising taxes."[75] Strong states begat other strong states. And the people targeted by these powerful revenue collectors, in turn, eventually amassed enough power to demand representation in those administrative systems. European colonies in Africa were also the products of conquest, but unlike in Europe, the conquerors did not shed blood over borders. The European rivals had an interest in avoiding war over Africa, and at the Conference of Berlin, they drew up mutually acceptable limits to one another's colonial expansion. It suited Britain and France to make room at the table for Germany, Portugal, and even the King of the Belgians, for the colonizers found that there was more than enough territory to go around. At Berlin the colonizing states acknowledged one another's sovereignty over the areas within the consensual borders, even when the colonizers' effective control of the African interior was non-existent. As long as a colonial power held the capital, it was convenient for everyone to assume it occupied the territory associated with it. The result was what Jeffrey Herbst calls fictions of power: "European colonialism was a combination of domestic administrative structures and a state system that went to elaborate lengths to uphold the notion that Europeans were actually ruling Africa."[76] Moreover, Chabal points out, "the division of Africa into colonies was done with no serious consideration for economic, particularly capitalist, economic logic,"[77] with the result that "a number of colonies were economically not viable and had no conceivable means of becoming viable independent countries,"[78] another reason state power could be described as fictional.

The weakness of the colonies and of their postcolonial successor states meant that the state, unable to impress its discipline on the psyches of subjects, had to rely on Foucauldian graphic violence.[79] The Prerogative State in most of Africa, unlike in its apotheosis in Nazi Germany, manifests itself especially where the state is too weak to establish a Normative State. Where the weakness of the sovereign power prevented it from asserting hegemony and making its presence seem legitimate or even natural, it had to rule by terror instead. Also, the thinness of the colonizers on the ground forced them to adopt the principles of Indirect Rule: rather than integrate colonial subjects into state institutions, they maintained in place traditional authorities such as chiefs and emirs.[80] This is the origin of the distinction Mamdani makes between subject and citizen: urban and educated Africans were ruled directly by the colonial state and could, as we have seen, imagine themselves seizing the state and becoming full citizens, but rural Africans were ruled by traditional (or supposedly traditional) authorities, and it was intended that they remain subjects. Under Indirect Rule, traditional authorities were no longer accountable to their subjects and instead owed their power to the British. Indirect Rule, as we shall see, posed an especial problem in stateless societies such as that of the Igbo, where there had never been chiefs and the British had had to invent them.

The expulsion of the colonizers at the time of decolonization posed conceptual problems for inheriting sovereignty. African states had been conquered by foreigners *who always remained foreign* and who never extended an invitation to subjects to identify with the sovereign in the way that a European Renaissance monarch's subjects could imagine themselves participating in his mystical body. Norman or Frankish conquerors became English or French; British colonizers did not become Nigerian or Ghanaian. Peter Ekeh notes that while "democracy developed historically in Western Europe in the context of the struggle for freedom from domestic repression," "African nationalism's democracy was concerned with the freedom of peoples and collectivities from *foreign* domination."[81] Instead of the revolutionary cry "the king is dead, long live the people," African nationalists proclaimed, "the colonizer is gone, long live the nation-state." The colonizers' justification for the continued tutelage of Africans had always had a basis in racism, and race became the nationalists' rallying cry for equal rights and self-determination. This produced the familiar oxymoron *African nationalism*: anti-colonial nationalists sought independence for the colony in the name of the race and the continent. African states were defined not against their neighbours, as European states were, but against the distant colonizers. Decolonization was a great body swap: the racially distinct bodies of the colonizers departed, leaving behind the sublime body of the state. But with the departure of the colonizers, some of their foreign racial charge may have adhered to the state that remained in place. The sublime body of the sovereign in the form of laws and administration bequeathed to the People at decolonization did not coincide with the sublime body of the continent or the race and may have continued to feel as foreign as the colonizer's mortal body had. The state continued to be associated with the foreigner; its institutions and its laws were felt to be neither transparent nor universal and were deeply mistrusted. When, a few years after independence, Ghana and Nigeria eliminated the British queen as the constitutional monarch and became republics, as Ireland, India, and South Africa had done before them, they did not solve the problem of the foreignness of the state's body but drew attention to it.

We can appreciate the weakness of the postcolonial state if we consider its inability to collect taxes. In Europe and in America the winning of rights from the absolute monarch entailed a long struggle by taxpayers for representation. "No taxation without representation" was the cry of democratic revolutionaries, be they English nobles, American colonists, or the French Third Estate. In Igboland, too, the Women's War of 1929 was against the imposition of taxes; however, this was a struggle not for representation but for the elimination of state burdens. Jane Guyer points out that in Nigeria, the tax system such as it was under the British collapsed in the years after independence because it was regarded as part of the oppression that independence would remove.[82] As Ekeh notes, during the anti-colonial struggle, the "African who evaded his tax was a hero."[83] Rather than replicate the story of the state as it has unfolded in other places, where citizens have insisted on representation and accountability as the price of their taxes, postcolonial Nigeria has featured instead what Guyer calls "representation without taxation."

The failure of new citizens in Africa to integrate the sovereignty of the state into their psyche is often blamed on the unnatural borders drawn up by the colonizers. Nigeria, it is said, has failed to cohere because it contains speakers of 250 different languages; Christians, Muslims, and animists; and the very different ecosystems of rainforest and savannah. Ofeimun points to the "pervasiveness of the view that 1914 was a mistake, and the fact that many Nigerians continue to act as if the mistake remains a mistake."[84] (In 1914 the Southern and Northern Nigerian Protectorates were merged to form the single colony of Nigeria.) The idea that artificial borders are a mistake ignores that most states, including Britain and France, emerged through conquest and assumes incorrectly that a state can have a true foundation and natural borders. Ofeimun writes: "The business of not taking Nigeria seriously was borrowed by the natives, North and South, from the British colonialists whose body language, and sometimes stated policy, was against ruling Nigeria as one country." Ofeimun notes that even though (or because) the British had experience of a multi-ethnic state at home, they tended to share "the very European idea that a nation state must be made up of people of only one language, one culture and one religion" and therefore did not believe that Nigeria could be a state.

The perceived cultural homogeneity of England, and of France, did not precede and underpin the state; rather, it was the product of centuries of state-building. Peasants needed to be taught to be Frenchmen,[85] and what began with the mass experience of the Revolution and of the Grande Armée continued with the development of universal education and a national curriculum. The problem with Nigeria and other states sometimes felt to be artificial is not objective artificiality – all states are artificial – but the *feeling*. Frantz Fanon, the Martiniquan psychiatrist who identified with the Algerian struggle for independence, looked forward to the day when Africans would become Kenyans, Senegalese, and Nigerians, meaning citizens of states defined by common ideals and goals. He conceived of the state as a collective project undertaken by a people to construct the society they want. Such a project could be undertaken even in a manifestly arbitrary nation such as Nigeria; indeed, artificiality aids in building such a nation because it acknowledges that inheritance is less important than the future people make together. Fanon did not want nations, as defined by language or religion or ethnicity, to become states; he wanted states to become nations.

Fanon also believed that, for psychological reasons, independence for the colonized required violence in the form of a revolution: "Violence is a cleansing force. It frees the native from his inferiority complex and from his despair and inaction; it makes him fearless and restores his self-respect."[86] It also dissolves groups based on kinship and smaller than the state "and introduces into each man's consciousness the ideas of a common cause, of a national destiny, and of a collective history."[87]

In Schmittian fashion, Fanon argued that decolonization requires an existential decision, struggle against an enemy, and sacrifice. In West Africa, however, independence was granted without a military struggle, and since decolonization, African states have behaved among themselves as the European colonizers did before them, by and large agreeing that if a "government is in control of the capital city, then it has the legitimate right to the full protection offered by the modern understanding of sovereignty."[88]

Decolonization, like colonization before it, was always a struggle for control of the centre; that struggle was never over borders. If, as suggested earlier, the Normative State was frequently the face of the European state at home, and if the Prerogative State reflected how it was experienced abroad in the colonies, decolonization did not so much abolish the Dual State as turn it inside out. A consensus after the Second World War upheld what Robert Jackson has called a "rights-model of international relations"[89]: the assumption that every state had a right to self-determination. State sovereignty, the political form at the core of world empires, became the forum and goal of the anti-colonial struggle, which appealed to the principles of rule of law and human rights in order to win international recognition for the self-determination of African states. Since then, African nation-states have in many ways been model members of the postwar United Nations, at least when it comes to respecting the borders and the sovereignty of neighbours; this amounts to acknowledgment that "there are sharp limits on what is appropriate for a nation to want or to dream of – not an empire, for example, or even conquest of an enemy or neighbor."[90] We have already noted the remarkable fixity of African state borders. The Charter of the Organization of African Unity affirms the "sovereign equality of all member states, noninterference in the internal affairs of member states, and respect for the states' sovereignty and territorial integrity."[91] Within their own borders, however, African states have shown notably less respect for human rights and democracy.

STATE AND NOVEL

Such is the state that is the setting for many of the first generation of West African novels. As noted above, one task faced by African writers has been to imagine the *nation*, a community sharing a common history and identity. The nation needed to be named in literature, its history written, a shared set of reference points established. But another task undertaken by African novelists – and my subject in this book – was *imagining* the postcolonial *state*, its laws and institutions. Where does the law get its authority from? What does the citizen owe to the state? How does one come to trust state institutions? To focus on states and citizenship rather than on nations and identity, as I am arguing Nigerian novelists do, is to raise important questions about legitimacy, succession, the virtues of different models of political organization, the nature of representation, and the relation of state to empire, colony, and the international system. These novelists make it possible to ask questions like "What is a state *for*?"

Of the first generation of West African novelists in English, the majority were Igbos or from other stateless peoples in southeastern Nigeria. One explanation for the "overrepresentation"[92] of the Anglo-Igbo novel is that Achebe's example inspired his fellow Igbos. Another is that Igbos took to Western education more than most other groups. Obi Nwakanma suggests that Igbo writers dominated the Nigerian novel because Igbos, being migrants spread throughout Nigeria, had a more developed national consciousness.[93] But those explanations simply restate the question at hand: *Why* did Achebe's example resonate with other novelists more than, say, Tutuola's? *Why* did Igbos take to Western education? *Why* did they migrate throughout the territory? Another explanation for the prevalence of Igbos among the first generation of novelists lies precisely in what I have described as the precolonial statelessness of southeastern Nigeria. As the heirs to stateless societies, Igbos and their immediate neighbours were arguably more distanced from the colonial state than were the Yoruba with their city-states or the Hausa with their emirates. Paradoxically, however, they also felt the presence of the colonial state more directly because the British could not rely on traditional authorities to mediate their rule. Indirect rule, the British policy of ruling through traditional rulers – and creating them where they did not exist, as in Igboland – merely reinforced the Igbos' experience of the arbitrariness of imperial rule. My argument is that the particular experience of the Igbo and their neighbours, for whom the colonial state was more novel and more direct than it was for others, raised political questions best addressed by the form of the novel.[94] The first generation of African novels, Achebe's but also Flora Nwapa's and Elechi Amadi's, make the state visible by hearkening back to a precolonial society that did without the sovereignty of the law. West African novelists, and those from southeastern Nigeria in particular, asked what is to be gained, and lost, when one becomes a sovereign citizen of a sovereign state.

This book focuses on four particular figures – Okonkwo in *Things Fall Apart*, Efuru in Nwapa's eponymous novel, Ezeulu in *Arrow of*

God, and Obi in *No Longer at Ease* – in order to explore a series of topics related to the state: the alternative to the state represented by precolonial democracy, the coming of the state in the form of conquest, the problematic inheritance of the state by erstwhile African subjects, and the psychic costs of integrating the state and its rule of law. Three themes recur as ways of measuring and understanding the modern state: (1) in stateless societies interpersonal debt was a hallmark of reciprocity, how people related to one another, but the state instituted a new notion of absolute and unrepayable debt to an impersonal creditor; (2) the state exercises a sovereign power experienced by people as subjection, but insofar as citizens identify with the sovereignty to which they are subject, they enjoy a sense of personal sovereignty; and (3) the impartiality and objectivity of the rule of law correspond to the ideals of transparency and comprehensibility characteristic of fictional realism.

The first three chapters consider Achebe's depiction in *Things Fall Apart* of a precolonial stateless world at the moment when his generation was about to inherit the colonial state from the British. I locate a tension in the novel between two systems of imagining relations among people in society: a horizontal system based on reciprocity, and a vertical one based on the rule of law. Achebe the citizen-to-be was writing realism in order to teach his fellow would-be citizens how to understand a society in which trust was based on a common submission to the law. At the same time, he remembered another way of imagining social relations. The novel is thus fraught with ambivalence, at the heart of which is the question of trust, which the novel thematizes in terms of credit and debt.

The realism of *Things Fall Apart* presumes the state of Nigeria that lies in the future of the fictive Umuofia, as seen in the sequel *No Longer at Ease*, which had been part of Achebe's conception of his novel from the beginning. Flora Nwapa, whose *Efuru* alludes directly to Achebe's novel, is set in the real, *non*-fictive town of Ugwuta and, even though set in the colonial period, assumes the validity of the world characterized by orality and traditional markets rather than modern Nigeria. This contrast can be tracked through Nwapa's treatment of gossip and markets and is reflected in her novel's very different perceptions of tricksters and confidence men. Where Achebe blames colonialism for having introduced a disconnect between words and the world that made room for tricksters, Nwapa considers tricksters essential for imagining the foundations of trust. The contrast between Achebe and Nwapa is the subject of Chapters 4 and 5.

Chapters 6 and 7 consider Achebe's *Arrow of God*, a tragedy that hinges on the problem of succession. Written, unlike its precursors, after independence, *Arrow of God* assumes that the peace established by force of arms by the British has no alternative. The problem then becomes how Igbos can inherit the rule of law. Achebe, who along with his fellow citizens has inherited the colonial state from the British, asks which of the sons of Ezeulu, the chief priest of Ulu, will inherit from him. Answering the question, which is of central importance to imagining Nigerians' relations as citizens to the state, involves also asking how the British inherit from each other, as well as what Ezeulu inherited from his parents, his mother as well as his father.

The only novel of Achebe's discussed here that is not set in the past, *No Longer at Ease*, set almost exactly when it was written, on the very eve of independence, is an exploration of the meaning of citizenship as imagined through a civil servant who owes rival duties: to his village group and family, and to the state that employs him. It thematizes many of the features of the modern state: bureaucracy, police, courts, and prison, but also corruption and denunciations of corruption. The notion of corruption implies an ideal that is not realized, but where do that ideal and the corruption that violates it originate? That is the burden of the final three chapters.

1

Crediting African Literature

As Chinua Achebe tells it, when he was twenty-six years old and had written what he fondly thought of as the first novel by a West African, he mailed his only manuscript to a London typing agency whose advertisement he had seen in *The Spectator*, along with a British postal order for £22[1] (or £32[2]; the story varies). The novice author did not hear back, and might never have, had a British friend returning to London not intervened. The London firm obviously did not believe that something mailed from Africa was worth their time or needed to be responded to. Achebe and his literary contemporaries had yet to establish the credit abroad and at home necessary for their work to have currency.

That novel was *Things Fall Apart*, eventually published in 1958 by Heinemann, the novel that established black African literature in English. A historical novel about the colonial encounter, *Things Fall Apart* attempted to account for the presence in southeastern Nigeria of the English language, writing and books, and the colonial administration and its rule of law – in other words, for the conditions of the novel's own existence. It also posed the question of the African novel's relationship to the Igbo language, Igbo oral culture, and the precolonial symbolic order. There had been West African novels before this, and Newell argues forcefully that it is unfair to regard *Things Fall Apart* as the first, in effect making its precursors appear to be merely awaiting Achebe.[3] I discuss some of those precursors in this monograph. For the most part, however, West African novelists in English before Achebe only ever wrote one book each and had no successors.[4] The first West African writers in English to write more than one novel and to inspire successors were the Nigerians Amos Tutuola and Cyprian Ekwensi in the 1950s. Critics of Tutuola, however, unfairly treat him as if he, too, wrote only one book or as if he wrote the same book eight times. Achebe and Soyinka, by contrast, self-consciously embarked on literary careers: they conceived of their first books as preparing the ground for their books to come. Unlike their precursors, they imagined themselves as part of a literary tradition they were setting out to define. Every African novelist before Achebe thought of himself as the first to write; Achebe, by contrast, was the first to cite a precursor: his protagonist, Obi Okonkwo, in the 1960 novel *No Longer at Ease*, has read Tutuola. It is because Achebe, unlike his precursors, conceives of himself as part of a literary tradition that we can locate him at the origins of the Nigerian novel.

What is remarkable about the anecdote of the manuscript sent to London is the confidence manifested by the young writer, who was launching a literary career in a soon-to-be independent colony on the imperial periphery. That confidence verged on naivety, as though Achebe did not know enough to mistrust. The young Nigerian had placed his faith in the postal system, the banking system, the advertisement for the typing service, and the London-based publishing industry, institutions that he believed would offer the same services to all customers and judge prospective authors fairly. As it happened, the vaunted objectivity and impartiality of the great institutions dealing with paper almost failed the racialized colonial subject. The first lesson to be drawn from the story of the manuscript is the need for mistrust. Without the personal intervention of a well-placed friend, Achebe's manuscript would have been lost. Achebe found, like many Nigerians before and since, that when facing massive institutions, one needs a person on the inside who can intercede on one's behalf. A second observation, however, no less important, is that the young Nigerian wanted to trust, and did.

Trust is a political question. Strong institutions make trust possible between strangers who do not know one another and have no personal relations. With large institutions that work primarily with paper, such as the postal system and publishing houses,[5] it is possible to imagine, even against all personal experience as a colonial in West Africa, that race and ethnicity are not factors in access. Of course, Achebe's trust was eventually vindicated: his novel succeeded on a world scale beyond the wildest dreams that the young man could have harboured, but before that could happen, he not only had to demand fair treatment from the typing company but also had to win credit from a publisher and from readers.

In telling this episode Achebe may have embroidered somewhat the precariousness of his original success,[6] but the story does reflect the enormous faith needed by his generation of African writers. The young man had only ever been a colonial subject, yet his education somehow made him desire the imminent boons of citizenship. Even as Achebe trusted that he could be accepted by readers in distant places as a full member of the worldwide Republic of Letters, he looked forward to no longer being a mere subject and becoming a citizen of an independent state. And the first criterion for citizenship is to act like a citizen.[7] A citizen is one who demands to be treated as such.

Before putting words to paper all writers need faith that what they write is what unknown and unseen readers will want to read, but in the mid-twentieth century the African writer faced more hurdles than most: he had to teach his fellow citizens *how* to read. In general, the realist novel is an invitation to reader-citizens to credit the rationality of the world underpinned by modern ideas and institutions. It reassures its audience that people are knowable and explicable because they accede to their subjection to state institutions and, in particular, to the law.

CREDIT AS A THEME IN *THINGS FALL APART*

To signal how central trust is for both writer and citizen, *Things Fall Apart* self-consciously opens with two scenes about credit, both set before the present of the narrative in precolonial Igboland around 1880. A creditor visits the chronic debtor Unoka to call in a long-standing debt of two hundred cowries (seashells that served as money), and Unoka's son, Okonkwo, the protagonist, gets his start as an independent householder by asking a wealthy neighbour for a loan of seed yams with which to expand his farm. Unoka the flute-player's pleasure-seeking ways have won him the goodwill of friends of his own age cohort, whom he can ask for small sums, but that same insouciance means he does not repay them. Okonkwo, by contrast, as serious and industrious as his father is dreamy and idle, is able to turn his renown as a wrestler, a warrior, and especially a worker into financial credit. In addition to borrowing four hundred seed yams from a friend of his father's, Okonkwo borrows twice that amount from Nwakibie, a man of means who decides the young man is worth the investment. The younger man contracts to repay the seed capital by sharecropping: he will give his creditor two-thirds of the resulting harvest.

Debt is something that Achebe can trust African readers to know well. Because many Africans find it so difficult to earn a livelihood, they often have to borrow small sums and, of course, larger ones, such as for children's school fees. But the historical novel reminds us that debt is nothing new. As David Graeber writes, "it cannot be overemphasized that in a small community, everyone normally was both lender and borrower."[8] Such debts bind people together in a web of mutual assistance and dependence.

Unoka's and his son's loans reinforce relations among people already known to one another. In Umuofia there are no strangers and all relations are face to face.[9] Like any Igbo host, Unoka offers a kola nut to Okoye, his guest and creditor, and they courteously dispute who has the right to break it. A conversation follows, much of it in the form of proverbs, about the weather and the crops, the next feast, the news, and music, a mutual passion. Only after the ritual exchange of food and words has reaffirmed the men's relationship to each other can the guest broach the topic of his outstanding debt. When Okonkwo seeks a loan he brings palm wine and a cock to the wealthy Nwakibie, who in turn sends for kola and pepper for his visitor, before a circuitous conversation sets the stage for the request. In other words, both loans are located within the larger exchange of small gifts and respectful rhetoric; in this way, people build relations.

Debt in Umuofia is related to the gift or prestation economy described by Marcel Mauss, according to which gifts always impose obligations of countergifts.[10] Marx defined gifts as inalienable objects exchanged between "transactors who are in a state of reciprocal dependence."[11] Gifts are "inalienable" because the giver is always implicated "in the thing given."[12] Gift exchange is about relations among people, not the things themselves.

The two loans appear, however, to belong to different economies. Okoye's loan to Unoka is an act of friendship based on mutual trust built by the shared activities of friends, in this case, making music together. The loan does not involve interest; Okoye is only asking for the return of his principal, and that only because he is calling on all his friends for their assistance with expenses of his own. He hopes to earn an *ozo* title, a mark of status that requires him to throw a great feast, a celebratory expenditure of resources in which the whole community will participate. Unoka would no doubt be invited to the feast, so the two hundred cowries Okoye asks him to return would come back to him in another form. The logic of Nwakibie's loan to Okonkwo is different. The rich man is in a position to make the loan because he has produced a surplus – that is, more yams than he can use himself – and they are best put to use by lending them to another who has labour to spare. Okonkwo will plant the seed yams he borrows in order to increase production. In the end, the odds are good that there will be more wealth in the world, Okonkwo's labour will increase the capital invested in him by the wealthy man, and both creditor and debtor will gain from the transaction. That is why Nwakibie asks for more than his principal in return: "For debts to be repaid, the objects produced by the use of the capital must thus be worth more than the original amount of the capital itself."[13]

To understand the difference between the two loans, we can turn to Anthony Giddens's important distinction between confidence and trust: when Okoye lent to Unoka he showed confidence, a "more or less taken-for-granted attitude that familiar things will remain the same"; while Nwakibie, who trusts Okonkwo, "presupposes awareness of circumstances of risk."[14] Confidence is needed by the members of an *esusu* savings group, in nearby Yorubaland, who contribute a fixed amount every month to a shared pool and then take turns receiving the entire proceeds, counting on those who have already received their share to continue to contribute. Where people live side by side and rely on one another, such confidence is necessary. Trust, by contrast, involves more than interpersonal relations and constitutes a wager on how situations may develop, including weather conditions and political circumstances like war. Nwakibie's trust in Okonkwo implies the possibility of *dis*trust: he refuses other young men who come to him for seed yams because he believes "they would just dump them in the earth and leave them to be choked by weeds" (22). Experience has taught him to be chary with his yams.

The loans to Unoka and Okonkwo thus appear to belong to different economies, the one a gift economy based on maintaining equilibrium, the other an investment-based economy based on constant growth (the characterization is Godbout's[15]). Okoye's loan to Unoka relies on reputation for enforcement: a debtor can commonly be counted on to repay his debts lest he gain a negative reputation in his community (which Unoka does). A corollary, however, is that Okoye's own reputation rests on his willingness to help out those who need to borrow.[16] Debtor and creditor are both embedded in a network of confidence, status, and mutual dependency. Nwakibie's investment in Okonkwo, on the other hand, rests more on a judgment of character: is Okonkwo worth the risk?

Father and son could be classic character options in game theory, the free rider and the high stakes bidder, as if Achebe's novel were a thought experiment in how to build trust in society, which is indeed what I am arguing it is. The two loans belong to different economies, but from its opening pages, the novel also makes credit a question to which there may be a right answer and to which there is certainly a wrong one. An irony of the novel is that Okoye's confidence in Unoka is misplaced, while Nwakibie's trust in Okonkwo is vindicated. The twinned scenes of collecting a debt and asking for a loan in the first and third chapters of *Things Fall Apart* divide the world into those worthy of credit and those who default and break the circulation of value and confidence. Unoka and Okonkwo form a contrast like that of the grasshopper and the ant in Aesop's fable or like the servants entrusted with talents (coins) in Jesus's parable.

We are told that "Unoka was, of course, a debtor" (4), a term of opprobrium. Unoka is not just a chronic debtor and therefore at the bottom of the status ladder; his debt is deplored as a moral failing. He is a "failure" because he "was poor and his wife and children had barely enough to eat. People laughed at him because he was a loafer" (5). Nietzsche describes the relationship between debtor and creditor as "the oldest and most basic personal relationship that there is": the moment when "individuals first met one another and *measured themselves* against one another."[17] He celebrates the appearance on the historical stage of a new man, one who "promises like a sovereign, with discretion, reluctantly, selectively and cautiously, who is sparing with his trust but confers honour to another by the very fact of trusting, who gives his word as something that can be relied on, because he knows himself to be strong enough to keep it even in the event of disaster, even in the 'face of fate.'"[18] Such a man is Okonkwo. The Nietzschean "sovereign individual" has "become *reliable*, *disciplined*, *predictable*, even for himself and his own conception of himself, so that, like a man making a promise, he could warrant himself for the future."[19] Such a man can have nothing but contempt for Unoka and "the annoying little pests who make promises when they have no business doing so, and his rod is ready for the liar who breaks his word the very moment he utters it."[20]

THE ACHIEVEMENT-BASED SOCIETY

Precolonial Igboland knew both confidence and trust, equilibrium and risk. And it knew both men who failed to repay their debts and men who succeeded in accumulating wealth. The village group of Umuofia is what Kent Flannery and Joyce Marcus in *The Creation of Inequality* would call an "achievement-based society," one in which social inequality is not inherited from previous generations but reflects personal merit and efforts,[21] or, as Achebe puts it, "where age was respected … but achievement was revered" (8). The narration in *Things Fall Apart* is aware that elsewhere a man might be judged by his lineage, but "fortunately, among these people a man was judged according to his worth and not according to the worth of his father" (8). Okonkwo, who starts with nothing, earns a position as one of the richest and most respected men in Umuofia, wealth and respect being largely synonymous. Okonkwo's success "was not luck" (27). Contrary to what jealous neighbours repeat, his palm kernels have not been cracked for him by benevolent spirits: "He had cracked them himself" (27).

Achievement-based societies "were remarkably stable societies, made up of descent groups that exchanged brides and gifts, honored their ancestors, considered everyone equal at birth, yet threw their support behind gifted kinsmen who sought to achieve renown."[22] They rewarded personal merit and hard work and blocked the inheritance of privilege that would install inequality on a permanent basis from generation to generation. A man who works becomes wealthy, a man who does not remains poor. It is not the case that those higher in status enjoy leisure while the work is done by those below them. At the start of the twentieth century, "village societies with achievement-based leadership were among the most common in the world."[23] They were never, however, the subjects of novels or written histories, so they do not loom as large in the world view of readers of books as their ubiquity would warrant.

In discussing Tutuola's *Palm-Wine Drinkard*, Simon Gikandi argues that, because the eponymous narrator schemes to be "richer than the rest of the people in the town," he is "a consummate capitalist" and not the embodiment of a traditional world view that he is commonly taken to be.[24] This is part of a larger argument Gikandi makes – that there is no pure tradition in African literature, and the project of creating an African literature is modern in inspiration – an argument that clearly resonates with mine. Nevertheless, Gikandi makes too sharp a distinction between tradition and modernity and is too ready to assume he can always recognize modernity when he sees it. Southern Nigeria in 1900 did not have the institutions associated with capitalism in Europe, especially the gold standard, fixed systems of counting, and regulatory and security frameworks overseen by a state,[25] but people did honour wealth and had systems in place whereby the wealthy could invest their wealth and profit from the labour of others.[26] Toyin Falola, writing about the Yoruba of the nineteenth century, long before Tutuola was born, explains that the "*olówó* (rich person) was contrasted with the *olòsì* (the poor) in material and derogatory terms. The *olòsì* had no power, little or no influence, and was expected to rely on the *olówó* for support."[27] The poor man often needed to "approach a lender for credit, in less than generous terms."[28] Karin Barber writes that "in the oral and written Yorùbá texts with which I am familiar, the image of money recurs constantly," and "what is most striking is the predominantly *positive* valuation placed on it."[29] "Money, the market, buying and selling, credit arrangements, interest and profit form a complex of metaphors by which the social and spiritual worlds are envisaged," and this is true even "in texts that are clearly of nineteenth-century provenance."[30] Money "is conceived of as constitutive of individual self-realization. It is the medium in which human potential becomes fulfilled. Energized by money, people can expand and fully occupy the space that they have chosen as their destiny."[31] Indeed, "people are constituted as members of a shared humanity by money, for everyone from the poorest to the richest, participates in its circulation."[32]

In *Things Fall Apart*, as a man proceeds through life and approaches the ultimate goal of ancestorhood, he increases his status by acquiring *ozo* titles, of which there are four in Umuofia. The worthless Unoka has not taken even the first title, a requisite for manhood; Okoye intends to take the third (6); Okonkwo's great ambition is to acquire the fourth (131), a rare achievement that would make him one of the "lords of the land" (123). Titles in Igboland constituted "steps up the ladder of conversion of money"[33]: an *ozo* title "corresponded exactly to the level of money spent to achieve it."[34] Igbo titles "were quantified in money and associated with competitive acquisitiveness. And yet they were so deeply spiritually meaningful and religiously sanctioned that continual conversions upward were intensely motivating to personal accumulation of monetary wealth, as evidenced in an unusually highly developed system of saving."[35]

In Achebe's later novel *Arrow of God*,[36] set in 1922, twenty or so years after the end of *Things Fall Apart*,[37] and in the same region though not the same village group, the highest title that a man can acquire is "Eru," after the god of wealth, the most popular of the gods (15), whose praise name is "the Magnificent, the One that gives wealth to those who find favour with him" (9). When Eru "likes a man wealth flows like a river into his house; his yams grow as big as human beings, his goats produce threes and his hens hatch nines" (9). Nwaka, one of only three men who have taken the Eru title, has a great Mask in which he dances on special occasions: "The Mask was called Ogalanya or Man of Riches, and at every Idemili festival crowds of people from all the villages and their neighbours came to the *ilo* of Umunneora to see this great Mask bedecked with mirrors and rich cloths of many colours" (39).

In Africa in general, still at the time of Achebe's writing, wealth was not a function of ownership of land, which was abundant on a still underpopulated continent,[38] but rather of the number of dependents a man had: his wives, children, clients, and pawn slaves. As an elder puts it in a prayer to the gods, "We do not ask for wealth because he that has health and children will also have wealth" (165). Wealth in yams can be converted into money, which can bring in more people in the form of wives and therefore children, sharecroppers, or pawn slaves, or it can be converted into titles. As Guyer writes, "wealth lay in followers, alliances, the breadth and prominence of one's social networks, all of which had to be cultivated by spending money. So status for the wealthy derived from the capacity to deal with needs, which derived from claims on goods, which in turn derived from money."[39] What Barber writes of nineteenth-century Yorubaland also applies to Igboland: "People and money were inseparable. The components that made up *ọlá*, the ultimate status aspired to by a big man or woman, were multiple. However, in all texts, their bedrock is the twinned pair: people and money ... Incantations, invocations, divination texts and *oríkì* all solicit the powers that be for *owó àti ọmọ* (money and children)."[40]

Marshall Sahlins explains about economies based on domestic production that once men of means have used their control over dependents to accumulate power over products and means of production, "then, usually the best move, as well as the most coveted right of property, is to give the stuff away."[41] Feasts so large that few guests will ever be able to reciprocate redound to the giver's honour: "Deploying his resources carefully, the emerging leader uses wealth to place others in his debt. Moving beyond his household, he constructs a following whose production may be harnassed [*sic*] to his ambition. The process of intensification in production is thus coupled to reciprocity in exchange."[42]

In Umuofia the feasts thrown in the process of earning titles ensure that wealth circulates and is not hoarded. Georges Bataille notes of gift-giving economies that "social rank is linked to the possession of a fortune, but only on the condition that the fortune be partially sacrificed in unproductive social expenditures such as festivals, spectacles, and games."[43] In Umuofia those who give have more status than those who receive, and their giving reinforces that status. As Jacques Godbout writes, "the gift between equals gives rise to equality, the gift between those who are unequal gives rise to inequality."[44]

The emphasis on accumulation in precolonial Umuofia was not the same as in modern capitalism. It was neither endless nor an end in itself. Money "was a medium for a relational life rather than a goal as a store of wealth."[45] According to Patrick Chabal, "in African pre-colonial modes of production, accumulation was the foundation of power rather than the means to further accumulation."[46] Accumulation establishes rank and status in the community; rather than being "an individual economic agent," a man is defined by the place he earns in the political economy.[47]

Donald Wehrs regards Unoka, the lazy man who treats loans as free gifts, as living proof of an "increasing coarsening and rigidity in Igbo life." He attributes this to the slave trade in previous centuries.[48] We do not, however, need this explanation. The achievement society in *Things Fall Apart* is not the corruption of some earlier ideal society but itself constitutes Igbo tradition in the two senses of preceding colonialism and constituting a coherent and viable world. That is not to say that slavery has not left a mark; it has, as we shall discuss in Chapter 3. But Flannery and Marcus show that agricultural societies that put a premium on the achievements of Big Men[49] presume the existence of a roughly equal percentage of "rubbish men."[50] The chronic debtor such as Unoka was an inevitable corollary of the achievement society. As Guyer writes, in Equatorial Africa, "valued work was a means of endorsing personhood, validating a dimension of reality, singularizing the producer," but where a person can realize himself by developing his potential, it is always also possible that "a human being could fail to be a person."[51] At the bottom of ranked society among the Beti of Cameroon "was the *zeze mot*, the empty person, one-dimensional man, a nobody who authored nothing."[52] Sahlins argues that the domestic mode of production tends to polarize people's relations to the productive process, "grouping on one side the big-men or would-be big-men and their followers, whose production they are able to galvanize, and on the other side those content to praise and live off the ambition of others."[53] There will always be "those who bring in wealth and those who scatter it," explains an elder in *Arrow of God* (123–4).

When Unoka goes to consult the oracle Agbala as to the reason he fails to prosper even though he makes the proper sacrifices, the priestess rebukes him: he has done nothing to offend the gods or the ancestors, she tells him, but is incorrigibly lazy. She orders him to "go home and work like a man" (18). But Unoka is also an "ill-fated man"; he has "a bad *chi* or personal god" (18). That is the Igbo explanation. The Yoruba of the time would have said that he suffers from àgbàná, a magic force that, as Falola explains, turns money against a person. Àgbàná was typically inflicted by an enemy and needed to be guarded against by rituals, but àgbàná was also related to moral character, especially "the weakness of the person in lavishing money on women and entertainment."[54] External forces and internal character were inseparable: "the unseen forces of àgbàná ... prevented the individual from being rational and prudent."[55] In other words, forces inside *and* outside a man conspired to make a man poor or collaborated to make him rich.

Unoka meets the fate appropriate to a chronic debtor: instead of becoming an ancestor, he dies of a swelling considered an abomination and is cast into the Evil Forest, his spirit doomed to wander, reduced to less than a person. What Jonathan Parry writes about gifts also applies to debts: a man's failure to return a gift "would destroy the source of his own productiveness and vitality, and [he] would therefore succumb to witchcraft or otherwise sicken and die": "for one who defaults on his exchanges will cease to be an acceptable partner, and will be excluded from this apparently magical source of growth and productivity."[56] Among the Yoruba at least, "when an habitual debtor or one for whose debts his relatives would not make themselves responsible died, his body was placed on a stretcher and left in the bush so that any of his creditors could be directed to it should the need arise."[57]

Things Fall Apart itself, however, expresses an ambivalence with regard to Unoka. Although people "swore never to lend him any more money," the profligate's charm, inseparable from his flute-playing, his good humour, and his love of good fellowship, is such "that he always succeeded in borrowing more" (5). His fondness for storytelling as well as his flute-playing, when his face would beam "with blessedness and peace" (4), ally him with the novel's authorial consciousness. In what is surely a figure for the novelist's own art, Unoka manifests a sensibility that allows him to

> hear in his mind's ear the blood-stirring and intricate rhythms of the *ekwe* and the *udu* and the *ogene*, and he could hear his own flute weaving in and out of them, decorating them with a colourful and plaintive tune. The total effect was gay and brisk, but if one picked out the flute as it went up and down and then broke up into short snatches, one saw that there was sorrow and grief there. (6)

Unoka even shares some of Achebe's personal memories: his delight in "the first kites that returned with the dry season, and the children who sang songs of welcome to them," prompts him to "remember his own childhood, how he had often wandered around looking for a kite sailing leisurely against the blue sky" (5).

Unoka travels to other village groups with his band, sometimes staying three or four months, and in another novel his music would be rewarded with a living. Guyer writes that in Equatorial Africa, wealth did not just mean material accumulation through exploitation and differential status; "the 'assets,' the pools of wealth, in such systems were ultimately the extraordinary people – the named heroes, the virtuoso performers and craftsmen, the most deeply concentrated of the spiritual adepts – whose self-realization careers skipped around the value register and then moved beyond its range into the domain of total singularity that, when it applies to people rather than goods, one could term charisma."[58] If gifted charismatic individuals are considered pools of wealth, then Unoka no less than Okonkwo might qualify.

The early realist Nigerian novels, however, those that set out to win credit for their characters (as, I argue, Achebe asks credit for Okonkwo), remain suspicious of the man who does not produce his own food. In Elechi Amadi's 1978 novel *The Slave*, set in the precolonial Niger Delta, a master wood carver, known for his wit and his ability to take pleasure, does not ask for money for his sculptures:

> Indeed he felt shy about asking for money. Why, he asked, should anyone earn money carving funny figures in wood? He had a farm and could support himself. It should never be said that he had to depend on carving to eat. It was, he thought, like living on the generosity of the public. Masquerades were fun, not serious affairs. Only a trickster would make money out of a thing like that.[59]

Dance groups ply the mask-maker with money and gifts, which he considers "money dropping from the sky,"[60] but despite his own experience, he wants to earn his living by the sweat of his brow, and he thinks of artists, whose images and words remake the world, as tricksters and of tricksters as characters to be condemned.

When Okoye asks for the return of his two hundred cowries, Unoka laughs and points at chalk marks on his wall, which represent his debts to several others: Okoye will have to get in line. Even small debts when not repaid can spoil friendship, and when Unoka mocks his creditor for expecting the return of his loan, he is putting at risk more than their friendship: the novel suggests that the productivity and vitality of the community and the world at large are involved. The wastrel who cares nothing for titles or status, whether his own or that of others, who refuses work and lives for the day, also consumes wealth: "if any money came his way," Unoka "bought gourds of palm wine, called round his neighbours and made merry" (4). Okoye hopes to earn a title by throwing a feast, while Unoka, through his consumption, dissipates energies rather than fostering them. Bataille writes that "only relative austerity and the absence of dissipation," such as are practised by Nwakibie and Okonkwo, "allow for the growth of the energy systems that living beings or societies constitute."[61]

INVENTING A FICTIONAL CHARACTER

Things Fall Apart centres on a moral judgment of character: Unoka deserves his failure, Okonkwo earns his success. Okonkwo, however, is a tragic hero whose rise to the status of one of the leading men of

Umuofia is followed by a fall. When in the second half of the novel the newly arrived Christian missionaries convert many, including his own son, dividing the community along religious lines, Okonkwo feels that his entire world and the place he had worked so hard to earn in it have collapsed. His entreaty to his fellow titled men to resist the colonizers fails because doing so would entail a war against fellow members of Umuofia. Faced with this failure, Okonkwo commits suicide. At the end of the novel, the British District Commissioner is led to the hanging body of Okonkwo and avers that the suicide's story would make an interesting anecdote in his ethnographic memoir, to be titled *The Pacification of the Primitive Tribes of the Lower Niger*. The colonial officer judges that Okonkwo's story will fill "perhaps not a whole chapter but a reasonable paragraph, at any rate" (209). Readers who have just read an entire novel about Okonkwo and felt the tragic force of his death appreciate the ironic disproportion here. The District Commissioner will reduce Africans to background and to illustrations of culture. Achebe, by contrast, insists that Okonkwo has a story of his own, just as all heroes of novels do.

Achebe conceived the character of Okonkwo in response to the depiction of Africans in a 1906 ethnographic memoir, *The Lower Niger and Its Tribes* by Major Arthur Glyn Leonard, a former District Commissioner in Igboland.[62] In his ethnography Leonard discusses several suicides, each in a single paragraph. One "distinctly luminous occurrence" is offered as proof of "the sensitive and phenomenally impulsive nature of these natural people,"[63] in this case, the Ijo (or Ijaw). The Ijo, according to Leonard, are a "very excitable, passionate, and quarrelsome race, not only with strangers, but among themselves," and would "commit self-murder on the slightest provocation, even when they have been only abused or chaffed."[64] Among the neighbouring Ibo, however, Leonard says, suicide is rarer and looked upon with "manifest deprecation and horror"[65] as God's retribution against "those people who are not at peace with themselves or their neighbours and who, maintaining a persistent attitude of evil, avail themselves of every opportunity by which they can commit an offense against the land and their fellow-men."[66] We must imagine that this is what Achebe's fictional District Commissioner will write about Okonkwo.

Leonard's inability or refusal to recognize a mind or a reason in the suicides that he encountered in southeastern Nigeria is of a piece with the British refusal to recognize African political sovereignty: the question of textual representation is also one of political representation. Achebe clearly felt it was a grievous misrepresentation for Leonard to suggest that the colonized had no motivation for despair. To correct this representation was a two-pronged task. Achebe needed to show, on the one hand, that the psychology of an Igbo suicide was explicable in terms that readers of novels everywhere would understand[67] – that is where trust comes in – and on the other hand, that the District Commissioner's was not the neutral account of an outside observer, however blinkered. Indeed, his very presence was responsible for the suicide that in his understanding appeared causeless. Achebe determined to show how an Igbo at the time might feel that the future had been closed – how colonialism itself could provoke suicidal despair.

Leonard in his book reduced tragic deaths to single paragraphs; Achebe, in effect, took one of those paragraphs and expanded it into a novel. To do this the aspiring author had to create an Igbo – not Igbos in general, but a particular man, a man, however, credible as an Igbo man – who commits suicide not on a whim or because of moral weakness, but as the result of the interplay of psychology and social context. The question Achebe faced was this: Given the character's drastic reaction to colonialism, what sort of disposition must he have had? In other words, he had to create a realistic character whose despair is understandable as the product of a personality forged over a lifetime. To win the credit of readers, he would have to make Okonkwo comprehensible in terms of psychology *and* history.

Leonard implies a disproportion in the African character: the Ijo commit suicide when "only abused or chaffed"; the Ibo suicide is motivated by "a persistent attitude of evil." Achebe needed to create a character and a world that observed the proportions approved by the conventions of verisimilitude: motivation must balance deed, individual must balance society, cause must balance effect. Where Leonard assumed that the Igbo suicide merely acts out his nature (or his culture, just as unchanging), Achebe's task is to show that the man who takes his own life proves thereby that he has a sovereign will. A character in a novel cannot commit suicide in an isolated fit of madness or as the result of a debilitating mental illness distinct from his personality. A fictional suicide is not random or unmotivated; rather, it is the ultimate existential act. The fictional character who commits suicide exercises the sovereign right, like Hamlet, to decide between life and death. Achebe's claim that Okonkwo be recognized as a sovereign individual is also a claim for the political sovereignty of Africans.

Okonkwo, more of an individual than Leonard's suicides, is also more typical. Not typical in the sense of average, for most Igbos did not commit suicide, but typical in the sense of fitting in a series: the novel records the case of a farmer who hanged himself when he lost his harvest to the rains (24), and Uchendu, Okonkwo's maternal uncle, declares that he might have hanged himself after he had buried six wives and twenty-two children (though he did not) (135). Okonkwo's own death is also typical in the sense of marking an important point in the line of variation that can be traced among Igbo reactions to colonization. As shown by Émile Durkheim, the father of sociology and author of *On Suicide*, suicide rates follow general rules and reveal the state of society. Suicides are more prevalent in times of crisis when accepted restraints are removed. The man who is the most personally invested in society's forms of reward and restraint will also feel the most loss and personal emptiness when these are cast aside.

Okonkwo is a fictional character intended to correct a lie that appeared in a non-fictional ethnographic memoir. Non-fiction can lie; fiction does not make the same truth-claims. Achebe's novel pretends that the name Okonkwo refers to an embodied individual, the man "well-known throughout the nine villages and even beyond" (3). His adopted son Ikemefuna, the tale states, is one "whose sad story is still told in Umuofia unto this day" (12). The name Okonkwo is credible as that of an actual person. It is not a name like Tortoise, the trickster hero of Igbo animal fables, whose name points both to his species and to a permanent character role he plays from story to story. Yet readers of novels also understand or must learn that there was no Okonkwo and no Ikemefuna, just as there is no Umuofia: these exist only in the pages of the novel. Novel readers must learn that "the human referent of the text was a generalization about and not an extratextual, embodied instance of a 'species.'"[68] Thus can the novel "be judged generally true even though all its particulars are merely imaginary."[69]

The name Okonkwo, which means "born on Nkwo," one of the four days of the Igbo market week, is as ordinary as Smith or Brown, the names of the English missionaries in Achebe's novel. So, too, Okoye and Nwoye were born on Oye. There is also a character called Okafo, born on Afo (50), and not one but two called Okeke, born on Eke (159, 189). The fact that these names may be carried by actual people ironically signals that they do not refer to individuals outside the novel but to fictional entities.[70] The one character that the novel does not deign to name but refers to only by his role, the District Commissioner, is also the one character based on a person who actually lived. Just as Leonard's memoir left the Ibo suicide unnamed, Achebe's novel reduces the real colonial officer to an absolute type.

Mary Poovey writes that over the course of the eighteenth century the European novel developed a "*problematic of representation*" that relied upon "recognizable and socially agreed-on criteria by which to judge fictional probability."[71] These "allowed one to evaluate the features internal to a text" without having to ask about "the relationship between the text and the ground of its referential system."[72] Achebe's readers, too, must recognize that Okonkwo did not exist but that he nonetheless tells us about Igbos who did. Among the protocols of verisimilitude that Achebe marshals in creating Okonkwo is what is now called the Theory of Mind, that is, the understanding that the behaviour of others reveals their internal motivations. The two debtors, Unoka and Okonkwo, belong to two different forms of narrative. Unoka remains a type in the sense of a flat character. Although his debts bind him in a web of relations with his neighbours, those relations have no effect on his character, which remains ever the same. Okonkwo is as consistent as his father, but with a difference: his character is not primordial but rather is willed in response to external stimuli. Okonkwo did not inherit his character or a propensity to suicide. The course of his life was not set from birth but was the result of a painful experience in childhood: the moment when he became aware of the contempt in which his father was held as a chronic debtor. Shame for his father motivates Okonkwo's obsession with strength. His masculinity is compensation for his father's perceived feminine traits, his industry for Unoka's laziness, his strict discipline of himself and his family for Unoka's dissipation. Okonkwo is the man who threw Amalinze the Cat in a wrestling contest and a warrior who brought home human heads, but he is defined not so much by an *agon* or physical struggle with another as by a struggle within. His character is generated by the contrast with his father: Unoka is a type, and single; Okonkwo is a reaction against a flat type, and therefore internally doubled. He always includes both Unoka and something else. And the original division, willing himself not to be his father, inevitably results in further divisions, as Okonkwo is forever haunted by the fear that he is like his father after all and later by guilt when his single-mindedness drives him to participate in the killing of the boy Ikemefuna.

Nancy Armstrong writes that to "create an individual ... still requires the novel to offer an interiority in excess of the social position that individual is supposed to occupy."[73] Okonkwo wears the mask of the strong man afraid of nothing but wants the mask to become his face and is afraid the mask will drop and reveal that it is not. Okonkwo never exists in the present moment the way Unoka does: shaped by the past, he faces the future that exists for him as a project: to make it as different from the past as possible. Okonkwo's character is predicated on growth, in wealth, respect, and status, as well as in distance from the past, and

Nwakibie judges him therefore a worthy credit risk. Readers must also judge him, both in terms of how effectively he responds to his circumstances and on moral grounds. Okonkwo can have a novel written about him, but no novel could be written about Unoka (though, as we shall see, Tutuola's Palm-Wine Drinkard, as the anti-hero of an anti-novel, shares some important qualities with Unoka).

Armstrong states baldly that in order to qualify as the protagonist of a novel, a character has "to harbor an acute dissatisfaction with his or her assigned position in the social world and feel compelled to find a better one."[74] Unoka does not need anything, but Okonkwo feels a lack that he must fill. Realist novels focus on individuals at once ordinary and unique, the same as everyone else in having desires particular to themselves. The protagonist of a novel, says Armstrong, "does not become an individual on the basis of what and how intensely he or she desires; individuality depends on how he or she chooses to displace what is a fundamentally asocial desire onto a socially appropriate object."[75] Okonkwo's need to prove his worth puts him in opposition to his father, but his excessive, inconvenient desire is directed toward becoming one of "the lords of the land" (110), a socially approved goal. Because he first rejects and resists inherited limits, his adherence to approved social values comes from within.

I am not discussing here Okonkwo's psychology as such, but his construction as a character. The nature of the judgment that readers must render on Okonkwo and Unoka at the start of *Things Fall Apart*, which demands that we credit the son and condemn the father on moral grounds, is the very dichotomy that is at the heart of Okonkwo's own self-definition. The qualities that make him deserving of Nwakibie's trust result from his rejection of his father. What I have been calling the realism of the character is inseparable from his creditworthiness. Nwakibie's loan to Okonkwo is a judgment of the latter's moral character, which is a function of something inherent in him and independent of his relations to others (indeed, he puts a distance between himself and other young men of his age, whom he characterizes as "afraid of hard work" [21]). Okonkwo has inner potential, which Nwakibie recognizes and which the extension of credit is intended to realize.

If we can derive Okonkwo's (interior) motivations from his (exterior) actions, it is because his motivations were originally inspired by his (exterior) context. Because he is himself inserted into time, determined as he is by the past and resolved to control his future, his personal story can resonate with history, the unfolding of larger events, especially the cataclysmic event of colonization. This resonance between personal lifetime and social history is fundamental to a realist character. In realism the development of character is set against a social background also undergoing change, and each can be read in terms of the other.[76] Okonkwo is a type in Georg Lukács's sense of the word: a character who, complete within himself, lives and acts "within a concrete, complexly stratified social reality and it is always the totality of the social process that is linked with the totality of the character."[77]

DEBT AND THE NOVEL

As we have seen, the self-made man was not new in the achievement society of Igboland in 1900, but Okonkwo the fictional character *was* something new in 1958. Precolonial Igboland combined both reciprocal exchange, based on the circulation of gifts, and investment for growth. It also knew both successes like Okonkwo and chronic failures like Unoka. But Achebe's novel correlates the two halves of the economic systems, the one based on reciprocity, the other on investment, with a judgment of moral character. The marked contrast between the debtor who defaults and the one who repays is a sign that the novel emphasizes the second form of economy. The first economy, the one based on reciprocity and equilibrium, appears frail because associated with Unoka. The second, based on investment and risk, appears validated because associated with Okonkwo.

Achebe's emphasis on trust rather than confidence, on investment rather than reciprocity, and on risk rather than equilibrium coincides with the interests of the novel as a genre as it developed in England and France in the eighteenth century. Craig Muldew reports of debts in Early Modern Europe, before the rise of centralized states or the novel genre, that "credit was sociality – an essential part of the network of bonds that held families and communities together. To be alive was thus to be in debt."[78] However, Elaine Lewinnek writes, starting in the late eighteenth century, "as older ideas of honor mixed with the burgeoning market economy and the newer surveillance systems of credit-rating agencies, the 'self-made man' faced the terror of becoming his own opposite: the 'failure,' the bankrupt, the loser."[79] According to Mary Poovey, in England over the course of the nineteenth century debt was transformed "from the ubiquitous feature of everyday life that it was in the period from the sixteenth through the middle of the eighteenth into a personal failing, which could – at least in theory – be avoided."[80] Unoka joins debtor fathers like Mr Tulliver in George Eliot's *The Mill on the Floss* or Dickens's Mr Dorrit, a prisoner in the Marshalsea Debtors' Prison, whose children, like Okonkwo, become painfully aware of their fathers' fiscal and even moral irresponsibility.

The novel as a genre developed in Europe in the early eighteenth century alongside the modern state and the capitalist economy, and, like the state and the new economy, it relied on credit. Poovey argues that the first novels in England, by creating characters in the sense of fictional personages who had never existed and showing them negotiating a world that bore an explicit relation to the world that readers lived in, encouraged readers to have trust not just in particular characters in the sense of moral types but in the entire system of laws and norms that characterized the new liberal governmentality of parliamentary democracy and the new world of investment capital. This trust that strangers would behave in predictable ways because they had absorbed the rules of a common world was necessary because modern states were so large that members perforce remained strangers to one another and the collective that they shared could therefore never be viewed whole and had to be "imagined," in Benedict Anderson's sense of the term. One did not need to know all one's fellow citizens personally in order to judge that the world one shared with them followed established parameters that made it possible to predict how strangers should behave and to judge them accordingly. Poovey describes Daniel Defoe's literary project at the beginning of the English novel tradition thus:

> Experimenting with print's ability to generate and sustain belief, Defoe helped cultivate in readers the mental habits they needed to negotiate the credit economy. At the same time, and without fully articulating the modern category of fiction, he also explored the possibility that print could generate belief in events and characters that had never existed but that were, nonetheless, valid.[81]

Poovey writes that authors like Defoe and Samuel Richardson created the "distinctive realm of fiction, in which writers and readers might explore uncomfortable cultural anxieties without suffering their consequences. Through the medium of fiction, a writer might teach a reader to believe once more in possibilities that could not be proved; in so doing, a writer could encourage readers to accept the deferral that was essential to credit, both private and public, without feeling imperiled by risk."[82]

Credit is a prominent theme whenever the novel develops in new circumstances. Benjamin Franklin's autobiography, written like *Things Fall Apart* on the eve of his nation's independence and self-consciously at the beginning of a new literary tradition,[83] is obsessed with the starter loans that enable the self-made man's career. Throughout Franklin is careful to record how much he owes to whom and judges other people by whether or not they repay their debts to him. Jennifer Baker writes: "Indebtedness provides the means for his own self-determination, and he uses this model, in turn, to solicit the reader's faith in the nation's own rise."[84] By contrast, to the north, in British North America on the eve of Confederation, Susannah Moodie's memoir *Roughing It in the Bush* (1852) records the overwhelming burden of debt that new immigrants to Upper Canada from England laboured under and decries the terrible habit of the Moodies' improvident neighbours, newcomers from the United States, of never returning what they have borrowed. Moodie could be talking of Unoka when she complains that her Yankee neighbours cheerily claim her property as a loan that they have no intention of returning: "This method of living upon their neighbours is a most convenient one to unprincipled people, as it does not involve the penalty of stealing; and they can keep the goods without the unpleasant necessity of returning them."[85] Moodie does not have Franklin's trust in the credit of the new nation. The title of Premchand's *Gift of a Cow* (1936), at the beginnings of Hindi fiction, refers to a debt of two hundred rupees a peasant incurs to acquire a milch cow. The landowners and dignitaries in the district are money-lenders who exploit the dependence and the illiteracy of peasants to charge exorbitant interest and cheat them. A son who has been to the town of Lucknow, however, returns with knowledge of modern ways of regularizing and taming debt and of the potential of courts and the threat of lawsuits to protect peasant debtors. Sam Selvon's *The Lonely Londoners*, at the origins of Black British literature in the 1950s, makes a distinction between West Indian immigrant men, forever on the move through London, who survive by hitting one another up for money, and the older Jamaican woman, Tanty Bessy, who makes herself a home in the metropole by compelling the local grocer to extend credit to his new customers.

When I say that credit is the major theme at the beginning of every new national tradition of prose fiction, I do not mean that African literature had to go through the same stages of development as all other literatures in order to arrive at the same terminus. The historical conditions are utterly different, and so are the novels and memoirs. I do mean that debt as a theme and realism as a mode appeal as solutions to questions of imagining how people relate to one another posed wherever there are new nation-states (or, as in Selvon, new groups of citizens). Europe, America, India, and Africa have faced similar questions about the modern state, albeit at different times. They have also worked out different solutions. African writers had to create a form, an audience, and a model for what the novel should be – and what they created could never be the same as had been created in Europe and America because conditions differed radically.

Things Fall Apart differs in at least one all-important way from the European and North American texts I have compared it to because it is a historical novel set in a precolonial village and not a modern credit economy. The debts that are the focus of attention at the beginning of *Things Fall Apart* differ from the debts in, say, Defoe or Franklin because they involve people from a single village group already closely related to one another. As a realist fictional character living around 1900 who is *not* a citizen of a modern state or even a colonial subject, Okonkwo is an almost complete anomaly. Few are the novels before Achebe anywhere in the world where none of the characters is a citizen of a state or a colonial subject.[86] Okonkwo lives in a world of subsistence farmers, and to associate him with characters in bourgeois novels as I have done risks absurdity. My justification is that, while Okonkwo is not a citizen of a modern state, Achebe will soon be, and he invents a realist character to test ideas of trust and moral judgment and to teach readers how to read fictional characters.

2

Reciprocity

The previous chapter established the contradiction in Okonkwo, at once a self-made man such as Umuofia has always valued and a new kind of realist character. I expressed the contradiction by saying that Okonkwo the self-made man was not new in the achievement society of Igboland in 1900, but Okonkwo the fictional character *was* something new in 1958. The contradiction arises because Achebe wants to honour precolonial Igboland, whose achievement society he admires as an alternative to the modern state, but also wants to satisfy his fellow citizens' need for a legible and trustworthy world. The realist novel implies the rule of law, a moral standard with which to judge debtors, and an objective system whereby other people can be credited but also judged. Achievement societies like Umuofia, however, were not governed by the rule of law, which treated all alike, but by personal relations that people forged with one another according to principles of reciprocity.

Jacques Godbout writes that "the system of the gift is not first and foremost an economic system but the social system concerned with personal relationships."[1] Relations among people in *Things Fall Apart* are determined by the principles outlined by Mauss: the receiver of a gift must respond with a countergift. A corollary, however, is that the receiver of a blow must respond with a counterblow. At the centre of social and political organization in Umuofia are two reciprocal exchanges between villages or village groups: bride price and blood price, that is, the exchange of women in marriage and the compensation demanded for a violent death.

Marriage requires that a suitor make a gift to the family of the bride. In keeping with terminology common at the time, the novel calls this gift "bride-price"; however, modern anthropology prefers the term "bridewealth" to make clear that this is not a market transaction but represents the circulation of wealth and, at least in principle, an acknowledgment by the man's family of the obligation to supply a wife in return. Not just any buyer can pay the price and receive the bride; nor does the bride go to the highest bidder; the most important thing is that the families involved embark upon a long-term relationship. Graeber is overstating the case but getting at an essential truth when he writes that "the underlying logic of bridewealth everywhere" is that

> the suitor presenting bridewealth is never paying for a woman, or even for the rights to claim her children. That would imply that brass rods, or whale's teeth, cowrie shells, or even cattle are somehow the equivalent of a human being, which by the logic of a human economy is obviously absurd. Only a human could ever be considered equivalent to another human. All the more so since, in the case of marriage, we are speaking of something even more valuable than one human life: we are speaking of a human life that also has the capacity to generate new lives.[2]

The exchange of brides, like the exchange of gifts more generally, looks forward rather than back: young men pay a "bride price" to the bride's father not to clear a debt once and for all but in acknowledgment of the ongoing relation between the two families *and* as a gage of the suitor's family's obligation to supply a wife in return. My reader will immediately note that reciprocity is between men and between families and that women are the exchanged.

The negotiations around the exchange of a bride take up two chapters in *Things Fall Apart*, three if one includes the case of the man whose wife left him and who wants the bride price returned to him. At the *uri* ceremony of Obierika's daughter Akueke, the oldest man in her suitor's family acknowledges the long-term pattern of reciprocal exchange of gifts and women:

> "It will be good for you and it will be good for us."
>
> *"Ee-e-e!"*
>
> "This is not the first time my people have come to marry your daughter. My mother was one of you."
>
> *"Ee-e-e!"*
>
> "And this will not be the last, because you understand us and we understand you. You are a great family." (117)

Exchanges, be they of gifts, brides, or injuries, always involve delay. When families exchange brides, one family must often wait for a son or a daughter in the other family to be old enough to be married for the exchange to be completed. Amadi's novel *The Concubine* revolves around the fact that two young people have been promised in marriage to each other from birth by their fathers, who want to solidify their own relations. The deferral of the countergift is the reason that money in the form of bridewealth is necessary: to represent the debt owed. The mediation of money facilitates exchange across time, where the relation is P – M – P' (where P stands for person and M for money). For a time one family has a bride and another awaits one. The deferral creates a debt. The debt creates inequality.

Meek writes of the Igbo that "failure to repay a debt was one of the commonest causes of fighting between two kinship or two local groups."[3] Delays mean imbalance, which involves risk, but on such risk is community built. Sahlins explains that "unequal benefit sustains the alliance as perfect balance could not," for equal and complete exchange "cancels debts and thus opens the possibility of contracting out": "If neither side is 'owing' then the bond between them is comparatively fragile."[4] Chuma Nwokolo has a character observe that if you offer a guest premium palm wine you must not accept inferior snuff from him, for then he will consider his debt acquitted and he will not feel obligated to offer you anything when you pay him a visit.[5] The immediate return of a gift "amounts to a refusal of the gift, with benefits and counter-benefits reduced to a simple transposition or exchange – to a barter."[6] A debt is a commitment to the prolongation of the self that has made a promise; the extension of a relation between people to their future selves and sometimes even future generations; and a wager on the possibilities contained in the unfolding future. But as time elapses, a debt can also become a chain around one's neck and a curse.

The deferral of reciprocity inevitably gives money a greater role than mere mediation would suggest. In Umuofia, bridewealth must be negotiated, but it is done in the spirit of reciprocal balance; the goal is precisely to avoid a quarrel. As Obierika tells his daughter's suitors, "marriage should be a play and not a fight" (73). Obierika asks for thirty bags of cowries for his daughter, her suitors offer fifteen, they settle on twenty. The bride price does, however, reflect the relative social worth of the relations between families. In other places, such as Abame, families "haggle and bargain as if they were buying a goat or a cow in the market" (73). In a neighbouring town, or so rumour in Umuofia has it, people take the priceless nature of human beings to a logical conclusion: "In Umunso they do not bargain at all, not even with broomsticks. The suitor just goes on bringing bags of cowries until his in-laws tell him to stop. It is a bad custom because it always leads to a quarrel" (74). In such cases, bride *price* seems like the appropriate term after all. Young and beautiful daughters from good families command higher bride prices. There is obvious potential for both honour and insult here. A common form of abuse is to tell someone how small a bride price was offered for his mother.[7]

In 1913 in the Gold Coast, a character in Obeng's *Eighteenpence* has paid a bride price (called a "dowry") of thirty pounds.[8] By the time of Nwapa's *Efuru*, set during the 1940s, average bride prices have risen to one hundred pounds in cash.[9] About the same time, Jagua Nana's bride price in Cyprian Ekwensi's eponymous novel was one hundred twenty pounds.[10] Bride wealth is a function of the status of the groom as well as the bride. In Achebe's *No Longer at Ease*, set in 1956, on the eve of Nigerian independence, a young man making a government salary can expect to pay five hundred pounds for a bride (37). In that novel British attempts to restrict bride price have only succeeded in driving it up further. What has happened is that whereas previously there had been distinct spheres of exchange – food items could be exchanged for food items, prestige items for prestige items, and women for women – the introduction of Western currency levelled the spheres so that women were no longer exchanged for women, an exchange for which bride wealth was the symbol, but were exchanged for bridewealth itself.[11] The introduction of capitalist accumulation under colonialism had created "a new moral economy in which the bride's father (rather than mother) sought to maximise his return on the production of a daughter."[12]

The principle of reciprocity epitomized by the exchange of brides makes allies and even kin out of other people, but it also implies that, were it not for the equilibrium maintained by reciprocal exchange, the relations among village groups would be hostile. The practice of exchanging brides among village groups makes war less likely; even so, the reciprocity of gifts can shift into that of blows, as in the case of the man Uzowulu, who beats his wife Mgbafo to the point that she miscarries and almost dies. His in-laws come to beat him and take away their daughter. In marriage as in war, everyone is alert to offence; indeed, the negotiations around bridewealth in the novel appear every bit as precarious as those concerning war. Meek reports of Igboland that "one of the commonest causes of fighting was the refusal or failure of the parents of a wife who had abandoned her husband to refund the bride-price. This frequently led to reprisals by the husband's kindred, and in due course a state of open hostility might supervene between the village of the husband and the village of the wife."[13]

In *Things Fall Apart*, when Uzowulu beats his wife and her family takes her away, husband and in-laws must appear before the *egwugwu*, the masked spirits of the clan, to decide what should be done about the original bride price. The *egwugwu* hold public "hearings," "not to blame this man or to praise that, but to settle the dispute" (93). The *egwugwu* base their decision on the "law of Umuofia" that "if a woman runs away from her husband her bride-price is returned" (92); this "law" affirms the principle of reciprocity. In calling such a principle a "law," Achebe is following the lead of Meek's *Law and Authority in a Nigerian Tribe* (1935), which describes and categorizes the Igbos' jural system, which colonial officers need to know if they are to administer Indirect Rule effectively.[14] Nọnso Okereafọezeke, author of *Law and Justice in Post-British Nigeria*, written sixty-five years after Meek, also discusses the Igbo systems of justice and social control as a form of "law." It must be noted, however, that although the hearings in Umuofia resemble a court of civil law, "no attempt is made to extract a true version from the conflicting accounts; no principles of traditional law are invoked to apportion blame."[15] The *egwugwu* do not assess guilt, but rather work out how to salvage the principle of reciprocity: "The refusal to rely upon absolute principles of law reflects the widespread scepticism of the people of Umuofia toward authority and custom."[16] In this case the judgment of the ancestors reaffirms the original bride exchange, thus averting the threat of reciprocal violence. (In Elechi Amadi's 1986 novel *The Estrangement*, a husband who has cast off his wife is called before Omirinya, the council of women, and ordered to reconcile. In this case, it is women and not the ancestors who are responsible for maintaining social equilibrium. Amadi's novel is set after the Biafran War and reflects not so much an increased participation of women as an increased awareness by male novelists of the political role of women.)

Before the present of the narrative a woman from Umuofia had been killed in Mbaino market and Umuofia threatened war in reprisal. Death is irreversible, but blood vengeance seeks to restore balance by exacting a violent death from the murderer's party.[17] Bridewealth and vindicatory violence are twin modes of reciprocity. "Vindicatory debt," explains Marcel Hénaff, "belongs to the logic of gift-exchange relationships; it is a debt of reply and a debt of honor. Reply is mandatory, as are the gestures of ceremonial gift exchange – offering, receiving, and reciprocating a gift. Debt is erased by the fulfillment of the procedure."[18]

By casting its gaze backward at the affront, retaliatory killing can risk careening forward in an endless spiral of killing.[19] In the case of the Umuofia woman killed in Mbaino, however, the decision to go to war is debated democratically by a council of the titled men and is approved by the Oracle of the Hills and Caves, who needs to be satisfied that the case for war is "clear and just" and not "what the Ibo call *a fight of blame*" (12). The existence of the notion of a war of blame suggests a jural community that includes the neighbouring village groups and acknowledges norms of exchange. The injured have the right to demand redress but must exact it themselves. Barkun explains of stateless societies that the implementation of agreed-upon rules "cannot very well depend solely upon force (it is nowhere sufficiently concentrated so that force can be effectively and invariably applied); instead self-help and self-restraint take the place of the sovereign."[20] Barkun calls this "law without sanctions":

> The norm, in this sense, is a rule that is accepted as binding by the society. Because the rule is binding and because there is nothing that even remotely resembles centralized sanctions, the obligation for redress of the breach falls to the injured party; he and his kinsmen can *legitimately* retaliate. Their right to retaliate is unquestioned, either by the society at large or by their antagonists. It is in the nature of a self-help system that retaliation is both a right and an obligation, binding the injured to avenge himself and giving moral sanction to his act.[21]

Justice here is imagined as restoring balance and repairing relations, not as punishing an offence against a central authority.

Mbaino, as represented by its council of titled men, is offered the choice between war and peace. The two groups manage to avert war when Mbaino accedes to Umuofia's demand that it hand over "a young man and a virgin" (11) as compensation for the woman killed. The elders of the two village groups are able to stand outside the cycles of vengeance in order to discuss them, thus affording themselves autonomy from the momentum of violence. Negotiation presumes reason, a parity in status, and some level of mutual trust. Sahlins could be describing Umuofia and Mbaino when he writes that, in the Maussian scheme of things, "the right to give battle is retained by the people in severalty. But this must be underlined: it is the right which endures, not the battle."[22] The gift "is Reason," "the triumph of human rationality over the folly of war."[23]

Mark Anspach argues that to reverse the cycle of revenge and embark upon the forward cycle of the gift, including the exchange of brides, requires sacrifice, a killing that is not revenge but a gift because it is of one's own.[24] Mbaino, the offending party, freely hands over the son of a man who "had taken a hand in killing a daughter of Umuofia" (15). In this case, the life of a member of the offending party is not sufficient compensation for the woman killed because a woman is more than a life; she is the potential for future lives. To avert war Mbaino must also give Udo a girl "to replace his murdered wife" (12), in effect recasting the debt of death in terms of bride-givers and bride-receivers. Compensation for a victim whose life has been taken and the exchange of a bride who will bear a new life are twin aspects of what Philippe Rospabé calls "a debt of life."[25]

It is no coincidence that the *casus belli* in this case was a woman killed in the market. The markets that rotate every four or eight days among the village groups create vitality and abundance, but as we shall see in the next chapter, those same energies carry dangers, especially associated with theft, cheating, rumour, the power of crowds, and the magic of marketing (Umuike has become the largest of the markets as the result of a powerful medicine that beckons people to it from all directions [113]). The market, however, is also the model for reciprocity, and the word "payment" etymologically means "making peace."[26] Mauss writes that where two groups meet, if they do not move apart, they must either fight each other or sit down and trade.[27] Lévi-Strauss elaborates: "Exchanges are peacefully resolved wars and wars are the result of unsuccessful transactions."[28]

When the people of Mbaino accede to Umuofia's demands for compensation for the woman killed in the market, they do so because they acknowledge the justice of Umuofia's grievance but also because they fear their neighbour's prowess in war. Umuofia has a famous "war-medicine" (11) in addition to men unafraid of blood. A village group needs to be able to instil respect in others if it is not to be taken advantage of. As Meek says, "in the absence of any strong central authority the best method of preventing outrage is to let every one see that you will give as good as you get."[29] The fear village groups have for one another is not, however, the terror Umuofia later learns to feel for the British: village groups do not go to war to subjugate one another or to take land from one another.

In the Igboland of *Things Fall Apart*, war itself is a process of maintaining equilibrium. Meek writes that "warfare among the Ibo ... was waged not with the object of winning markets or annexing territory, but with the purely practical purpose of keeping one's neighbours in order."[30] The wars between neighbouring village groups, each constituted symmetrically, none subordinate to the others, have inherent limits. "Generally, fights expand until the forces engaged are roughly equivalent," explains

Barkun.[31] The historian Elizabeth Isichei notes that among Igbo village groups, the same principle of an eye for an eye that regularly led to war also constrained the spiral of violence: "the combatants knew that at the end of the war, a balance sheet would be drawn up, and the side with the lower casualty list would have to give the other side victims to equalize."[32] Meek reports the same.[33] Winners must compensate losers. The gift represents neither "the victory of one" nor "the submission of all," but "*mutual surrender*."[34] "The gift is alliance, solidarity, communion – in brief, peace, the great virtue that earlier philosophers, Hobbes notably, had discovered in the State."[35]

PRECOLONIAL DEMOCRACY

In its potential for war, the Maussian world of gift and countergift, blow and counterblow, might resemble the world of violence and insecurity that Hobbes says characterizes the state of nature before the establishment of the sovereign – each village group is surrounded by enemies – with this key difference: unlike in Hobbes's natural state, the village groups always already have political links to one another. Sahlins writes: "The state of nature is already a kind of society."[36] Gifts that maintain a balance over time make strangers or enemies into allies.

For Hobbes, Locke, and Rousseau the social contract is an agreement whereby individuals agree to surrender private force to a single public power. The classic social contract is "a structure of submission, and sometimes of terror."[37] Reciprocity, by contrast, "is a 'between' relation": "It does not dissolve the separate parties within a higher unity, but on the contrary, in correlating their opposition, perpetuates it. Neither does the gift specify a third party standing over and above the separate interests of those who contract."[38] Abélès summarizes: "Unlike the social contract of the philosophers where, in a single move, partners ally themselves and surrender their power to a third party that constitutes the State, the Maussian pact does not imply the dissolution of the parties involved nor their submission to an all-encompassing state."[39] Anspach argues that there *is* a third party involved in reciprocity – the reciprocal relation itself: "A relation of reciprocity cannot be reduced to an exchange between two individuals. A transcendent third emerges each time, even if this third is nothing but the relation itself that imposes itself as a full actor."[40]

To account for the origins of the state, political philosophers like Hobbes, Locke, Rousseau, and Marx posit two moments: a time before the state and a moment the state was founded. They all assume that history starts with the state (and with writing) and is divided from prehistory by a gulf. Achebe, too, emphasizes a break between the state and a time before, but he makes the break an end instead of a beginning. In this he is close in inspiration to anthropology, which defined itself against political philosophy as the study of societies without states.[41] Anthropologists accept the great divide drawn by political philosophers between societies with states and those without, between societies organized on the basis of kinship and those organized on the basis of territory, but they insist that politics did not begin with the state. Mauss and Malinowski assumed that "the political tie is a given in primitive society."[42] I am not arguing that anthropology supplies the cultural key to *Things Fall Apart*; rather, I am saying that Achebe is interested in how Igbo political life worked, not just because it represents tradition, but also because it represents a viable social order. As Christopher Wise suggests, *Things Fall Apart* contains a strong utopian element: it is an examination of what *should be* the case as much as of what *was* the case.[43]

On the eve of becoming a citizen of a new state, Achebe was writing a novel about a past epoch of statelessness. His concern was with the viability – and more, the value – of precolonial village democracy as a political model:

> My world – the one that interests me more than any other – is the world of the village. It is one, not the only, reality, but it's the one that the Igbo people, who are my people, have preferred to all others. It was as if they had a choice of creating empire or cities or large communities and they looked at them and said, "No, we think that what is safest and best is a system in which everybody knows everybody else." In other words, a village. So you'll find that, politically, the Igbos preferred the small community; they had nothing to do – until recently – with kings and kingdoms.[44]

Achebe often declared his admiration for the village world with its limited scale, where human relations remain face to face and political association does not rely on representation of the many by the one or the few but rather on direct democracy, so that every citizen has a say, decisions are negotiated, the ideal of all transactions is balance, and relations among people are created and reinforced by reciprocal exchange.

Democracy in Achebe's depiction of precolonial Igboland is inspired not by what Hannah Arendt calls "mere" liberation from an oppressor but rather by "freedom as the political way of life."[45] Freedom requires a political space where people can assemble and engage in certain properly political activities together, "the agora, the market-place, or the *polis*, the political space proper."[46] Such a space was the *ilo*, where the titled men of the Igbo village group met to make decisions in council. In Umuofia, all citizens, meaning free adult males, meet to debate and decide on a collective course of action. Authority attaches to age, eloquence, and achievement, but people can and do disagree with one another. Umuofia therefore realizes the classical Greek notion of liberty, "the opportunity to do your best to bend the sovereign judgement of your fellows to your own will by pressing your views upon them in public,"[47] or, as John Munonye puts it, "the difficult art of conducting meetings democratically and yet having one's way in the end."[48] The author of *Things Fall Apart* believes, with Aristotle, that "no one could be called either happy or free without participating, and having a share, in public power."[49] Again like Aristotle, Achebe regarded the chief merit of such deliberative democracy to be "its capacity to reach out to, and bring into play, the full breadth of knowledge and awareness of the entire citizen body."[50] In Achebe's *Arrow of God*, an elder is even described as wearing a "toga" at the assembly (143), an indication that Achebe has the classical world (or at least Rome) in mind.

Such direct democracy is only possible in a small face-to-face community such as the Greek polis or the Igbo village group, not in the large-scale modern state where citizens are perforce strangers and decisions must be made by elected representatives. Aristotle thought that ten thousand citizens (free adult males) was the ideal size of the polis;[51] not coincidentally, ten thousand is the number of men who gather in Umuofia's *ilo* to debate going to war with neighbouring Mbaino (10).[52]

Umuofia should properly be called not democracy but isonomy, "a form of political organization in which the citizens lived together under conditions of no-rule, without a division between rulers and ruled."[53] In Umuofia there are the unfree, as there were in Athens, but no kings and no division into nobles and plebeians. The freedom that men in Umuofia enjoy requires equality; put another way, the ruled are the rulers, not because all are equal in merit or in wealth – as we have seen, they are not – but because freedom is exercised in certain activities during which men make themselves seen, judged, and remembered. "The life of a free man needed the presence of others," says Arendt.[54] But women and slaves do not enjoy the same equality or potential to participate in decisions.

THE LIMITS OF RECIPROCITY

It will not have escaped my reader, however, that there is a problem with the principle of reciprocity when it comes to human beings: people are unique individuals who cannot substitute for one another. Lévi-Strauss concludes: "But woman could never become just a sign and nothing more, since even in a man's world she is still a person, and since insofar as she is defined as a sign she must be recognized as a generator of signs."[55] In a system in which women are not exchangers but only the exchanged, not givers but merely gifts, half the members are oppressed, as Gayle Rubin shows in "The Traffic in Women." Graeber, discussing reciprocity, reminds us that "human beings can never be equivalent to anything – even, ultimately, to one another."[56] "Bridewealth money," therefore, "is presented not to settle a debt, but as a kind of acknowledgment that there exists a debt that *cannot* be settled by means of money."[57]

The reciprocity that binds Umuofia and Mbaino in violent death and in marriage alike can be woefully indifferent to those persons who are the objects of exchange as brides, debt pawns, or sacrificial victims. Ikemefuna, the victim given to Umuofia to compensate for the death of Udo's wife, is an example of the unfairness of reciprocity to the individuals being exchanged. The boy's death would repay Mbaino's debt, but the boy is not killed right away. He does not have to be, for slavery is already, in the words of Orlando Patterson, a form of social death.[58] Slavery, writes Graeber, "is the ultimate form of being ripped from one's context, and thus from all the social relationships that make one a human being. Another way to put this is that the slave is, in a very real sense, dead."[59] Ikemefuna has lost his family and the ties to others that defined him.

The case of Ikemefuna poses the question of how to imagine reciprocity in the case of a violent death. Must repayment involve inflicting a loss equal to the first loss on the other party?, or can repayment take the form of a living person whose labour will replace that of the person lost? This kind of dilemma was often faced in Igboland in previous centuries, during the era of the transatlantic slave trade, when people faced "the pecuniary choice between selling people for material proceeds or retaining them for labor purposes; the juridical choice of imposing enslavement or another form of punishment; the social and ideological choice of whom to sell and whom to retain; and the cultural choice of which group or gender to incorporate and which to sell."[60] When in the nineteenth century there were no longer overseas buyers of slaves, the surplus of slaves in West Africa resulted in an increase in human sacrifice.[61]

Slavery in Igboland was paradoxical: it represented social death but could often take the form of "incorporation based on acculturation and accumulation."[62] Over the course of three years, Ikemefuna becomes a member of Okonkwo's family; the boy who has lost his ties to his lineage and its protection, and in that sense has died, is treated like a son and restored to life. In Umuofia the human context reasserts its warmth and its capacity to overcome death. Ikemefuna's new life as a son in Okonkwo's household may, however, threaten to violate the original exchange of a death for a death. Much as the *egwugwu* did in the case of the man who beat his wife, the oracle decrees a return to the original terms of exchange, that is, to the execution of the sacrificial victim.

The sacrifice that resolved the exchange of violence between Mbaino and Umuofia becomes, however, a different thing when the victim has learned to feel himself a son of Umuofia. Violence between village groups can be managed by reciprocity, but violence is much harder to adjust for when it breaks out *within* the family or village group. Reciprocity works to make families into allies, but when violence breaks out in a man's compound or within the village, it cannot be reciprocated, for each blow would strike against the life of the group as a whole.[63] In Nwapa's *Efuru*, for instance, conflict *within* a family is passed on as a debt from father to son without end (145). One man is still atoning for the murder committed by his grandfather in the course of a feud between two brothers, a murder that will only be cleansed when the murderer's lineage dies out (151). In Amadi's *The Slave*, conflict among the constituent villages of the village group of Erekwi cannot erupt into open violence, so it festers in the form of witchcraft and accusations of witchcraft from one generation to the next. In Munonye's *Bridge to a Wedding*, one man, having accidentally caused the death of a cousin's wife, must go into exile as punishment and put distance between him and his cousin: "The two must be kept well apart – out of sight and out of hearing – lest some vengeful spirit should drive the injured to acts of vengeance, thus drawing yet more blood within the family and leaving a streak that might lead to extinction in no distant future."[64]

Violence *internal* to the family or the village group, because it cannot be reciprocated except at cost to the self, must be deflected to a crime against the gods. When the short-tempered Okonkwo beats one of his wives during the Week of Peace, a time when everyone is supposed to refrain from offences against their neighbours in honour of Ani, the goddess of the earth, it is not his wife who is compensated but the goddess, who through her priest demands a she-goat, a hen, a length of cloth, and one hundred cowries so that she will in turn bless the crops (31). The goddess is "the ultimate judge of morality and conduct" (36). We could regard this sacrifice, however, as another form of reciprocity, this time between the human and the divine: obedience or sacrifice in return for blessing; sacrifice to atone for an offence. Before planting, a farmer will "sacrifice a cock to Ani" and another "at the shrine of Ifejioku, the god of yams" (17).

Later, in a grievous accident, Okonkwo's gun explodes and kills the son of Ezeudu, an elder. Because this event takes place *within* the village group, even within Okonkwo's own village, Iguedo, the offence cannot be cancelled out by paying compensation. It is considered not an offence against another but "a crime against the earth goddess" (124), albeit a lesser, "female" crime because inadvertent. The earth itself needs to be cleansed. Okonkwo must go into exile, and in a reversal of the feast given by a man taking a title, during which everyone revels in the abundance to be consumed, now the men of the village come together in a frenzy of destruction to tear down the walls of his compound, burn his houses, and kill his animals. The villagers in this way take on a collective responsibility intended to preclude the possibility of revenge and to placate the wrath of the goddess.[65]

After Ikemefuna becomes a son to Okonkwo, the sacrifice to restore the equilibrium with Mbaino threatens to disturb Umuofia's own internal equilibrium. *Things Fall Apart* deplores the ultimate fate of the boy, whom readers come to know not just as a sacrificial countertoken given in compensation for a murder but as a person of admirable character loved by Okonkwo and his son Nwoye. However well-suited the principle of reciprocity is to regulating relations among groups who recognize themselves in one another, *Things Fall Apart* makes clear why some in Umuofia might prefer a law based on a transcendent morality and enforceable by an objective authority in order to protect individuals. In a world governed by principles of reciprocity, Nietzsche suggests, justice itself is defined as the balance among equal powers "who come to terms with one another, who come to an 'understanding' once again by means of a settlement."[66] The question of intention, and thus of guilt or innocence, is irrelevant. No one asks whether the death of the woman in Mbaino market was an accident. When Okonkwo is sentenced to exile for an accidental death, his friend Obierika does wonder, "Why should a man suffer so grievously for an offence he had committed inadvertently?" (125). There is an incipient desire on the part of Obierika for an outside judgment that would remove violence from reciprocal exchange and make it a matter of morality, that would weigh the guilt of the individual rather than calibrate the honour at stake in interpersonal or intergroup relations. Okonkwo's son Nwoye, who bitterly feels the death of Ikemefuna his foster brother, registers the bonds of reciprocity as chains and longs for another mode of justice, one based on a recognition of the worth of the individual.

THE COMING OF BRITISH RULE OF LAW

The principles of reciprocity apply only between groups and not within the family or the village group, where it is the "justice of the earth goddess" that must be satisfied, not principles of retaliation or equilibrium (125). The modern state is more like the family than it is like a village group, for when it comes to violence within the state, retaliation is not allowed and an offence is considered a crime against the justice of the queen. However, between the justice of Umuofia and that of the modern state there is not a continuum but a great gulf. Unlike the family or the extended family, the modern state and its rule of law were originally imposed by overwhelming force.

The second half of *Things Fall Apart* offers a parable-sized depiction of the essence of colonialism. The British military conquest of Igboland is crystallized in a single incident – the killing of a white man on a bicycle in the village group of Abame – inspired by an actual incident involving a Mr. Stewart in Ahiara, Mbaise, in 1905.[67] The British do not acknowledge any parity with those whose land they are invading. When an Englishman is killed, they do not seek compensation in the form of a life for a life. They do not send a delegation to explain to Abame how it has offended and negotiate compensation. They simply attack on a market day, when normally war would be forbidden, and smash the village group with the aim of teaching it and its neighbours a lesson. From the British point of view, Abame's "crime" does not demand compensation or even proportionate punishment, but must be met with a display of strength so severe it will be registered throughout the region. The later Collective Punishment Ordinance of 1909 would codify the principle that colonial officers could punish a group for the "transgressions" of a member.[68] "I do not regret the loss of life among the aggressors," wrote Governor Lugard in 1915, "for these people hold life so cheap that the only way to prevent a recurrence of the outbreak is to make them understand that it will be severely dealt with."[69] For that reason, the British response at Abame is more accurately characterized as revenge than is the reciprocal violence between Igbo village groups.[70]

To read Achebe's novel one would not know that the incident of the man on the bicycle occurred in the context of British military expeditions that took more than a decade and a half to subdue Igboland in the face of fierce resistance. From 1900 to 1914, the British launched twenty-one military expeditions into Igboland.[71] The British conquest of Igboland was a shock-and-awe campaign made possible by modern artillery. The disproportionate violence spread terror,[72] and the British retained the capacity for that violence as long as they ruled. Frederick Cooper writes that "Empires perpetrated violence because they were strong and because they were weak. Terror tactics – mass slaughter during conquests, collective punishments on villages and kinship groups thereafter – were hallmarks of colonization and lasting features of maintaining control."[73] The British were less concerned with retribution against Abame than with performing their own power: their object was not specific to Abame; rather, as with the infamous massacre at Amritsar in India in 1919, "it was a *specific action taken to establish rather than merely enforce a general rule*."[74]

The lack of parity between Abame and Britain reflected a difference in scale that the British cast in moral terms.[75] The invaders regarded the stateless world of autonomous village groups along the Lower Niger, as they did Africa at large, as a field in which morality did not apply until they, the British, imposed the law. From this point of view, the British conquest was itself neither legal nor moral, as befits the amoral field in which it saw itself intervening; rather, the British claimed legitimacy retrospectively on the basis of introducing a system of laws that claimed to bear a relation to a would-be transcendent morality. The British justified their own violence as putting an end to what they perceived as the anarchic violence in which they themselves had perforce participated. The British thus claimed to be rescuing Africans (not yet Nigerians) from an anarchy they projected as endemic to Africa and intolerable even to Africans.

At the end of *Things Fall Apart* the District Commissioner invites six leaders of Umuofia, including Okonkwo, for a palaver after the destruction of the Anglican mission church by the *egwugwu*: "I have been told a few things but I cannot believe them until I have heard your own side" (193). "Let us talk about it like friends and find a way of ensuring that it does not happen again," says the DC. "We have brought a peaceful administration to you and your people so that you may be happy. If any man ill-treats you we shall come to your rescue. But we will not allow you to ill-treat others. We have a court of law where we judge cases and administer justice just as it is done in my own country under a great queen" (194). The new rule of law presents itself as rational and just: it listens to both sides; it protects all equally against ill-treatment; it presumes that all will give their consent to its manifest neutrality.

Whereas before injuries were considered offences against the injured party and that party's kinship group, the new law will treat injuries as offences against the mighty state. Justice will no longer be a question of adequately compensating victims – that is, of balance – but rather one of identifying and punishing guilt. As Nietzsche writes,

> while, after the establishment of law, the authorities treat the aggressive and arbitrary acts of individuals, or of whole groups, as a violation of law, and as resistance to the authorities themselves, they distract their subjects' attention from the immediate injury inflicted by such a violation, and thus eventually achieve the very opposite result to that always desired by revenge, which sees and recognizes nothing but the standpoint of the injured party.[76]

When a man is killed in a land dispute that had been settled in the white man's court in favour of the one who bribed the messengers and interpreter, the killer is imprisoned along with all his family and eventually hanged (177). This death, however, is presented not as compensation but as transcendent justice: the offence was not against the victim but against the state.

The elders who listen to the District Commissioner's speech about the magnanimous impartiality of the justice he upholds have, however, been forcibly seized and sit in handcuffs. The new law, which derives its claim to legitimacy from the consent of the governed, the impartiality of its judgments, and the manifest reasonableness of its decisions, does not seek the consent of the elders, whom it regards as irrational and in need of coercion until they comply with reason. The elders will have their heads shaved, be locked up, and be denied water (195); they will be whipped (199); and they will only be freed once Umuofia has paid a huge ransom, or rather fine.

John Sifton quotes an anonymous seventeenth-century philosopher who may have been Hobbes to the effect that kings regard the sheer awesomeness of explosives as "a mark of their sovereignty."[77] Locke, however, writes that "no man can, by agreement, pass over to another that which he hath not in himself, a power over his own life."[78] That is "the perfect condition of slavery," which is "but the state of war continued" unless conqueror and captive "make an agreement for a limited power on one side, and obedience on the other."[79] True, "such have been the disorders ambition has filled the world with, that in the noise of war … many have mistaken the force of arms for the consent of the people," but "conquest is as far from setting up any government, as demolishing an house is from building a new one in the place."[80] To justify their conquest, the colonizers, however, needed to pretend that such a compact between conquerors and captives existed. That compact is the law.

Robert Cover argues that "[all] judges are people of violence."[81] Courts rely on armed men to enforce their verdicts. Étienne Balibar calls the state's monopoly on violence "preventive counterviolence": "In the final analysis, state power can keep the peace in the social body only if it is virtually at war with it. The state is the bosom enemy of the society it protects."[82] However, where the authority of legal and judicial institutions is accepted as part of the authority of the state, the violence of the state may be forgotten. The moment of colonialism reveals the violence that founded the law in the first place. Pacification by the British meant everyone was treated equally and rationally, *except* those the empire deemed primitive and irrational, which is to say, the colonized. The new administration thus hides from itself how much it is itself based on violence and on arbitrariness.

In a reading of *Things Fall Apart* consonant with mine, Adélékè Adéẹ̀kọ́ considers the crisis created by the colonial encounter not as a clash between cultures – "the precolonial societies are not governed from one uncontested 'cultural point' and … the colonial presence added another center to hitherto existing multiple sources of forceful power" – but as "the consolidation of law-making power and law enforcement violence amidst the uncertainties of regime change."[83] Jacques Derrida, discussing Walter Benjamin, reminds us that the rule of law, which proscribes violence within the territory of the state and underwrites a seemingly universal morality that the state itself must adhere to, always requires an original violence of its own for its establishment: "the operation that consists of founding, inaugurating, justifying law [*droit*], making law, would consist of a *coup de force*, of a performative and therefore interpretative violence that in itself is neither just nor unjust and that no justice and no previous law with its founding anterior moment could guarantee or contradict or invalidate."[84] This "law to come" retrospectively legitimates the violence needed to bring it into being: "its future anterior already justifies it."[85] Derrida the Frenchman imagines that the "foundation of all states occurs in a situation that we can thus call revolutionary. It inaugurates a new law, it always does so in violence."[86] He overlooks the fact that the origin of many, perhaps most, states was not in revolution from within but in conquest and colonization from without. It could be said of *Things Fall Apart* what Foucault says of the Norman Invasion: "Formulated from on high and in a foreign language, the law was the stigmata of the foreign presence, the mark of another nation."[87]

When the British consolidate their rule, Okonkwo summons Umuofia to resist, but his call goes unheeded. Umuofia has many reasons for not fighting: the new religion has divided its members; the new British order opens up attractive economic opportunities; and some, like Nwoye, feel that the new law will put an end to a reciprocal violence that unjustly ignores the moral innocence of the individual. Mainly, however, people in Umuofia fear that they will "be like Abame" (176). Umuofia chooses to live rather than to die. Foucault writes that "for sovereignty to exist, there must be – and this is all there must be – a certain radical will that makes us want to live, even though we cannot do so unless the other is willing to let us live."[88] Sovereignty historically arises not from within, from a decision or a social contract, but from surrender to forces without. Hobbes wrote that "preservation of life being the end for which one man becomes subject to another, every man is supposed to promise obedience, to him, in which power it is to save or destroy him,"[89] and Foucault concurs: "It is fear, the renunciation of fear, and the renunciation of the risk of death" that "introduces us into the order of sovereignty and into a juridical regime: that of absolute power. The will to prefer life to death: that is what founds sovereignty."[90]

The conquest by the British introduced Igbos to the modern experience of the state, which now so fills the social universe that we "define politics in terms of command and obedience."[91] Citizens, who participate in sovereignty insofar as they identify with it and are willing to die for it, are also always subjects, whose refusal to die prompts their submission to the sovereign power that now rules them.

3

Sovereign Debt

We have explained the principles of reciprocity that originally demanded Ikemefuna's death or his social death as a slave, as well as the conundrum that arises when the warmth of Igbo society integrates the slave into the life of the household. In Umuofia, human sacrifice is limited to reciprocity between neighbouring village groups – a life is given for a life – and has no function *within* the village group. Newborn twins are killed because they are an abomination, not offered as a sacrifice to the gods. As we have seen, when the boy Ikemefuna comes to Umuofia from Mbaino as a sacrificial hostage in compensation for the death of a woman in the market, sacrifice permits vindicatory violence to be transformed into the reciprocity of gift and countergift. This changes when the three-year delay means that Ikemefuna has been integrated into Okonkwo's family. When the oracle renews a call for Ikemefuna's death, the boy's dual status – he is at once a stranger and a son of Umuofia – alters the logic of killing. Ikemefuna's death was originally a horizontal gift by Mbaino to Umuofia, albeit an awkwardly delayed one, but once the boy becomes a son of Umuofia his death becomes a sacrifice in the sense of a vertical gift to the gods. The sacrifice is now not of the enemy but of what is closest to the self.

The elders who bring Okonkwo the news of the oracle's belated demand for the sacrifice of Ikemefuna recognize that it is inappropriate for the boy's surrogate father to participate. Okonkwo insists on taking part regardless, a decision that, fully as much as the advent of the colonizers, is the crux of his tragedy. Okonkwo's identification with the social order is such that he puts it above his relations with other people based on reciprocity or on familial ties. His participation in the killing of his foster son is a form of obedience abhorrent to the earth goddess, "the kind of action for which the goddess wipes out whole families" (67).

Critics have commonly read the sacrifice of Ikemefuna as traditional practice, like the killing of twins. The sacrifice of a son by a father, however, represents something unforeseen by tradition and catastrophically new. Sacrificing what one holds dearest is how one acknowledges a transcendental creditor. Okonkwo kills Ikemefuna for the same reason the Biblical Abraham is prepared to sacrifice Isaac: to show that he places his ties to the transcendent above the ties that bind humans to one another. He casts himself as the upholder of a divine law that is superior to, and can even contravene, natural moral law. The sacrifice is a proof of his faith.

"Faith," of course, is a word borrowed from the Christians and not usually applied to traditional spirituality. Robert Wren, for instance, assumes that precolonial Africans did not need faith: "The priest of Ani in 'Dead Man's Path' [an early Achebe story] ... needs to prove nothing, to argue nothing, because he knows something beyond proof. And Achebe had become aware that he himself, mission schoolboy, university educated, had lost that same ancestral knowledge."[1] Precolonial Africans, Wren assumes, did not have to believe; they simply *knew*. *Things Fall Apart* suggests, however, on the contrary, that precolonial Igbos lived comfortably (though sometimes uncomfortably) with a gap in the mortal apprehension of the spiritual. The doubts that Obierika and Nwoye each have about the morality of the gods predate the coming of the missionaries and, we understand, are what some Igbos may always have felt. When, as an *egwugwu* masquerade, Okonkwo literally becomes "one of the dead fathers of the clan," the women can easily still recognize their husband by his gait, though they respectfully refrain from pointing out what they are not supposed to notice (88). Women's double consciousness when it comes to masquerades is a commonplace: the Yoruba historian the Rev. Samuel Johnson notes of the ancestral masquerade of the Yoruba that "the women believe (or rather feign to believe) that the Egunguns come from the spirit world."[2]

Achebe suggests that what is new is precisely the desire to *close* the gap between mortal apprehension and the divine that tradition tolerated. "Faith" is the right word to apply to Okonkwo when he obeys the oracle and participates in the execution of his foster son. As with Abraham, the patriarch of monotheism, Okonkwo's concern is to fulfil the divine will at all costs, without qualification or equivocation. Okonkwo's is the behaviour of someone afraid of doubting. His obedience to the oracle is the opposite of, and the *corollary* of, doubt. He accompanies the sacrificial party and even brings his own matchet down on the boy because "he was afraid of being thought weak" (61). While others find the will of the oracle lamentable but acquiesce to it, Okonkwo resolves to serve that will to the letter. His role in the sacrifice of Ikemefuna fulfills an image of himself in his own and others' eyes: the man who performs whatever the oracle commands, unafraid of blood and indifferent to personal emotion. Okonkwo may be afraid of being thought weak but not, it seems, of being thought disrespectful or irrational. His is a stiff-necked, unreasoning faith that mistrusts itself. As Slavoj Žižek explains, "*sacrifice is a guarantee that 'the Other exists'*: that there *is* an Other who can be appeased by means of the sacrifice."[3] There is in sacrifice to the gods always an element of defying the gods, or measuring that their force is still strong.[4]

A father's power of life and death over his son is the *patria potestas*, the power that a Roman paterfamilias exercised over his family and an emblem of sovereignty. The sovereign possesses the natural force of the father, says Hobbes, "as when a man maketh his children, to submit themselves, and their children to his government, as being able to destroy them if they refuse."[5] Paul Kahn explains that sacrifice creates sovereign power: "Killing and being killed is a demand that only the state can make on its members. It is the 'sovereign prerogative' to demand a life. To act on that demand is more than accepting a delegation of sovereign power. It is to participate in sovereignty; it is to be an instance of the sovereign."[6]

Nkiru Uwechia Nzegwu argues that precolonial Igbo society did not actually accord fathers the right over the life and death of their sons. The model of "overbearing patriarch, subordinate wives, and numerous children"[7] we find in Achebe's novel is, she says, not traditional; rather, it reflects "the pater familias principle of the nuclear family" propagated by the Christian missionaries that Achebe himself grew up with in the household of a catechist.[8] Precolonial family heads "lacked the sort of jural mandate and autocratic power that characterized nuclear families,"[9] and families divided power between the matrilineal and patrilineal lines. It was colonialism that transformed consanguineal families into "hybrids of the nuclear family in which a family is a man's personal domain, where he rules as head and his wife or wives are subject to his laws, and overall supervision and control."[10] Colonialism and Christianity "turned Igbo husbands into sovereigns," writes Nzegwu, by assigning them "the civic duties of maintaining law and order within the family units, effectively transforming fathers and husbands into quasi-administrative officers who implemented in family spaces the wage and tax policies and the local ordinances and edicts of the colonial administration."[11]

If Nzegwu is right about precolonial Igbo society (and she makes a strong case), then *Things Fall Apart* would appear to founder on a contradiction: Okonkwo, the upholder of tradition, himself embodies what has happened to Igbo society and the Igbo psyche *as a result of colonization.* Nzegwu's challenge underscores the peculiarity and even the wilfulness of Achebe's depiction of tradition. Her study highlights and deepens a contradiction already manifest in the novel: Okonkwo's fall represents at once the tragic passing of the old order *and* the perversity of someone who, in order to counter an external threat, would transform the traditional order into a transcendent absolute such as it had never been. I am arguing that the novel thus juxtaposes two moments: the historical moment when Igboland was violently folded into another's empire, and the fictional moment when one man in the village group acquires the ambition to represent the whole and thus to change the nature of power and authority.

Sacrifice is "a means of consecrating, of participating in the sacred. Short of that, sacrifice is either suicide or murder, which is exactly how it will appear to those not enthralled by the sovereign god of the sacrificial community."[12] Murder is how Okonkwo's killing of Ikemefuna appears to his other son Nwoye (and to readers). The killing of Ikemefuna drives Nwoye, a sensitive young man, to seek an alternative among the Christian missionaries. In Christian eyes blood sacrifice is but a vestige of paganism or the primitive. When God intervened with Abraham to replace Isaac as sacrificial victim with a ram, he replaced the practice of actual child sacrifice with a symbolic sacrifice. The Christian God later sacrificed his own son to remove sins once and for all, putting an end to any further need for blood sacrifice to atone for sins and to balance accounts. "Blood sacrifice does not even make sense in contemporary industrial society, where separate individuals, joined in temporary, voluntary association, are thought of as the basic units of society; where social institutions are not conceived as integrated by descent, real or metaphorical."[13]

In *No Longer at Ease,* the sequel to *Things Fall Apart*, the family still tells with horror the story of Ikemefuna (125–6). Okonkwo's son Nwoye, now called Isaac in commemoration of his foster brother, could not accept the logic of Ikemefuna's sacrifice and rejoiced when he heard of his father's death by hanging, invoking the words of Jesus that "those who live by the sword must perish by the sword" (125). The shedding of blood is felt to be wrong because it leads only to more blood. All readers will agree that Ikemefuna's sacrifice is a tragedy, however skeptical they are that Christianity provides an escape from the logic of sacrifice. Christianity, after all, cannot pretend it does not understand the need for sacrifice: the logic of the atonement is based on it. In modern times, when the state has absorbed much of the sacredness associated with religion, the state still demands that its citizens be prepared to sacrifice, most commonly in the form of death on the battlefield, a point made by Olunde in Wole Soyinka's play *Death and the King's Horseman.* And as with Christ's sacrifice, the absolute debt the state can demand from citizens is removed from any association with reciprocity and made something beyond anyone's ability to repay.

OF KINGS AND FATHERS

Things Fall Apart and Achebe's later novel *Arrow of God* both focus on the moment when the precolonial village group appears about to produce a pretender to kingship from within its own ranks. Would achievement societies, left to their own devices, have developed into chiefdoms and even kingdoms? The archaeologists Kent Flannery and Joyce Marcus argue that political development has historically been in the direction of larger societies, more social complexity, and more inequality, but that that path of development has not been inevitable. In the historical line they trace, inequality first entered the world with agriculture and settlement. The first agricultural communities were "achievement societies" that rewarded merit and effort but had not developed distinct classes because inequality was not inherited. Only when the honour a man earned in his lifetime could be inherited by his sons did achievement-based societies become rank societies with unequal classes.

As we have seen, Okonkwo is fortunate to live in a world in which a man is judged by his accomplishments and not by his parentage. However, he is also a new kind of man, an Oedipal patriarch in the making. In order to become the man he wants to be, he establishes what Claude Meillassoux calls "vertical affiliation," based on the debt repaid by one generation of harvesters to their predecessors. As we have seen, as a young man Okonkwo borrows seed yams from Nwakibie, whom he then calls "Our father," "Nna ayi" (19). Meillassoux explains that agricultural activity, in which "the workers of one season would advance subsistence food and seed to those who will work the following season whose product they would consume and store in the next season," leads to "a *change of generation.*"[14] Meillassoux goes on to explain:

> The management and redistribution of the product establishes the eldest man in the productive cycle at the apex of the productive community. In this position he acts as the provisioning "father" of all the younger men to whom he redistributes the subsistence goods

> necessary to continue and re-prime the agricultural cycle. "Father" does not in fact mean *genitor* but ***he who nourishes*** and protects you, and who claims your produce and labour in return.[15]

Wealth is in the hands of the older generation (although not all of that generation are wealthy), leaving young men in need of loans to get started as farmers. Debt becomes the way that wealth circulates from one generation to the next.

By contrast, hunter-gatherers, writes Meillassoux, "do not place themselves in reference to a common ancestor, nor do they classify themselves according to a formal genealogy. Whether some or all the members are biologically related is a matter of secondary importance: such ties *in themselves* create no permanent reciprocal obligations, nor do they define the status or even the rank of individuals."[16] Okonkwo's own father appears to him to be an embarrassing relic from a time when age did not determine status. Unoka is described in the way that agriculturalists have always described pastoralists and the colonizers described Africans: "he was lazy and improvident and was quite incapable of thinking about tomorrow" (4).

Agricultural work in small-scale communities does not have to be patriarchal, Meillassoux explains. Because it involves working side by side and sharing the harvest, it also encourages "*lateral* filiation, from elders to juniors, from 'brother' to 'brother' according to the order of access to the productive cycle."[17] In what is the novel's happiest moment involving Okonkwo, father and sons work together thatching the outer walls of the compound, passing a rope or *tie-tie* through "little holes from one side to the other in the upper levels of the wall": "Okonkwo passed to the boys and they passed it round the wooden stays and then back to him; and in this way the cover was strengthened on the wall" (55). The task of weaving a roof for the compound that a son will inherit is emblematic of a succession that is not based on paternal authority: one generation hands something on to the next, who respectfully reciprocate, and the bonds thus created protect the house, both the physical structure and the family line. In this scene, relations in time are imagined as relations in space, vertical affiliation as lateral affiliation, the generations as sharing the same moment. The scene of weaving is matched in bliss by the scene in which Ekwefi tells stories to her daughter Ezinma. Theirs, too, is a "companionship of equals" (77), and Ekwefi does "not call her mother *Nne* like all children," but rather by "her name, Ekwefi, as her father and other grown-up people did" (76).

"However," Meillassoux continues, "once the conditions of social inequality have appeared, and a dominant aristocratic class emerges, reproducing itself according to its own norms (and preoccupied with political succession and with the conditions of reproduction of its dominance), vertical succession tends gradually to be imposed upon collateral succession."[18] Whereas Unoka remained always a child and a "woman," on a level with his own wives and children, Okonkwo sets himself up as the progenitor of a new family line. The man who had rejected his own father has ambitions to take the highest title in Umuofia, which would mean initiating his sons into the *ozo* society (171). He is determined to convert the esteem his wealth has earned him into a hereditary principle. When frustrated with his sons, he repeatedly imagines himself as an ancestor looking back in rage on the living.

The scene of thatching is first interrupted by the spontaneous feast of a swarm of locusts, which are relished as food that has not been worked for and cannot be predicted. That moment of bounty and domestic harmony is, however, a mere interlude. In a miniature version of the tragic hero's rise and fall, the feast enjoyed by father and sons is interrupted by the elder Ezeudu, who brings the message from the oracle that Ikemefuna is to be sacrificed (57). The gods, it would seem, are jealous of human happiness. Certainly, they are as disapproving as their Greek counterparts of the levelling of the generations. The scene of domestic harmony represents a happy unfallen state before the intervention of the sovereign with its demand for sacrifice.

"NOW APPOINT A KING TO LEAD US SUCH AS ALL THE OTHER NATIONS HAVE" (1 SAMUEL 8:5)

To behave as if the oracle were sovereign, as I am arguing Okonkwo does, is to make it sovereign – to recognize a will that can demand the death of the subject – *and* to make the man who carries out that will a modern individual who derives his identity from the larger polity. In an earlier chapter I described Okonkwo's psychological self-division as what made him a realist character. His character is based on contradiction: he is strong because he is afraid of appearing weak. In his case, courage is a form of fear, submission to the gods a form of autonomy, fear of weakness a tragic flaw. Now I am arguing that this self-division has also to do with sovereignty, the representation of the collective in a single person. His friend Obierika reminds Okonkwo that, when it comes to sacrificing Ikemefuna, he need not perform the oracle's mandate himself: the oracle needs someone to carry out his wishes, but that could be anyone and need not be a particular person. Yet Okonkwo insists on his oneness with a larger will. In order to prove that he deserves to be one of the lords of the land, Okonkwo makes himself an obedient servant of the gods.

In *Arrow of God*, we learn that "long, long ago there had been a fifth title in Umuaro – the title of king. But the conditions for its attainment had been so severe that no man had ever taken it, one of the conditions being that the man aspiring to be king must first pay the debts of every man and every woman in Umuaro" (209). The idea of kingship implies service, even sacrifice. The coming of a king would be marked by a great jubilee, a general forgiveness of debts, but at the expense of putting everyone in one man's debt. Something like this absolute title of king is Okonkwo's unspoken aspiration: to relieve all debts among men and thus to replace them with a single debt, to society as a whole and, in effect, to himself, the man prepared to sacrifice what he holds dearest in order to enact the collective will.

According to Engels, the difference between the primitive chief and the modern man of state is that the latter is obliged to represent something outside and above himself.[19] The chief or, for that matter, the titled man or elder carries authority but does not represent the collective will. He is defined by his relations with others, often relations of protection or subordination, but he does not speak *for* others. Sovereignty, by contrast, is the concentration of society into a single will, represented as a person to whom everyone surrenders their will. The Sovereign of Hobbes is "One Person, of whose Acts a great Multitude, by mutuall Covenants one with another, have made themselves every one the Author, to the end he may use the strength and means of them all, as he shall think expedient, for their Peace and Common Defence."[20] The closest thing that Umuofia has to a representative of a collective will is when Okonkwo is sent to carry a message of war to neighbouring Mbaino, and such is that community's fear of Umuofia that they treat him as a king.

There is great irony in the ambition I am identifying here, of course: the people of Umuofia are proud that they do without kings. As Axel Harneit-Sievers notes, the "common proverb, *Igbo enwe(ghi) eze* (or *Igbo ama eze*, 'the Igbo have no kings'), plays with the ostensible paradox that the Igbo language has a term for an institution that did not exist in most precolonial Igbo communities."[21] To define oneself by the absence of a king presumes that one knows about kings. In *Things Fall Apart*, a young woman is praised as "the bride for a king" (116) and yam is called "the king of crops" (23, 33), and in *Arrow of God*, the Ikolo is "the king of all drums" (69). One resentful man says of Okonkwo that "looking at a king's mouth, one would think he never sucked at his mother's breast" (26) – a proverb that says explicitly that a king is a man like others who just puts on superior airs, but that also acknowledges a kingly bearing in Okonkwo. A proverb cited in praise of social mobility has it that "if a child washed his hands he could eat with kings" (8), which presumes both that a child can become anything he aspires to *and* that there are kings. Kingship is central to the Igbo imagination, even if, as Achebe himself told Jonathan Cott, the Igbos chose to do without kings:

> Some people look at the Igbos and assert that they didn't evolve to the stage of having kings and kingdoms. But this isn't true – the Igbos have a name for "king," they have names for all the paraphernalia of kingship – it isn't as if they didn't know about kings. I think it's simply that, looking at the way the world operates, they seemed to have said to themselves, "Of all the possible political systems, we shall insist on the one where there are only so many people.[22]

The Igbo define themselves against kings because, like Roman Republicans and the prophets of ancient Israel, they are afraid of kings. Pierre Clastres has gone so far as to argue that "there are no societies without the State, only societies against the State."[23] The term "statelessness," implying the absence of a state, may be appropriate after all. The Igbo "hero" would be like Udemezue of the Burning Eyes, a man remembered in "Umudiobia of ten villages and two" who "had dictated terms of peace and war to the neighbours, and made and unmade rules, and yet would not be a ruler himself."[24] Udemezue did not appropriate land to himself, so "no bitterness, following a desire for redress, had developed on his death."[25]

Colonialism was riven by contradiction, none perhaps greater than the fact that the colonizing nations believed they were more civilized than Africans because they had democracy, yet preferred dealing with African kings and emirs rather than with village democracies. The British appreciated kingdoms like Buganda and emirates like Sokoto and Kano because they saw in them the potential to become states. Such polities had absolute rulers with whom the British could make treaties and through whom they later found it expedient to rule. Acephalous, segmented societies like the Igbo, the Nuer, and the Gikuyu, on the other hand, struck the British as more primitive and as lacking something essential. The explanation for this contradiction is that the colonizers' own understanding of democracy, as we have seen, was not inherited from the Greek polis so much as from the overthrow or sidelining of the absolute monarch. The colonizers felt that the highest form of democracy retained the notion of sovereignty, the embodiment of the collective in a single will, the will of the people having been substituted for that of the king.

The British and the French believed they were the epitome of democracy, yet their states preserved the sovereignty of the monarch. This is a truth about themselves that the colonizers had trouble recognizing but the colonized could never forget, because European states that were democracies at home behaved as undisguised monarchies abroad. As Hobbes had already declared in the seventeenth century, "provinces which are in subjection to a Democracie, or Aristocracie of another Common-wealth, are not Democratically, or Aristocratically governed, but Monarchically."[26]

Confounded as they were in Igboland by the absence of kings, the British issued warrants to create "traditional" rulers. Unlike titled men, the new warrant chiefs did not derive their authority from the acknowledgment of their worthiness by their peers and by those below them; rather, they were entirely dependent on the powers above them. They acknowledged the authority of no law or no spirit, only that of their colonial masters, whom they could manipulate. Power, instead of moving between above and below, between spirits and humans, chiefs and their subjects, elders and their sons, now came down entirely from above. The result was "a thinning of the patrimonial relation *and* the gradual emergence of a non-accountable form of clientelism – that is, a clientelism narrowed to the strictly instrumental, increasingly divorced from the moral and ethical dimensions of pre-colonial rulership."[27]

The system of warrants and native courts was therefore, not surprisingly, a gross failure. It was one cause of the Women's War of 1929, the largest resistance mounted in Igboland after the original conquest. As a result of that war, the British had largely withdrawn the warrant chief system by the 1930s, eventually replacing it with customary courts and elected councils.[28] On the eve of Nigeria's independence, however, chieftaincy once again became an issue in Igboland, but this time it was Igbos themselves who instituted chiefs.[29] The other two regions of Nigeria, the Northern and Western, both had houses of chiefs that served as second legislative chambers on the Westminster model, and the Eastern Region demanded such a house as well, even if it meant creating the chiefs to fill it, lest they lose in prestige relative to the other regions.[30] In 1955, Azikiwe's NCNC government created a house of chiefs in the Eastern Region, in effect reintroducing "an institution that had been both created and abolished by the colonial rulers."[31]

The impetus for the new house of chiefs came not just from above, and the chiefs were not merely ceremonial. Village groups themselves wanted chiefs in order to enhance their prestige. Some of these new chiefs even inherited their titles from the warrant chiefs whose warrants the colonizers had abolished in the 1930s.[32] In other words, at the time Achebe was writing, sovereignty was a question not just for the new nation but for the self-governing region and even for the local council.

On the eve of Nigerian independence there were two models available to Igbos for the conception of democracy. The precolonial model represented by Umuofia does without kings in favour of direct democracy. In the modern state model imported from Britain, the king's sovereignty passes to the people. In the latter model, sovereignty, the notion that the community has a single will that overrides that of members, is retained from monarchy but has become popular sovereignty. The two kinds of democracy, that which resists the consolidation of a monarch and that which supplants a monarch, share an ideal of equality and liberty. The difference is that the former is without a state and the latter is a state that was formerly a kingdom. There are also two corresponding models for the founding of a kingship: acephalous achievement societies develop leaders and become chieftaincies, or African societies are invaded and forcibly integrated into a colony ruled by foreigners.

UNPAYABLE DEBTS AND CLEARED DEBTS

The risk that Nwakibie took in lending Okonkwo eight hundred seed yams involves more than the young man's capacity for hard work: it also involves the natural world and Okonkwo's *chi* or "personal god," the external will that complements or thwarts a man's own will. In Okonkwo's first year of farming, rain "as it had never fallen before" and drought "more fierce than it had ever been known" conspired to ruin the young man's harvest (24). The "earth burned like hot coals and roasted all the yams that had been sown," and, in an ominous foreshadowing, one ruined farmer hanged himself in despair (24). Subsistence farmers who rely entirely on the rain and do not make use of cooperative methods such as irrigation will be at the mercy of the elements. Strangely, the novel never tells us whether, after those natural disasters, Okonkwo was able to repay Nwakibie's starter loan or how he did so. Was the creditor content to receive a two-thirds share of a meagre harvest, in effect sharing Okonkwo's misfortune? Or did Okonkwo's hard labour and perseverance eventually allow him to repay Nwakibie's investment regardless? The novel's indifference to the question suggests that the meaning of the loan is not as a relationship between two men, but rather as a measure of Okonkwo's resilience and his determination to be a sovereign individual dependent on no one. Okonkwo remembered "with a cold shiver throughout the rest of his life" the tragic year at the start of his career when flood and drought colluded to destroy his harvest (24). That cold shiver is the horror of a debt so large that it cannot be repaid. A similar "cold shiver descended" on Okonkwo after he killed Ikemefuna (63), and again when he hears that Ezeudu, the man who told him to have no part in the boy's death, has died (121). As we shall see, a half century later, his grandson Obi Okonkwo feels a similar sensation of horror.

The young farmer's experience of failure served to strengthen his resolve, but the spectre of permanent debt may also have frightened him from ever going into debt to others again. Certainly, in the present of the novel Okonkwo's ideal is not the interdependence of mutual credit that allows neighbours to assist one another and mitigate the risks of subsistence farming, but rather the autonomy that comes from clearing all debts and standing outside debt. His desire to stand free of debt is of a piece with his need to prove that he has inherited nothing from his father, of whom he is ashamed. Okonkwo's resolution neither to inherit nor to owe ironically means, however, that he is always burdened by the past. He behaves as if his father's spiritual and literal bankruptcy had placed on his own shoulders a debt he can never clear. His debt becomes almost metaphysical. *Things Fall Apart* leaves readers with the contradictory sense of Okonkwo as someone who refuses to owe anyone anything and someone with an unlimited and unpayable debt.

When Okonkwo accidentally kills Ezeudu's son, he is forced into exile and his ambition to acquire the highest title in the land lies in ruins. At first he is so embittered that it appears he will never raise his head again. He is intensely conscious of the wasted years ahead and of his loss of the right to lead Umuofia. In exile in his mother's village group, Mbanta, he is assigned two or three pieces of land to farm, and his five cousins lend him three hundred seed yams each. Back in Umuofia his friend Obierika lends out Okonkwo's own yams to sharecroppers and brings him the proceeds of the sales. On the surface, therefore, the exile does not seem so terrible: it can be survived by borrowing and lending. Okonkwo, however, resents the forceful reminder of his dependence on others. As a young man, Okonkwo had needed a loan to get him started, but as an established man with two titles, he finds it intolerable to have to acknowledge a continued reliance on others.

When Obierika brings the two bags of cowries that are the proceeds from Okonkwo's yams, Okonkwo says he does not know how to thank his friend. "Kill one of your sons for me," jokes Obierika, meaning that thanks should not be extravagant but observe the principles of proportion (142). "That will not be enough," replies Okonkwo. "Then kill yourself," replies Obierika. Okonkwo finally understands his friend's joke and asks forgiveness: he will not talk about unrepayable debts any more. Readers catch the joke's sinister underside planted by the narrator: Okonkwo, after all, has already killed a son, and Obierika knows it. Later Okonkwo will kill himself. Obierika's joke points to the extreme side of Okonkwo's need to clear debts at the most extreme of costs.

An entire chapter of Achebe's novel is devoted to the feast that Okonkwo, once again prosperous, throws at the end of the seven years of his exile to thank his maternal relatives for hosting him. Okonkwo "never did things by halves" (165), but he also cares not for reciprocity and scorns balance. His wife protests that two goats would be sufficient, but, no, Okonkwo insists on slaughtering three (165). He repays his kinsmen's generosity with his own, but, being Okonkwo, also wants to do more: he wants to clear his debt for good. He gives the greatest feast anyone in Mbanta has seen, but he refuses to marry his daughters to men from Mbanta. His own father had married a woman from Mbanta, and as we have seen, bridewealth is the marker of an intention eventually to return the gift, but Okonkwo instructs Ekwefu and her sister that they will not marry until the family has returned to Umuofia. Okonkwo does not want to say, as the Akueke's suitors had said to Obierika's family, "this is not the first time my people have come to marry your daughter. My mother was one of you ... And this will not be the last, because you understand us and we understand you. You are a great family" (117). To owe a debt that can never be repaid (such as one's life), and to clear one's debts once and for all (as Okonkwo wants to do here), are both contrary to the circulation of ordinary debts that establish ongoing horizontal relations among people.

European and American literature, of course, features cosmic debtors, like Faust, and cosmic debt collectors, like Shylock or Melville's Ahab, for whom debt transcends their relations to other human beings. Okonkwo is neither of these, but I am arguing he does bear a resemblance to another kind of debtor, one that has appeared in the last two centuries on a realist scale in a bourgeois economy – the man who reconfigures his debt so that it is no longer to other men but to society as a whole.

Benjamin Franklin is full of high praise for a patron, Mr. Denham, who, having once failed in business in Bristol and gone to America to start afresh and made a fortune, insists on returning to England to clear his debts. Denham invites all his old creditors to a dinner at which he thanks them, "and, when they expected nothing but the treat, every man at the first remove found under his plate an order on a banker for the full amount of the unpaid remainder with interest."[33] Okonkwo would fully appreciate the significance of the feast Mr Denham throws for his creditors. The money orders that his creditors find under their plates are a display of the host's wealth and generosity and a vindication of the judgment of those who had once trusted him, but they also settle the American's score with his British past. He does not just restore his reputation by repairing the human bonds broken by an unpaid debt but puts a glorious end to those bonds, clearing the slate.

Balzac's César Birotteau, a perfumer in Paris just after the restoration of the monarchy, feels a similar compulsion to clear his debts. Forced to declare insolvency, Birotteau had dissolved his debts, paying his creditors only 60 percent of what he owed them. From the point of view of the law, he has released himself from debt by paying all he has, albeit not all he owes, and the chastened perfumer can legally resume business on his own account. Not satisfied, however, with the line drawn by legal convention through his debts, he, his wife, and his daughter scrimp and save until, with the help of allies, they repay all the monies ever owed. The duty that Birotteau feels is a matter not of repairing relations with creditors, who are for the most part jealous people who have cheated him and do not deserve his repayment, but of restoring his honour. Birotteau's self-image presumes a field larger than his relations with others: "Nourished by religious ideas, Birotteau believed in Justice as it should be in human eyes, as the representation of society itself, the majestic expression of consent to the law, independent of the form under which it was produced."[34] This concern with repaying money that one is not obliged to is so rare as to deserve special notice. Everywhere the newly restored debtor is greeted with "Voilà un homme d'honneur!"[35] This "héros de probité commercial"[36] becomes that oxymoron, the bourgeois tragic hero.

For Birotteau, as for Mr. Denham, and, I am arguing, Okonkwo, debt can never be forgotten or forgiven. It has been internalized as an absolute measure of the self. Graeber argues that it is a modern idea that one owes a primordial debt to society and that this debt is the essence of society, subsuming and overriding one's debts to neighbours: "the notion that there is this thing called society, that we have a debt to it, that governments can speak for it, that it can be imagined as a sort of secular god – all of these ideas emerged together around the time of the French Revolution, or in its immediate wake. In other words, it was born alongside the idea of the modern nation-state."[37] That explains why Franklin's Mr. Denham, just before the American Revolution, and Balzac's César Birotteau, just after the French Revolution, feel that debt transcends human relations, but not why Okonkwo, living in an Igbo village group around 1900, at the moment of the cataclysmic intrusion of the colonizers, clears the slate of his debts at Mbanta and behaves as if he has transferred all his debts to Umuofia as a whole, which he is now prepared to defend to the death regardless of what his neighbours think.

Achebe's Umuofia is a village society characterized by reciprocity and achievement, but, as the setting of a novel, it must also represent the traditional past that the modern nation-state can inherit, a coherent whole greater than the interpersonal relations of its members. Okonkwo the self-made man in an achievement society is not anachronistic, but Okonkwo the realist character and tragic hero is new. For an explanation of Okonkwo, we need to look at the needs of the young Achebe, soon to be a citizen of an independent nation and self-consciously assuming the mantle of the father of African literature.

WHY OKONKWO STANDS AT THE ORIGINS OF WEST AFRICAN LITERATURE

Okonkwo prefers to acknowledge a debt to an idea of himself, inseparable from his idea of the collective whole, rather than debts of reciprocity to the people around him. This makes him a more consistently realist character than can be found in any of the other contenders for the title of the first African novel. We may better understand his newness by comparing him to characters in precursor African novels. Achebe's obsession with debt is shared not just with Franklin and Moodie, Premchand, and Selvon, but also with R.E. (Richard Emmanuel) Obeng's *Eighteenpence* and Tutuola's *The Palm-Wine Drinkard*.

One candidate for the claim to being the first West African novel, championed as such by Newell, is Obeng's *Eighteenpence*, written in 1938 and published in 1943 in the Gold Coast.[38] The title refers to a debt that launches the action. As "poor as a church rat" but determined to get married, Obeng-Akrofi decides to set up as a farmer. But colonial subjects find it hard to secure credit, which banks rarely extend to Africans. Refused a loan by a well-to-do neighbour, Akrofi buys a cutlass costing eighteenpence on credit. With that cutlass he is able to clear forest, turn bush into a farm, and grow crops according to the modern agricultural methods introduced by the British.

Eighteenpence, as its name suggests, turns on money. Newell writes that Obeng "manifests an intense consciousness of money, accounting for every penny spent, lost and gained by the protagonists. No previous (Gold Coast) novel pays such detailed attention to the prices paid for goods and the cash earned from cocoa sales and wage labour."[39] Akrofi's original loan bears fruit, allowing him to marry and then to educate his children. His success is premised on a rational world whose rules can be relied upon when making plans, where scientific principles hold true and virtue in the form of hard work is rewarded in British currency. In the final pages Akrofi builds himself a house crowned by two gold replicas of a cutlass; he names it Eighteenpence in honour of the modest sum that gave him his start (137). The house that marks his triumph is an emblem of the novel itself, which bears the same name and provides Akrofi the space in which to exist.

Akrofi resembles the heroes of eighteenth- and nineteenth-century European fiction in his self-conscious modernity, his self-reliance, and his openness to new markets reaching around the globe.[40] His initial loan of eighteenpence generates a forward propulsion permitting the debtor's self-actualization. His debt also, however, generates a resistance to that forward movement that repeatedly derails the plot and, for the length of the story, defers the ending. Newell characterizes the two opposing forces as the principle of "political order, rationality, truth-telling, the achievement of justice and civil stability" and "the chaotic element," embodied in particular by a very strong-minded woman, the wife of Akrofi's creditor.[41] Akrofi's loan also has a distinctly non-modern aspect. Because two weeks, the term of the loan of eighteenpence, is not enough time to produce a harvest on land that must first be cleared, Akrofi offers to work for his creditor for free until the harvest comes in. A condition of his subsequent rise is that he accept the condition of a "slave." That Akrofi accepts debt peonage as a condition of material progress is surely part of the reason that Obeng's novel has not inspired successors as Achebe's has.

Debt peonage was a common method of paying off a loan: similarly, a character called the Invisible-Pawn proposes to Tutuola's Palm-Wine Drinkard that he work "as a 'pawn' or as [a] permanent hired labourer" (86) in return for a loan of sixpence. Debt peonage in West Africa had long been part of a continuum of involuntary servitude that extended in one direction to chattel slavery and even ritual sacrifice, but in the other direction included domestic servitude and quasi-familial relations. Ikemefuna, sent to repay Mbaino's debt to Umuofia, exemplifies both poles: he is adopted into Okonkwo's family *and* sacrificed.

Debt peonage, which puts a debtor in another's power, is, in Africa, closely related to slavery, and it shadows African literature. The transatlantic slave trade changed everything by making the slave mere chattel, but even then, at least at sea, slavery sometimes retained its connection to notions of debt that could be cleared. Olaudah Equiano, who wrote an account of his life as a slave in the Americas in the eighteenth century, tells how his industry and prowess in trade enabled him, during voyages around the West Indies in the service of a ship's captain, to buy goods cheaply in one port to sell them at a profit in another. Equiano's own condition as a slave and an African prompts many of those who do business with him to cheat or rob him. Nevertheless, his astute dealing earns him the forty pounds necessary to buy his freedom. His master, initially reluctant, is reconciled to the loss of his slave by the consideration that, all things considered, Equiano has proven a worthwhile investment and that he has "received good interest for it all this time, and here is now the principal at last."[42] Equiano, the slave who builds his capital through trade in order to buy himself, and Akrofi, the poor man who becomes a slave in order to build up capital, are both self-made men. Together they illustrate how slavery, away from the plantations of the New World, could be a commercial transaction like debt. But they also remind us that debt could be like slavery, an exploitative burden and a form of inhuman social death.

In *Omenuko* by Pita Nwana, published in 1935, two decades before *Things Fall Apart*, and often hailed as the first Igbo-language novel, the protagonist, a prominent and successful trader to whom others have entrusted their sons as apprentices, loses all his trade goods in a flooded river. In order to recuperate his losses and preserve his business, Omenuko sells his apprentices, some of whom are his kinsmen, in the market where he had been bringing his goods. This betrayal of those entrusted to him by their parents restores his capital but spoils his reputation at home, and Omenuko is forced into exile. The sale converts a mutual relation based on personal trust into an inhuman treatment of others as commodities. The guilty Omenuko cannot rest until he has amassed sufficient wealth to redeem those he had sold and he is able to return them to their own people and restore his reputation.

Where *Things Fall Apart* makes debt peonage a problem and ritual sacrifice the climax of Okonkwo's tragedy, Obeng's *Eighteenpence* conflates what we commonly understand as distinct social and moral economies: one centred on the self-made man and the other on the debt pawn. The confusion is surely Obeng's, but it reflects a larger contradiction associated with the moral regime established by British colonialism. Akrofi makes his arrangement to pawn himself in 1913, five years after the British in the Gold Coast had made debt peonage illegal and punishable by seven years' imprisonment.[43] In Britain itself, indentured servitude had once been a potential punishment for crimes, and Daniel Defoe's Moll Flanders was sentenced to work alongside African slaves in a plantation in Virginia in the seventeenth century. In West Africa in the twentieth century, however, the British made involuntary servitude itself a crime punishable by imprisonment. British colonialism in Africa, which began after the abolition of slavery, found ideological self-justification in waging a campaign against what it deemed local forms of slavery. In Achebe's Igboland, the British tried to outlaw domestic slavery through a series of laws beginning in 1900.[44] Indeed, the British undertook the massive invasion of Igboland with the declared purpose "to abolish the slave trade which is actively carried out throughout the entire territories."[45] Any form of involuntary servitude that looked like slavery would fail to pass the "repugnancy test," the limit to British tolerance of indigenous custom.[46] Akrofi the self-made man becomes a slave and *thereby* breaks the law.

Colonial conquest in order to end slavery is contradictory on its face. In the Gold Coast in the late nineteenth century, "colonial administrators feared a premature abolition of slavery,"[47] for they doubted that the transition to free labour could be made without great disruption:

> the colonial states thus constructed an alternative to free labour. As long as they could rely on chiefs to recruit labour and impose discipline, labour shortages could be met. The failure to create a working class could even be turned into an achievement, as later officials warned of the dangers of proletarianization and presented the alternative labour system as a happy symbiosis of the old and the new.[48]

In Igboland the British replaced slavery with an apprenticeship system and called on chiefs to provide forced labour for colonial projects such as road-building. The Roads and Creeks Proclamation no. 15 of 1903 had decreed that chiefs could be forced to supply forced labour, with or without pay, from "all able-bodied men between the ages of 15 and 50 and all able-bodied women between the ages of 15 and 40": "Anyone who refused to comply was to be punished by fine, imprisonment, or flogging."[49] In Achebe's *Arrow of God*, set in 1922, the village group of Umuaro is required to supply labour to build a road. It cannot have been clear to Britain's new subjects where the difference lay between slavery, which had often existed on a continuum with kinship ties but was now condemned, and the new forms of coercion.[50]

Obeng's novel manifests other contradictions attributable to the experience of colonialism. The policy of indirect rule, which entailed deliberately preserving and working through traditional authorities, fostered overlapping courts, mutually contradictory legal systems, and "self-cancelling agencies of authority and legitimacy."[51] It did something more, however: it "led to the antidemocratic principle that the public domain is the sole property of rulers and that it is theirs to control as they please."[52] In relying on traditional chiefs for their own authority (and investing their authority in those chiefs), the British retained the precolonial land tenure system. That system, developed at a time of a low population density and readily available land, offered willing farmers like Akrofi and Okonkwo as much land as they had the strength and the dependents to clear and to farm on their own account. As the priestess Chika screams at Unoka, good farmers "go out with their ax to cut down virgin forests," whereas Unoka sows his yams "on exhausted farms that take no labor to clear" (17). But the same system of land tenure prevented the development of a wage labour market and threatened the prolongation of coerced labour. Eventually, Anne Phillips explains, in the first decades of the twentieth century, "trapped between the impossibility of a working class on the one hand, and the many difficulties of forced labour on the other," the British in West Africa lighted upon "the magical solution of a thriving peasantry."[53] Large corporations like Cadbury and the British Cotton Growing Association, discouraged from attracting and disciplining their own wage labour, did not invest in plantations but "preferred to 'mimic' mercantile capital, and leave production in the hands of African peasants."[54] Akrofi becomes a debt pawn and invests borrowed capital in order to generate wealth and become a better peasant.

Anne Phillips characterizes British colonialism in twentieth-century West Africa as an "enigma" for the way it deliberately fostered the existence of a self-sufficient peasantry instead of the development of a wage labour force. Historically, elsewhere, in order to harness production to the ends of accumulation, capitalism needed "workers who are, in Marx's ironic term, 'freed' from the ownership of means of production, freed from control over the production process, freed to sell their labour-power as a commodity."[55] In Southern Africa and Latin America, colonialism produced the conditions for this new labouring class by dispossessing millions of their land, requiring them to pay taxes in currency, and thereby forcing them to toil for wages as migrant workers in mines or on plantations. In West Africa, however, the British colonial administration was too weak to reorganize society on such a scale and came to rely on traditional chiefs both for extracting taxes and securing labour for infrastructure projects like roads. The British rejected Lord Leverhulme's proposal for palm oil plantations[56] and preserved the indigenous system of land tenure.[57] The result was what Hyden calls an "uncaptured peasantry,"[58] a peasantry that remained largely self-sufficient and that could rely on the support of urban family members and thus was able to escape being subordinated to the needs of capital or the state.

Akrofi's confusing status as a debt pawn paying off the loan he took out in order to become a self-sufficient peasant thus exposes the contradiction in the colonial economy. Akrofi grows onions and groundnuts as cash crops, later expanding to cocoa, which he sells to the United Africa Company, and fruit trees (99). When later he becomes rich, he acquires a labour force for himself by purchasing the freedom of other indebted people and then taking the cost of their redemption out of their wages. Colonialism integrated West Africa disadvantageously into the world economy as the site of peripheral processes, but the economic order, as opposed to the political oppression, was experienced by West Africans in more contradictory ways than it was in settler colonies or in Marxist theory.

At the end of the novel, in a further confusion, this time of genre, Akrofi's efforts are rewarded not only with abundant harvests but also with buried gold. Obeng concludes that "Mother Earth had indeed repaid Akrofi amply for his industry" (110), for it "was obvious that the central power of Akrofi's personal magnetism, which held together all what he possessed was nothing but industry which brought fortune in its train" (137). The gold that Akrofi finds is not mineral wealth but a jar buried by the Omanhene, the traditional ruler of Kwahu (114). Gold is, of course, the emblematic form of wealth in the Gold Coast,[59] but underground treasure is also a common element in imperialist romance, such as in Rider Haggard's *King Solomon's Mines* (1885) and John Buchan's *Prester John* (1910), where gold and diamonds hoarded underground by others and entirely divorced from the labour needed to mine them become the legitimate property of a character who deserves them merely because he is the protagonist, the man with a story. This is the dream of mercantilist capitalism, pure accumulation divorced from labour, productivity, or efficiency.

Obeng's novel revolves largely around a series of court cases, shifting between the traditional court and the District Commissioner's court and involving large outlays in the form of surety, bail, fines, and court expenses. *Eighteenpence* expresses a limitless interest in the new financial system of the colonizers and in the larger regime that has redefined law, justice, marriage, labour, and property. Akrofi, however, does not understand the workings of these. His triumph at the end of the novel is that the Chief Justice of the Gold Coast Colony and its dependencies upholds his legal right to keep the gold instead of surrendering it to the current Omanhene, as he would have had to do under the precolonial land tenure system. After being provided with land to farm by the Omanhene, he had subsequently bought it and become its proper owner. According to the British judge, then, even the wealth below the land is now Akrofi's property. Akrofi has thus benefited from two systems of land tenure – traditional title and private property – without registering the contradiction.

In *Eighteenpence*, set in 1913, thirty-five years before its publication, we find little awareness of historical change. The confusion the novel displays regarding court jurisdictions is not clearly demarcated as belonging to the past and might well be the author's own. *Things Fall Apart*, by contrast, written two decades later, on the eve of Nigeria's independence, but set a decade and more earlier, at the initial moment of colonial encounter, is able to imagine an *outside* to colonialism, a before and, by implication, an after. That all stories begin with their end is an implication of the past tense in which they are told and something that Achebe appreciated more than any of his precursors. He made the end from which the story is told central to the understanding of the African past: the precolonial can only be understood from the point of view of colonialism; colonialism from the point of view of decolonization. A position at the limit of colonialism, from which he is able to cast a look backward *and* forward, allows Achebe to locate colonialism in history. Colonialism had limits. It can be seen around and fitted into a story that the soon-to-be formerly colonized tell themselves. Achebe evades the confusion associated with the colony by suggesting that there is a clear moral distinction to be made between different kinds of debt *and* by projecting that distinction onto precolonial society.

Obeng's Akrofi has no interiority and no psychology. He is rewarded in part because he is a good credit risk but primarily because he is the protagonist. Where Akrofi is a mass of contradictions – a successful peasant and a debt slave, a peasant farmer who inherits the gold of a king – Achebe divides similar contradictions neatly into what Okonkwo desires and what he fears. Slavery, in the person of the young hostage and eventual sacrificial victim Ikemefuna, poses a moral issue. Okonkwo the self-made man is a peasant farmer who represents tradition rather than modernity. He, like Akrofi, becomes rich as a result of his strategic loans and his own efforts, but colonialism is not what makes this possible; indeed, colonialism brings about his downfall. Okonkwo's virtues brought him success before colonialism and may be the virtues Achebe believes are needed after colonialism, but under colonialism they spell ruin.

Tutuola's *The Palm-Wine Drinkard*, published six years before *Things Fall Apart* and thus another legitimate contender for the claim to be the first West African novel, ignores colonialism almost entirely, but, as we might expect, debt and credit figure prominently in it. Among the many adventures the eponymous protagonist and his wife have is a year-long stay with Faithful-Mother, an interlude of perfect bliss during which the couple are able to "sell their death" for £70.18.6d and "lend their fear" to someone who pays interest of £3.10.0d per month (67). This is an image of clearing one's own debts for good and becoming an eternal creditor. It is, however, too good to last. When the year comes to an end, the couple's fear is returned to them.

The Drinkard is also asked to judge a court case involving a chronic debtor who sounds like no one so much as Unoka:

> There were two friends, one of these two friends was money borrower, he had no other work than to borrow and he was feeding on any money that he was borrowing. One day he borrowed £1 from his friend. After a year his friend who lent him the money, asked him to refund the £1 to him, but the borrower said he would not pay the £1 and said that he had never paid any debit since he was borrowing money and since he was born. (111)

The desperate creditor then hires a debt collector, who boasts that "*he* never failed to collect debits from any debitor since *he* had begun the work" (111). The Drinkard is asked to judge between the two men. The case comes across as a comical version of Okoye's case against Unoka, except that £1 is much bigger than Unoka's debt.[60] As always in Tutuola, however, farce retains an aspect of terror. Debtor and debt collector fight, until the debtor pulls out a knife and stabs not his harrier but himself – committing suicide over a £1 debt! – whereupon the debt collector, determined to pursue what is owed him into the next world, pulls out a knife as well and kills himself (112).

The Drinkard assumes it is perfectly normal that that there be borrowers and therefore lenders. Also to be expected is that debtors will try not to repay and that creditors will pursue them. He registers confusion, however, when it comes to the colonial court system's moral judgment of debt. The Drinkard is not asked to decide to whom the £1 belongs but rather to assign "guilt," a moral notion marked as foreign. He cannot blame the "collector, because he was doing his work and also the debitor himself because he was struggling for what he was living on," so, unable to understand what guilt might mean here or why debt should be a crime, the Drinkard adjourns the trial for a year (113). Is this a lawsuit or a criminal case? The Drinkard finally asks readers of his book to help him judge by sending him their opinion (115). The Drinkard cannot pry borrower and lender apart but trusts that his readers will know the answer because they have read books and books teach whom to credit. Of course, readers are likely to feel that the Drinkard also does not understand the contract between writer and readers, which does not allow for two-way communication (except in the case of pamphlet-writing such as Onitsha market literature) any more than he understands the criminal code's attitude toward debt.

Achebe himself read Tutuola's imaginative tale against the grain as a stern moral fable in which the hero must forsake his pleasure-seeking ways and work for a living. According to Achebe, the Drinkard's fault is that "he attempted to reverse the order of things and put play in the place of work."[61] He has "an appetite which knows no limit or boundary,"[62] and he must learn these. The Drinkard's adventures, according to Achebe, change "him from a social parasite to a leader and a teacher whose abiding gift to his people is to create the condition in which they can overcome want and reliance on magic and return to the arts of agriculture and husbandry."[63] This is a puritanical misreading of Tutuola, who does indeed say that work is an unfortunate necessity and that suffering is inescapable, but who sees no virtue in this harsh reality and who values eating, singing, drumming, and dancing as what make life worth living. While it is true that, in Tutuola's novel, feasting always ends, it is not true, as Achebe the critic suggests, that work is rewarded. On the contrary, drought and famine in *The Palm-Wine Drinkard* are brought on by insatiable monsters who must be outwitted and killed, or by Heaven's displeasure, which must be placated by sacrifice. The three "good" creatures Drum, Dance, and Song are able to rid the narrator and his wife of the terrible baby with the limitless appetite who is eating all their food. Drum, Dance, and Song have disappeared from the world, and people "are only hearing their names about in the world" (85), but that is the world's loss. The Drinkard, himself a mass of appetites, reacts to events and to others in a way that does not reflect character but rather his status as the novel's protagonist. He is a trickster, able to change shape and become a bird or a fire and smoke, able to deceive and trap Death and the people of Dead Town. And, as we shall see, Achebe the realist novelist has moral reservations about tricksters.

Critical misreadings are themselves illuminating. Achebe defends Tutuola as "the most moralistic of all Nigerian writers,"[64] one who teaches that "play, though a necessary restorative, is not only a temporary but even an illusory escape from the reality of waking life which is work with its attendant pain and suffering."[65] Achebe deliberately does not invoke in defence of Tutuola the "misguided," even dangerous notion that literature "should be solely enjoyed for its own sake,"[66] even though another reading of *The Palm-Wine Drinkard* would conclude that the novel has the serious purpose of celebrating the healthy and humane value of play in all its forms.

When Achebe defends "agriculture and husbandry" and abhors the "illusory escape" of play, he sounds like no one so much as Okonkwo, who has no patience for women's stories and cannot abide leisure. Okonkwo stammers, lacks eloquence, and has none of his father's winning ways. Yet the author of *Things Fall Apart*, almost in spite of himself, asks that readers, like the wealthy Nwakibie, put their money on the surly, violent, but industrious self-made man and warns them against Unoka. The young Achebe was writing what he thought new citizens needed to read: it was not a question of pleasing readers but of creating them.[67]

Because of the success with which Achebe answered the questions he asked of himself, *Things Fall Apart* stands at the origin of a literary tradition that has inspired two subsequent generations of African readers and novelists and their readers. Nevertheless, wherever one finds the realist novel, one also finds an anti-novel that focuses on characters who remain without projects for the self: think of Sterne's *Tristram Shandy*, or Goncharov's *Oblomov*. *The Palm-Wine Drinkard* can best be read as an anti-novel *avant la lettre*, the inspiration for an anti-tradition of its own that, after the military coups of 1966, would inspire Ben Okri.

THE FORGIVENESS OF DEBTS

To take the measure of the new state of which he will be a citizen, Achebe considers the alternatives, especially the reciprocity that governed the precolonial achievement society, and the costs, as seen in the case of Okonkwo, who transfers all of his debts to others into a single transcendent debt to the collective. I have argued that Achebe creates this new man, who more resembles a citizen of a modern state than a traditional member of an achievement society, in order to explore the implications of realism and citizenship.

Flora Nwapa's 1966 novel *Efuru*, frequently considered the first West African novel by a woman, reminds us that there always was an alternative to Okonkwo's sacrifice of Ikemefuna. Nwapa has readily admitted that she had *Things Fall Apart* in mind when she wrote.[68]

The eponymous protagonist, a wealthy trader in colonial Igboland, is approached by her in-law Nwosu, a man fully as improvident as Unoka, for a loan of ten pounds. Nwosu offers his daughter to serve Efuru as a maid and promises to repay the loan at the end of the year with four pounds interest, at which point his daughter will return home (38). The sentence "That was how Ogea came to live with Efuru and her husband" (40) echoes the sentence "That was how Ikemefuna came to live with Okonkwo."

The "pawning" (98) of a family member to secure a debt was only made illegal in Nigeria in the 1930s,[69] much later than in the Gold Coast that Obeng wrote about. Indeed, colonialism at first exacerbated debt pawnship by imposing taxes; in order to earn money, some people had to pawn their children.[70] "Poor men would borrow from the rich, pledging their lands or their own persons, or the person of a kinsman as collateral. The labor of the pawn or the usufruct of the land thus acquired merely satisfied the interest obligation of the debtor, and would end only when the debt was fully paid."[71] Pawns in Igboland were classified as *ohu*, the same generic term applied to slaves, but the situation of the pawns was not as dire as that of others; some were accepted as members of the family and so were better off than in their own homes.[72] Unlike Ikemefuna, debt pawns retained their connections to their lineages and could not be resold, sacrificed, or killed. They could always be redeemed by repaying the loan they had secured.[73]

In Nwapa's *Efuru*, the feckless Nwosu's willingness to pawn his daughter is part of a larger pattern of irresponsibility: at the feast of the new yam, instead of using his harvest to repay his loan, he liberally dispenses money to the singing and dancing children until soon he has nothing left. To him it "did not matter whether a farmer had paid for the money borrowed for his farm or not. All that mattered was that the year's work had come to an end and it was time for feasting" (102). Later, he spends the fruits of his harvest on earning a title instead of redeeming his daughter. Taking a title was a common reason for pawning a child,[74] but it involved a fatal illogic: taking a title is a celebration of wealth and status, but Nwosu's wealth is not his own.

Ogea and Ikemefuna, the unfortunate pawns of the debts owed by adults, both cry when they first arrive at their new homes until their respective masters, Efuru and Okonkwo, flog them. Eventually, however, both children settle down; Ikemefuna calls Okonkwo father, and Ogea comes to regard Efuru as her mother (90). It is a mark of Efuru's goodness that she treats Ogea as a member of her family, indeed as the child she herself does not yet have. She supplies Ogea with cloth and food and teaches her the skills associated with being a woman. In the end Efuru even encourages the idea of having Ogea as a co-wife.

In rewriting *Things Fall Apart*, Nwapa also rewrote the sacrifice of Ikemefuna, which I have read as an assertion of Okonkwo's sovereignty. Whereas Okonkwo insists on his fidelity to the will of the oracle and participates in the sacrifice of the boy, Efuru forgives Nwosu his debt, thereby freeing Ogea. The creditor turns Nwosu's loan into a pure gift, just as earlier she had treated Ogea, the debt pawn, as a daughter. She does not abstract financial principles from personal relations; rather, she converts debts to the human scale. As Graeber puts it, "'redemption' is no longer about buying something back. It's really more a matter of destroying the entire system of accounting."[75] Hobbes writes that "men are freed of their Covenants two ways; by Performing; or by being Forgiven. For Performance, is the naturall end of obligation; and Forgivenesse, the restitution of liberty; as being a retransferring of that Right, in which the obligation consisted."[76] The equilibrium that is the ideal of reciprocity occasionally requires a sacrifice – in this case, of the debt to which one is entitled – in order to restore a baseline for future relations. This is the sacrifice not of a child by a parent but of an entitlement; the goal is not transcendence but ongoing interpersonal relations. Debts in Nwapa's novel remain on a human scale and based on reciprocity. When debt threatens to oppress, debt can even be forgiven. We shall have more to say about Efuru and female accounting in Chapter 5.

4

Of Confidence and Markets

There is another way of thinking about the contrast between Okonkwo and his father Unoka. Okonkwo's loan from Nwakibie took the form of seed yams, which directly reward labour by producing more yams that can be eaten or planted. Achebe's novel emphasizes the wealth generated by self-sufficient agriculture, wealth that takes the form of yams amassed in barns. Unoka, by contrast, who owes cowries – that is, money – dodges his creditor Okoye by spinning a story about chalk marks on the wall that record his debts. Achebe's novel is mistrustful of money, and Unoka, who brazenly shirks his debts, is the character closest to an actual trickster (as opposed to Tortoise, the trickster of folk tales) in precolonial Umuofia.[1]

The scene where Unoka welcomes Okoye is the only occasion in precolonial Umuofia in which we see graphic writing on something other than the body. The chalk marks that Unoka shows Okoye, like the first historical use of writing, have as their purpose the keeping of accounts, but in this case, they serve as a deceptive alternative to the actual payment of debts. Each of the chalk marks supposedly records a particular debt between the period it is contracted and the time it is repaid. Given Unoka's cavalier attitude toward debt, however, we understand that the marks are never cleared, only added to, and that Okoye will never be paid. The chalk marks are arranged in five groups, the smallest of which has ten strokes, each stroke representing one hundred cowries; in other words, Unoka has not even registered Okoye's two-hundred-cowrie loan! This written record kept by the debtor is intended to convince his creditors that a written record is an adequate substitute for and safeguard of the material wealth represented, but Okoye surely takes away the opposite lesson: that writing has no inherent tie to what it represents but is only the trace of its absence.

Unoka displays some of the trickster's gift for representing the world with such ungainsayable plausibility that others must acquiesce to his version: Obi Nwakanma refers admiringly to Unoka's "self-assurance that is associated with the Igbo cultural psychology and notions of the self."[2] Nevertheless, as we have noted, the novel deplores his fecklessness. Instead of tokens of the trust among friends, Unoka's chalk marks fold his debts into a larger, more abstract and depersonalized representation of his entire debt. Each mark on Unoka's wall indicates that, as with the writing on later Bank of Nigeria notes, he "promises to pay on demand the sum of" one hundred cowries, but it also signals that he will do nothing of the kind. The scene of debt collection in *Things Fall Apart* thus bears a family resemblance to another genre altogether: the treatise on political economy, an eighteenth- and nineteenth-century European genre that deployed allegory to understand money. William Cobbett, writing in 1815 to protest the issuing of paper money, asks what happens when money comes untied from gold and silver and instead represents something as amorphous and as difficult to understand as the national debt:

> Let us suppose, then, that the Government wants a *loan* ... and ... [that] the money is lent, by Mssrs. Muckworm and Company ... Well: what does Muckworm get in return? Why, *his name is written in a book; against his name is written, that he is entitled to receive interest for a million of money*; which book is kept at the Bank Company's house, or shop, in Threadneedle Street, London ... "Well," you will say, "but *what becomes of the money?*" Why, the Government *expends* it, to be sure ... "What? Then the money all *vanishes*; and *nothing remains in lieu of it but the lender's name written in a book?*" Even so: and this, my good neighbours, is the way, that "*money is put into the Funds.*"[3]

Like Cobbett's bank, Unoka takes another's wealth and, should the creditor come to collect, welcomes him with ceremony and reassures him that the debt has been dutifully recorded.

I see in the novel's insistence on use-value and suspicion of money a nostalgia that has less to do with precolonial tradition and more to do with the anxieties of the modern citizen. At the heart of the ontological and moral distinction that *Things Fall Apart* draws between Unoka and Okonkwo is a modern anxiety about the foundations upon which money rests. I have argued that *Things Fall Apart* deploys realism to secure the credit of readers in the world it depicts. Yet paradoxically, it anchors that credit not in modern institutions but in subsistence farming. Is there some absolute value such as yams that money merely represents and that secures the value of money? Or is there nothing more underwriting money than faith in social relations? In which case, what is to stop money from encouraging confidence men and charlatans?

In highlighting the importance of subsistence agriculture, Achebe's novel radically downplays the network of markets linking Umuofia to its immediate neighbours, including Mbaino, Abame, and the more distant Umuike. Umuofia and its neighbours each host markets on a regular rotating basis at four-day intervals called a "market week." On market days, the villages fill with strangers. A market in full swing, we are repeatedly told, is the greatest noise that the Igbo know (88, 202). Umuike, the largest market of them all (surely based on Onitsha), is "a wonderful place," where people are so many "that if you threw up a grain of sand it would not find a way to fall to earth again" (113). Yet the market is almost entirely absent from the narrated scenes in *Things Fall Apart*: we are only shown people discussing Umuike.

The novel's mistrust of markets is gendered. The yam harvest that is the source of men's wealth and status faces risks from flood and drought. To balance those risks, women grow other crops, such as cocoyams, beans, and cassava. They trade in order to cover shortfalls. Okonkwo's wife Ekwefi and her friend Chielo, the priestess of the Oracle, keep adjoining stalls in the market. Because it is associated with women, trade appears less than honourable to Okonkwo. There has been much critical commentary on Achebe's failure to do justice to the role of women in precolonial Igbo society, and the relative absence of the market is of a piece with this imbalance.[4]

MONEY

Markets have always been part of Africa. Except "in the European fantasy of the 'Dark Continent,' there never was in pre-colonial Africa production without exchange."[5] As Chabal notes, "other than agricultural production for food, the bulk of Africa's economic activities are concerned with commerce – formal or informal, legal or illegal – which essentially boils down to the exchange of goods for money."[6] As anyone who has travelled through Africa knows, villages are also markets, roads through towns are lined with stalls and stores, city pavements are taken over by goods for sale, and hawkers, strolling between cars stopped in traffic jams, sell all manner of goods. In any urban scene it can seem as if half the people are trying to sell to the other half. An Igbo proverb quoted by Tess Onwueme has it that "the World is a market place. If you bargain well, you profit. If you do not you lose."[7] The Yoruba also considered that "the world itself is a market; abstract values such as truth and falsehood are bought and sold there; anything that is highly prized – including good behavior or profound thought – is described as being 'worth money.'"[8]

Tutuola's Palm-Wine Drinkard explains that at the time his adventures began (sometime in the twentieth century, that is, after the events of *Things Fall Apart*), "we did not know other money, except COWRIES" (7). Gikandi writes that the lack of "money, the modern standard of exchange," signals that the world of Tutuola's narrator is premodern.[9] He assumes that precolonial Africa did without money. But no society anywhere has ever been based on barter; Graeber argues that a barter economy is an invention of economics textbooks.[10] Certainly "barter was never a central feature of the southern Nigerian economic system."[11] The Palm-Wine Drinkard does not say that they did not have money, but that their only money had been cowries. The British did not introduce money, the "general equivalent," to a land of innocence where debts took the form of seed yams; cowrie shells had been established as currency for centuries in West Africa. In Igboland a group of six cowries was called an *ego*, which is now the word for all money, including coins and banknotes. *Things Fall Apart* itself refers repeatedly to "money" (4, 90, 142, 163, 165).

During the slave trade, the major imports to West Africa were textiles and money.[12] Cowrie shells, imported since the sixteenth century by European traders from the Maldive Islands in the Indian Ocean to the west coast of Africa and by Arab traders to the Sahel region long before that, were the chief form of currency throughout Yorubaland and northern and western Igboland.[13] In the nineteenth century, cowries circulated alongside iron bars, manillas (horseshoe-shaped metal bars used as currency in southern Igboland),[14] and European coins. The slave trade did not introduce markets and money to a society without, but during the period of the slave trade, more than a half century before the events of *Things Fall Apart*, "the money supply increased, cash transactions became easier, a larger proportion of output was oriented toward the market, and goods and services flowed more smoothly and over a wider area than before."[15] This increase in money did not improve economic welfare: Africa lost millions of prime workers; piracy and raiding became rampant; and there was a terrible coarsening of morality, for "any person could be reduced to a monetary value."[16] There is therefore good reason for West Africans to mistrust the market, as Achebe does.

As argued in a previous chapter, however, it would be an error to view Umuofia to be a deformed society created by the slave trade and fallen from a pristine wholeness. Its citizens see their world as whole and consistent and, as the title of Achebe's novel suggests, something that tragically collapses with the coming of colonialism. Since cowries had had centuries to gain acceptance as the order of the world and were only displaced in the twentieth century – quite suddenly and forcibly – they feel like the order of things to the people of Umuofia and like a vestigial tradition to the Palm-Wine Drinkard.

The British officially prohibited the use of cowries as legal tender in 1902 (presumably just after the events of *Things Fall Apart*, where even the colonial administration charges fines in cowries), but "it required over fifty years of coercive legislations for the older currencies to be fully retired."[17] That is why Tutuola characterizes the past not as *when* there were cowries – from his point of view that was just yesterday – but as when there were *only* cowries. In *Arrow of God*, set in 1922 in a village group close to Umuofia, a woman buyer offers a seller three *ego* (eighteen cowries) for some prepared cassava, intending, after bargaining, to go as high as four (211). By contrast, the colonial authorities pay the labourers building a road (when they pay them at all) threepence a day, a wage that an overseer may unilaterally reduce to two (75). Twopence is the price of a full-grown cock (105) and roughly what Unoka owed Okoye in *Things Fall Apart*.

Unlike coins, cowries "were not centrally minted and were not amenable to centralized manipulation."[18] They did not carry the validation of a sovereign, a state, or a bank, and they circulated in a field much larger than any political entity. The title of David Northrup's book, *Trade without Rulers*, summarizes what had been the most salient characteristic of the cowrie economy. The area where cowries held sway in the nineteenth century was not politically united, and no one in the West African hinterland at the time would have had an exact idea of how far it extended. Markets were like international free zones where people from everywhere congregated. As Northrup writes, "in this land of small political units important markets became islands of political neutrality as well, and the preservation of order and justice in them became an exercise in international law."[19] Specially created deities had responsibility for keeping the peace in the market and punishing those who violated it.[20] It remained the case, however, that traders had to make their own security arrangements: "There simply did not exist a public force charged with and capable of safeguarding travelers. This is in very clear contrast to the situation in the more centralized societies of West Africa where, from an early date, traders and other travelers had been charged tolls on roads and in markets for which in return they could expect the protection of the public authorities."[21] Trade was not *within* a state but *between* village groups, and given the absence of an overarching authority that could ensure the security of travellers, traders moved along a chain of relays, from one known and trusted host to the next.[22] Trust in these cases was established by gift exchange, by marriage, and by rituals and solemn oaths of alliance.[23] In this world, there was a need for trust, and as a corollary, mistrust was ever-present – which is what inspired trickster tales.

Cowries remained popular in West Africa for as long as they did because small market traders, generally women, dealt in sums too small to be measured in coins. There was a sizable gap between the value of a single cowrie and that of the smallest coin, an *anini* or one tenth of a penny, first introduced in West Africa in 1906.[24] There were 120 *anini* to the shilling, but 1,500 cowries to the shilling in Igboland in 1902.[25] The fact that cowries came in only one denomination was a drawback, of course, for larger debts: the value of cowries was a direct function of their number (the time to count them was an integral part of transactions) and weight.[26] For large sums, therefore, coins or bills, whose value is a function not of size but of what is written upon them, were more convenient. (In times of hyperinflation, when even the largest-denomination bills are almost worthless, as in Zimbabwe after 2000, even paper money may need to be carried in suitcases or wheelbarrows, just as cowries were in bags.)

In the closing decades of the nineteenth century, cowries had fallen to one tenth of what their worth had been at the beginning of the century.[27] Okonkwo, who borrows seed yams rather than money, and Achebe, the author of *Things Fall Apart*, may not have known of this devaluation but they might well have sensed it. Herbst writes that it would be hard to find a more dramatic example than the devaluation of the cowrie "of how difficult it was for these states to mediate pressures from the international environment."[28] That said, however, the devaluation did not make cowries worthless, and in "no part of West Africa was the collapse as complete as it was for the Revolutionary Continentals, or Confederate States Dollars, or the German mark in 1923."[29]

The British spent five decades trying to remove cowries and manillas from West Africa and install their own coins and notes, not because they thought the latter were money and the former were not, but because cowries were not accepted as currency in Europe and therefore were not attractive to the British as payment for taxes in Nigeria. Ben Naanen writes: "From the point of view of colonialism the continuing circulation of the traditional currencies was not conducive to the establishment of the close and unequal economic ties between the colonial periphery and the metropolitan core which were necessary for the transfer of surplus from the former to the latter."[30]

At first the colonial administration introduced British currency to West Africa, but when the amount in West Africa outstripped that in Britain itself, Britain feared losing control of its money, so in 1912 it introduced the West African pound, which would circulate only in West Africa.[31] British West African currency was backed by sterling, which was in turn backed by gold reserves,[32] which meant that supply was severely restricted. The shortage was only alleviated when the new Central Bank of Nigeria introduced a new currency in 1959, an event reflected in Munonye's 1978 novel *Bridge to a Wedding*, set on the eve of independence. In that novel, the prospect of the new nation is accompanied by a building boom, attributable to the fact that "money was coming into the land at a fast rate, from where nobody knew for sure. The most popular guess however was that the Government, at long last alive to its responsibilities, had bought four additional minting machines, a thing that ought to have been done long before now."[33] Another cause of the increase in liquidity was that the major banks, which had previously dealt primarily with European and Syrian traders and refused credit to Africans, changed their policies when independence loomed.[34]

The economic zone once defined by the use of cowries, and not identified with any state, continues to be relevant today, in the absence of cowries. Informal trading, "the central economic activity in Africa,"[35] has always persisted alongside the official economy, ignoring state borders. In the colony of Nigeria the British never fully succeeded in setting up a banking system thoroughly tied to the state.[36] A large part of the Nigerian economy always has been and still is informal, beyond the surveillance or control of the state and, of course, beyond taxes and tariffs. As Chabal notes, "the bulk of the African population is active in the informal sector and operates according to the rules of the informal economy," where "the priority is the maximization of security rather than income and the time frame is the present rather than the future."[37]

THE TRICKSTER

In *Things Fall Apart* Achebe writes *about* the moment just before British coins displace cowries shells as money, but writes *at* the moment when British West African currency is about to be replaced by Nigerian currency. He displays an anxiety about market exchange and its trickster values and implicitly wants to anchor value in something intrinsically valuable, like labour or yams. He also writes realism, which, I have argued, makes trust a question of transpersonal institutions that render people and transactions knowable and able to be judged. But the market in West Africa did not have such transpersonal institutions that could enforce consistent rules; rather, it required relations of trust that had always to be negotiated anew by people alive to the risks and the need for mistrust. This circumstance inspired trickster stories such as are told even in Achebe's Umuofia.

As David Carroll notes, the men of Umuofia "enjoy testing each other's credulity to the utmost."[38] They tell with horror (but also some pleasure) of the man who went to sell a goat in the large market of Umuike, a place that the narrative itself never travels to: "He led it on a thick rope which he tied round his wrist. But as he walked through the market he realized that people were pointing at him as they do to a madman. He could not understand it until he looked back and saw that what he led at the end of the tether was not a goat but a heavy log of wood" (113–14). Modern stories tell of genitals disappearing in Onitsha market in the same way. Such stories are part of the stock in trade of market traders to make newcomers to the market fearful and persuade them to rely on their services as go-betweens. The trickster tale can serve a trickster's purposes. Tutuola also warns of the need to mistrust people met in the market: the Palm-Wine Drinkard tells of meeting a curious creature there, a "complete gentleman" of irresistible beauty, who is, however, merely a Skull with rented body parts attached. Defeating such a trickster requires vigilance as well as tricks of one's own.

In *Things Fall Apart*, Igbo verbal culture is primarily represented by proverbs and by a tale of the trickster Tortoise told by Okonkwo's wife Ekwefi to her daughter, a fable about borrowing, trust, and the abuse of trust that resonates with many of the themes of the novel in which it appears. Tortoise, the hero of many tales, is an expert in reading others and in making them misread him. In Ekwefi's tale, when the birds paint their bodies with cam wood and *uli*, the trickster knows they have been invited to a feast in the sky thrown by the sky-people. The earthbound Tortoise asks to join them, but they are initially wary because they have been burned by this smooth talker before. When the birds reply that they know him "too well," he declares, "You do not know me," which is both a lie and a truth, because with these very words he is deceiving them. Tortoise has a "sweet tongue" (97), and as always, he convinces them he is a changed man. There would be no story otherwise. The birds are persuaded to give him a feather each, with which he makes wings to join them on the trip to the sky.

The birds give to Tortoise for the same reason that Unoka's friends lend to him: because in a subsistence economy, where survival is the first priority, forging alliances by giving to neighbours is necessary. The birds' gift of the feathers is part of a larger circulation of gifts, as is the feast thrown by the sky-people. Their gift of feathers is a literalization of Godbout's principle: "Every gift is a gift of the self,"[39] marking the gift's inalienable tie to the giver. Nevertheless, if a listener to the story is sure of anything, it is that the trust of the birds will be betrayed. One of the delights of Ekwefi's story is the improvisational skill that allows the trickster to satisfy his hunger.

The trickster tale has a premise directly opposed to that of novelistic realism: it warns that all relations require trust but also mistrust because no larger institutions exist to render other people's behaviour predictable. And even if there were, the rules they established would be broken. In a society in which oratory, the power to persuade others, is the greatest talent, everyone needs to cultivate the skills of Tortoise and to guard against those same skills. Trickster tales notoriously do not make moral judgments: the cleverness of the trickster is admired even as his selfishness invites a comeuppance. The tales warn against foolishness as much as they condemn trickery – the birds are all gulls as it were – but they are concerned not with judgment or with admonishment so much as with what Lewis Hyde calls "invigorating experiences of transgression, salutary dunkings in ambivalence."[40]

Tortoise in Ekwefi's story is a cultural mediator, "a widely-travelled man who knew the customs of different peoples" (97). He exploits the point at which the animals meet strangers with whom they do not as yet have relations. On their flight to the sky, Tortoise explains to his avian fellow travellers the "age-old custom" of taking new names when attending a feast. He himself will take the name All-of-you. Because the birds are aware that their knowledge has limits that coincide with their community, Tortoise convinces them he knows something they do not: how to explain the sky-people. He can convince them of this because the birds already assume that the sky-people are knowable and explicable, which is the premise of novelistic realism. The birds "know" that Tortoise, a well-travelled man, "knows" the customs in other places. Once at the feast, he acts as the birds' spokesman and invites their hosts to assume that he is the king of the birds. Tortoise is "happy," the sky-people are "happy," and the birds are "glad": with words, he has created a reality that satisfies everyone. But not for long. When Tortoise asks who the great feast is for and the hosts reply that it is "for all of you," he claims all the food for himself. Tortoise explains to the suddenly unhappy birds that "the custom here is to serve the spokesman first and the others later"; at the same time, he allows the sky-people to assume that it is some strange "custom" of the birds "to leave all the food for their king" (98). He behaves toward the sky-people throwing the feast like a native informant manipulating ethnologists: he knows that when people encounter others from distant parts, they expect to witness behaviour they cannot read, and they will assume it is coherent and consistent. But this trickster has invented the cultural differences he is now exploiting.

In Ekwefi's tale the angry birds take back their feathers, leaving Tortoise stranded in the sky. He must make the hazardous leap back to earth, at which point one of his victims plays a trick on the trickster himself. Parrot, who usually can be trusted to do no more than repeat words, carries a message from Tortoise to his wife below on earth but tells her to bring out not soft things with which to break her husband's fall but hard things. Parrot, in other words – literally, in other words – repeats not Tortoise's message but his behaviour. The trickster tale is a reminder that the exchange of gift and countergift can be turned into the reciprocity of injuries and blows. The gift of feathers has been replaced by a collision with the hardest metal objects.

The trickster falls to earth and cracks his shell, but this is by no means the last of Tortoise. He will pick himself up. His ascent to the sky and fall to earth are a parody of the tragic arc traced by Okonkwo, but he is not psychically scarred by his experience, as Okonkwo is. His cracked shell does not correspond to a traumatic split in the self. It is impossible to imagine him committing suicide.

THE TRICKSTER IN THE COLONY

After her mother's tale, Ezinma starts to tell the story of when Tortoise and Cat went to wrestle against Yams (100). (Yams might almost be Okonkwo's ring name, for as a young man, he won fame for throwing Amalinze the Cat.) Wrestlers, like tricksters, need to study how an antagonist thinks in order to throw him. Achebe's novel delights in retelling a bout between two evenly matched wrestlers who have faced each other so often that "the one knew what the other was thinking" (50). That match ends when one of them miscalculates and goes down on one knee, and the other swings his leg over his head to claim victory. The victor is then acclaimed by the village group, for wrestlers, again like tricksters, are cultural heroes. There are limits, however, to the comparison, for

Okonkwo, the greatest wrestler of his time, has nothing of the trickster about him. As we have seen, his father is more like a trickster. From Okonkwo's point of view, tricksters are the subject of women's tales and to be scorned.

The tale of Tortoise the cultural mediator has an ironic and sinister echo outside Ekwefi's story in the world of Umuofia itself. In the last third of the novel, the District Commissioner sends a messenger, "sweet-tongued" like Tortoise, to invite a delegation of elders of Umuofia to talk "like friends" (193). At the "palaver," the DC asks whether his men, non-local Igbos, could be allowed to attend so that they might learn, because "although they speak your tongue they are ignorant of your customs" (193). Like the birds in Ekwefi's story, the men of Umuofia are aware that they do not know how the strangers think. It is not their ignorance, however, but their assumption that they are ignorant that leaves them open to exploitation. Once admitted, the DC's men forcibly arrest the elders in an egregious abuse of trust such as we have not previously seen in the novel. The DC speaks to the treacherously handcuffed elders of "a peaceful administration" that will administer justice impartially "to you and your people so that you may be happy" (194), but his words ring sour. There is no court to which one might protest the DC's own arbitrary violence.

The colonizers introduce a disconnect between words and the world that tricksters can exploit. The DC charges Umuofia an exorbitant collective fine (or ransom) of 200 bags of cowries (remember that a bride price is twenty bags), but the court messengers, Igbos mediating between the British and the villagers, twist his words and tell Umuofia that the fine is 250 bags, intending to pocket the difference (196). The DC must rely on a host of local authorities, chiefs, court messengers, and customary courts to carry out his will, and these derive their power not from the people they control nor even from the law, but from the fact that the DC depends on them. In the colony, as in the sky of Ekwefi's story, access to resources depends on manipulating blinkered foreign authorities located so high above that they do not see what is happening below. Colonialism makes for a knowledge differential that requires cultural mediation (not one of Okonkwo's skills), and this opens the door to abuse.

Things Fall Apart blames the increased potential for crafty manipulation directly on a new instability in language introduced by the imposition of British rule with its foreign language, laws, and God. The presence of the crafty court messengers in the last part of the novel recasts the meaning of Ekwefi's tale. Tortoise had first pretended to be a bird and an invitee, but then pretends to the sky-people to be the king of those who had brought him. He foresaw that the sky-people would assume that the birds have a king, just as later the missionaries arriving in Umuofia immediately ask who the king is (148). That there is a king is the default assumption people make when meeting another group. Tortoise's words create the very reality they name: by declaring himself the one able to speak, he really does become the spokesman of the birds. This shell of a king does not acknowledge that he is beholden to those who have given him their feathers. Tortoise behaves as though he owes nothing to those below him and misappropriates the feast for himself, cheating not only the birds, who go hungry, but also the sky-people, whose generosity fails to reach their guests. Tortoise, who speaks for "all of you," is a forerunner of those colonial and postcolonial politicians who argue that they *are* the constituency they are supposed to represent and who appropriate for themselves the resources meant for their constituents.[41]

Representative democracy such as the British have at home and will eventually establish in Nigeria requires someone who speaks for "All-of-you," but a "spokesman" who serves as the voice of others can reverse the relation of words to world and appear as the "king" whose voice silences others. Tortoise, the grotesque effigy of a bird, half earth-bound carapace and half invention of the birds themselves, has the gall to claim that he is their sovereign, Hobbes's famous "Artificiall Man." This king has appointed himself to the role, recognizes no reciprocal duties, and eats at the expense of his "subjects." The birds in the tale do not remember having accorded Tortoise sovereignty and discover they have done so either when they each give him a feather or when the sky-people recognize him as the birds' king. It is the mystery of sovereignty that the covenant that institutes it has always already been assented to; the moment at which sovereignty came into being only exists in retrospect. Sovereignty is based on the paradox that the sovereign and the community he embodies come into being together. If the community already existed, there would be no need for the sovereign. If the sovereign did not already represent the will of the community, he could not bring it into being. Bourdieu finds in this "alchemy of representation a true circularity whereby the representative makes the group who appoints him: the spokesperson is awarded the full power to speak and to act in the name of the group and, in the first instance, on the group … and is the substitute of the group who exists only by this process."[42] In Ekwefi's tale, which resonates with Hans Christian Andersen's tale of the Emperor's New Clothes, the birds stage a revolution, take back their feathers, and leave the would-be king stranded without his sublime avian body and its powers of flight, and with just the shell of his mortal terrestrial body.[43]

TRICKSTER AS HERO AND VILLAIN

There is thus a strange doubleness to the story of Tortoise in *Things Fall Apart*. That story is at once an emblem of traditional verbal culture *and* an allegory of the disturbance in the order of things introduced by colonialism.[44] Does the trickster reflect a traditional understanding of the need for trust but also mistrust in human relations, or does he mark a new disjunction that colonialism opened between words and the world? The colonizer's law purports to impose a new transparency and objectivity, but from the start it faces challenges arising from its opacity and ambiguity. The newcomers have "built a court where the District Commissioner judged cases in ignorance" (174). He cannot understand the "custom about land" because he does not speak the tongue (176) and must work through interpreters, the much-hated court messengers (174). Colonialism has thus introduced limitless new potential for tricksterish exploitation.

Steven Pierce writes that colonial law in Nigeria quickly needed to institute legal provisions against confidence scams:

> Termed generically "personation," the earliest versions involved people who dressed up in army uniforms or presented themselves as interpreters for British colonial officers and extorted money on the basis of their assumed positions. The colonial regime considered personation to be a particular threat to the legitimacy of the new British government and treated it severely. Attempting to install a political order that was culturally alien, the British had every reason to fear criminals who appeared to be state actors. From the start the state reacted with particular ferocity to Nigerians who threatened the legitimacy of the new political order.[45]

The distance that the law imposed from above opened between words and world and between words and understanding was ripe for both exploitation and subversion. Newell relates how the journalist and early nationalist T.A. Wallace-Johnson, at his trial for unauthorized possession of official documents in Accra in 1938, rested his defence on a distinction between his private persona and his public one.[46] Because he had been subpoenaed as Wallace-Johnson of 4 Bombay Lane, he denied that he could speak for Wallace-Johnson, Organising Secretary of the West African Youth League, who had been charged with the offence. Wallace-Johnson used the distinction that British law relies upon between the private individual with rights and the public persona with duties in a way that the prosecutors found unanswerable: they were forced to drop the charges against him. Wallace-Johnson ducked the seemingly straightforward questions asked of him by the all-powerful authorities and refused to speak truth to power because to do so would have been to accept the correspondence between the imperialists' word and the world. He was acting in the spirit of Tortoise, who adopted the moniker "All-of-you," and of Tutuola's Palm-Wine Drinkard, who told a god that his own name was "Father of gods" (10).

Nnamdi Azikiwe, editor of the Accra-based *African Morning Post*, which had published Wallace-Johnson, was able successfully to appeal his own conviction for publishing sedition because, his attorney argued, while he admitted to being editor on the *Post* on 23 May 1936, when he was arrested, the prosecution had not proven that he was the editor on 15 May.[47] When, later, in 1945, Azikiwe's Lagos newspaper the *West African Pilot* was banned for three months for fomenting rebellion, he immediately began publishing it as the *Southern Nigeria Defender*.[48] A truth of trickster tales, however, is that tricks often redound on the trickster. In 1947, the appeal of a verdict of libel against one of Azikiwe's papers was thrown out because it was judged that the appellant, "A.K. Blanksom, General Manager, Zik's Press Limited," had not himself been convicted of libel and had not, as he should have, signed the appeal "A.K. Blanksom, general Manager, *for and on behalf of* Zik's Press Limited."[49] Azikiwe also lost a 1951 appeal of another libel suit, one he had brought against a rival newspaper, because he had not proven that the "Ben Azikiwe" referred to in the publication was "Nnamdi Azikiwe," the respondent.[50]

If, as I have been arguing, realism invites trust in rules of verisimilitude that render the world and other people knowable, and if this is related to the promise of objectivity upheld by the ideal of the rule of law, then trickster tales, by contrast, suggest that that plausibility is itself a projection onto the world that allows others to be manipulated. The truth is what the trickster can make people believe. In his 1857 novel *The Confidence*-Man, Herman Melville conducts an experiment by conflating two kinds of trust: trust in the solidity of the world created by state institutions, and trust in the words and appearance of particular strangers. He then asks just how much crediting the social order requires also crediting strangers. In controlled conditions aboard a steamboat on the Mississippi, on the frontier of a new nation on the verge of civil war, a series of suspicious strangers who may all be the same man ask others to overcome their natural misgivings and to trust that they are who they say they are. They then ask for money for their own need or for a charity catering to others, or they try to sell a new patent medicine. Skeptics on the riverboat loudly cast doubt on these "confidence men," but readers cannot be sure. All the while, the confidence men repeatedly try to convince their interlocutors (and the readers) not just that they are trustworthy but that they *must* be trusted because unless people trust that strangers are who they present themselves to be, society itself will collapse. Of course, the trust that upholds society is precisely what enables tricksters to cheat people *and* the reason that people on the boat are suspicious. Melville's novel offers no guarantees and does not reveal whether the readers' confidence has been warranted or misplaced.

Where colonialism is newly and imperfectly established, tricksters appear as sinister figures of disorder. The character of Bonaparte Blenkins in Olive Schreiner's *The Story of an African Farm*, commonly recognized as the first South African novel, is a confidence man more sinister and dangerous than Mark Twain's Duke and Dauphin or Faulkner's Flem Snopes. On the colonial frontier, tricksters are strangers who come from elsewhere and flourish in spaces where those who can read are able to manipulate those who cannot; multiple legal systems vie for legitimacy; laws are not always known or understood; and their enforcement cannot be appealed.

Yet tricksters are presented as heroes in modern black African literature, in which their transgressions are admired or laughed at rather than feared. Soyinka's Brother Jero plays, Nkem Nwankwo's *Danda*, Efua Sutherland's *The Marriage of Anansewa*, Amadou Hampâté Bâ's *L'étrange destin de Wangrin*, Charles Mangua's *Son of Woman*, Munonye's *A Dancer of Fortune*, and Ngũgĩ's *Wizard of the Crow* are each named after a trickster hero. Wangrin, in particular, is adept at manipulating the distance between words and the world opened up by colonialism, and the book in which he appears purports to be non-fiction. The law is clearly not the rational and objective realm of justice that the ideal would have it be, but a field created by words that gives free play to the trickster.

The novelist T.M. Aluko, like Achebe, deplores the space that colonialism opened up for tricksters. His 1965 novel *One Man, One Matchet*, set, like so many post-independence novels, in the last decade of colonialism, presumes that the British have introduced a rational administration marked by the efficiency and transparency associated with science, democracy, and modern agriculture. However, an anti-imperialist rabble-rouser called Benjamin Benjamin takes advantage of the mediated communication introduced by the colonizer to manipulate illiterate peasant farmers. In the colony, farmers do not know whom to trust: the colonial administration, the Church, the press, the educated youth, the traditional elders, or the spirits of the land. Benjamin sets out to discredit among the uneducated villagers those people whom readers of the novel trust, in particular the black District Officer and the black Anglican minister. When the British Agricultural Officer announces a plan to cull diseased cocoa trees, the farmers are wary. Benjamin flatters the chiefs and tells people what they want to hear: that they do not need to cut down trees or pay the taxes they have been assessed, and that they can win back land lost to a neighbouring district before the British came. He has enough education to mistranslate the English of colonial officers, plagiarize and bowdlerize the rhetoric of famous texts, secure secret colonial records, obtain copies of colonial policy in advance of their publication, and publish libellous falsehoods in the newspaper. Like Wallace-Johnson, he also takes full advantage of the complicated and self-defeating justice system introduced by the British. In a stratagem worthy of Tortoise, Benjamin raises funds for legal campaigns but then appropriates all the money for himself. Like the novels of Achebe and Obeng, Aluko's satire is stuffed with references to monetary sums, but his trickster makes sure they do not add up. Benjamin takes the District Officer to court to have the excessive taxes reassessed, but the poor people of Ijapa end up paying more for the lawyers than they would have paid in taxes. Finally, like Wallace-Johnson and Azikiwe, Benjamin is acquitted at his trial for fraud because he has been arraigned according to the wrong article of the criminal code.

One way of eliminating the space for tricksters would be to restore the connection of words to world by transforming the African world so that it more closely corresponds to English words. For many of West Africa's elites on the eve of independence, especially those in the churches, the schools, the hospitals, the courts, and the bureaucracy, the trusted model of rationality was the Normative State enunciated by the colonial administration, based on the rule of law and supposedly backed by science and modern medicine, expressed by the English language, and confirmed by Christianity. In Aluko's novel, the black District Officer, an educated man whose views are those of the author, wants progress and the common good but is unfortunately unable to win the people's trust. And in any case, there are limits to what he knows and even to the objectivity of science. He finds himself betrayed by the administration he serves when the British rulers first withhold and then release news of a cure for the cocoa blight that will not require cutting down trees after all. As a consequence, having advocated culling, he stands discredited in the eyes of those he administers.

Aluko stages the contradiction between two sets of heirs to the colonial state: civil servants and nationalist politicians, who inherit what Giorgio Agamben calls the Government and the Kingdom respectively.[51] Benjamin's illegitimate politicking threatens the welfare of a community best cared for by a government dedicated to applying the latest techniques of rural development. If the lower-level colonial administrators – Africans soon to take charge of the administration of the new state – could win the people's confidence, they would be able to realize their worthy and progressive goals of abolishing domestic slavery, modernizing the economy, and educating the populace. But the most objective science and the best intentions of the administration are frustrated because the uneducated farmers do not know whom to trust. Instead of winning hearts, the British have introduced legalities and procedures that most people do not understand and that a trickster can manipulate.

Udo Akpan, the black District Officer and hero of Aluko's novel, tells his white superior that "Before you came to this country with Pax Britannica, a citizen of proved anti-community activities like Benjamin Benjamin was easily disposed of. He just vanished."[52] Akpan feels "fettered by General Orders, Financial Instructions, and other aspects of Civil Service bureaucracy."[53] Benjamin's capacity for damage is only contained when he is shot by a man "who had not heard of the British sense of fair play and justice and in any case had no use for it."[54] Vigilantism is necessary because British law cannot deal with the trickster who knows and can manipulate the law. Aluko's realist novel wants to secure readers' trust in the fundamental knowability of the world, based on laws that all acknowledge, and therefore condemns the trickster.

Things Fall Apart, too, registers the instability of the colonial regime's foundations in the law, which opens the way for exploitation. Achebe does not celebrate the potential for tricksterish subversion but writes realism and tragedy. His aim, like Aluko's, is to restore a connection between words and world that people can put their faith in. Other novelists, however, like Tutuola, and also like Flora Nwapa, whom we consider in the next chapter, believe the world is always characterized by the sort of instability that trickster tales appreciate and express.

5

Women and the Cowrie Zone

What would a novel that paid more attention to women look like? As we noted in the previous chapter, it would give more weight to the market and therefore to the cowrie zone and less to the village group (or the state). Women, who have always come as wives from a village other than the one they now live in and often from another village group altogether, enjoy the exchange of news and the meetings with outsiders afforded by the market. Susan Andrade notes that "it is in trade (and thus through relations with each other) as much as in marriage and childbirth that women obtain power in Igbo society."[1] The eponymous protagonist of Nwapa's *Efuru*,[2] set in the 1940s, is a trader who moves far more widely than do Unoka and Okonkwo, travelling up and down the Great River (the Niger on extratextual maps) and its tributaries in search of foodstuffs, especially yams, for sale more cheaply than they are at home. The village group of Ugwuta needs to import staples, and since "there is no organization for export from the districts which have a surplus" in Igboland at this time,[3] women traders travel to those areas to buy what they require.

Efuru acts as a third party, mediating between producer and consumer, who will never know each other. Her profits are a function of her ability to convert between incommensurate scales. We can represent her trade as M – C – M', where the Commodity, transported across distance, mediates between two different scales of Money. Gikandi finds in Efuru's arbitrage yet another sign of encroaching modernity,[4] as if it were the British who introduced trade. Efuru, however, does not deal in cash crops, instead importing yams and food items for her local market. Her activities are a reminder that trade has been central to the economy of West Africa for as long as we know, perhaps forever. True, by the 1940s, the British had secured the trade routes and made them safer – Lucy

Mair notes that "the women who from time immemorial have taken their small surpluses to market travelled farther and farther afield as means of transport became easier"[5] – but the colonial state only made safer what was already the practice.

The commodity, an alienable object exchanged between independent transactors, is the opposite of the gift[6]: once sold, it ceases to carry any residue of the previous owner. After the commodity has been paid for, buyer and seller have no further relationship. The market is therefore "an extraordinary machine for the cancellation of debt."[7] Although we commonly associate gift exchange with the premodern and commodity exchange with the modern, the distinction is seldom clear-cut, nor can it be mapped reliably on an evolutionary timeline. Gregory is careful to point out that "gift" and "commodity" do not exist in separate spheres but are analytical terms derived in retrospect in order to explain history. The gift is not the ancestor of the commodity; nor do the two categories represent mutually exclusive phases in economic development. It is probable that every society has always had both in one form or another, albeit in differing proportions and serving different functions. Certainly, in West and Central Africa, Guyer writes, "history suggests that parts of the gift lexicon and parts of the commodity lexicon are both relevant: in particular, the concepts of authorship, singularity and pathway from the former, and alienability and currency from the latter."[8]

Nietzsche writes that "establishing prices, assessing values, determining equivalents, trading – all this preoccupied the primal thoughts of man to such an extent that in a certain sense it *constituted* thinking itself."[9] If so, Efuru is one of the best thinkers: "Anything she touches is money. If she begins to sell pepper in the market, she will make money out of it. If in salt, money will flow in" (125). She has inherited these gifts from her late mother: "When she sold pepper, she made huge profits; when she sold yam or fish, she made profits also" (149–50).

The trader adds value by carrying goods across a distance, but the value depends on maintaining that distance. It is in Efuru's interest to keep producers and buyers apart and dependent on her. A suitor impresses Efuru with his suitability when he tells her of a deal he has found:

> You have to paddle upstream along the Great River. After paddling for four days, you get to the place. The natives don't know what to do with yams. Some yams are so big that two men cannot lift one. In the mornings when you see wives pounding fufu for their husbands and children, you would think that they are inviting a whole village to feast. It is so in the afternoon and at night also. They don't

> eat cassava though they have plenty of it. If a woman takes cassava to the market and she does not sell it, she leaves it in the market, because it is a great trouble carrying it back to her home when they have plenty at home. I did about five trips and made quite a profit. Many people don't know about this. Next year I am going again. (112)

The trade opportunity is described here in terms that sound like the finding of treasure or the invitation to a feast in traditional tales. As in European tales of cultural encounter, much of the success depends on strangers not fully appreciating the worth of what they have. Compare Efuru's trade with that of her contemporary, the protagonist of Munonye's novel *Obi*, who has bought eight bags of salt for trade:

> When he reached Obizi he saw very many people, old and young, rushing towards a small shop where salt was sold. A cup of salt cost as much as two pence there, and yet there was so much scramble! On enquiry, he discovered what had happened. Somebody, probably the owner of the shop, had started a rumour that the Germans had just sunk ten big ships which were loaded with salt, and which were bound for Ania; and that there would be no further supply for another four months. He himself also took advantage of the rumour and sold the eight bags, making a profit of two pounds fifteen shillings.[10]

Trade, like gossip, the other prominent theme in Nwapa's novel, relies on a knowledge differential. The successful trader needs to know the difference in the price of yams in different areas *and* has to keep this knowledge to herself. Should others find out, the trade will be flooded, the price be beaten down, and the profit margin disappear. Efuru and her first husband realize a fantastic profit of "over a hundred per cent" buying crayfish in Agbor on the Great River and selling them in Ugwuta, but when the trade attracts others, competition brings down the profits and the traders barely "recovered their capital" (21). Efuru says with some disgust: "These women spoil trade so easily. When they see you making a profit in one trade they leave the trade they know and join yours and of course in no time it is no longer profitable" (21).

Exchange value is determined by supply and demand but is also a function of convincing others to see things in a particular way. The price is whatever a seller can manage to convince a buyer to pay or that a buyer can convince a seller to accept. The market therefore favours the skills of reading others' minds and manipulating appearances associated with Tortoise. Efuru pursues her own profit, but she does not cheat anyone. She withholds knowledge from rival traders but not knowledge that, if a seller had it, would change her willingness to sell. Buyer and seller agree on a price that suits both and is therefore considered the just price. Janet Roitman writes that among the Fulfulde of northern Cameroon, a price is "true" (*gaskiiya*) if "it suits you,"[11] and it suits if it conforms to *narral*, or "confidence in the market."[12]

Efuru is a self-made woman, and in that sense the female equivalent of Okonkwo. As if to signal that she owes nothing to anyone else, at the start of the novel she uses her profits from trade to pay the bride price that her indigent husband owes for her. This recalls not just Okonkwo, who inherits nothing from his father, but also Equiano, the slave who two centuries earlier earned and paid his own redemption price. Unlike Okonkwo the farmer, however, a trader can never imagine that she is self-sufficient. As a condition of selling her goods, Efuru must extend credit to her women customers. To an extent far exceeding *Eighteenpence* and *Things Fall Apart*, *Efuru* is a novel about debt, regarded, however, from the perspective of the creditor. Efuru must at every moment put her trust in others, very often in strangers, and she must in turn win their trust.

Andrade has justly celebrated the network of trust among the women in Nwapa's novel. A corollary of the need for trust, however, is the need for mistrust. When Efuru is not buying, selling, or travelling in search of opportunities, she is chasing those who owe her money.[13] In *Efuru* there is no institutional power to support the "feminine art" of debt collection,[14] only the force of one's personality. The most formidable collector of debts in African literature (after the debt collector in *The Palm-Wine Drinkard*, who kills himself in pursuit of a dead debtor) is Efuru's friend Ajanapu, a fearless, plain-speaking defender of her due who refuses to be embarrassed. Ajanapu is prepared to camp out in a debtor's house and publicly call on witnesses, incurring shame herself in order to shame the one who owes her money.

Borrower or creditor, the one who visits another to ask for money always cedes some power to his host. Although borrowers come as supplicants, once they receive a loan, some power shifts and creditors must now call on those who owe them. Come back tomorrow, Unoka tells gullible creditors. People to whom one has lent money can, through procrastination, become slow-motion non-secret thieves. Ajanapu asserts her power as a creditor by flagrantly overstaying the welcome that visitors are entitled to, in effect, by proclaiming that the debt owed her has nothing to do with honour or hospitality. Neighbours complain about her tactics, saying, "That's how the newly rich behave" (48), but collecting debts is as old as debt itself. The Reverend Samuel Johnson in his nineteenth-century *History of the Yoruba* might be describing Ajanapu when he describes licensed "distrainors" of debt in the city-states of Yorubaland:

> This individual is called Ogo, he is said to *d'ogo ti* i.e. to sit on the debtor (as it were). For that purpose he enters the premises, seeks out the debtor, or ensconces himself in his apartment until he makes his appearance, and then he makes himself an intolerable nuisance to him and to the members of the house generally until the money is paid.
>
> The distrainor is a man of imperturbable temper, but of foul tongue, a veritable Thersites. He adopts any measures he likes, sometimes by inflicting his presence and attention on the debtor everywhere and anywhere he may go, denying him privacy of any kind, and in the meantime using his tongue most foully upon him.[15]

That Ajanapu is an attractive character, admired for her forcefulness rather than scorned for her crassness, is a mark of how much Nwapa's novel sees from the perspective of the trader. Efuru offers her friend ten shillings to collect a debt of five pounds for her (46). This debt collector, however, is herself a debtor: when Ajanapu returns from successfully collecting a debt of five pounds and finds someone at her own doorstep to whom she owes five shillings, she resists her creditor's claim every bit as fiercely as she herself had insisted on her own claims on others. In Ugwuta everyone is both borrower and lender: borrowers are forever trying to get away without repaying, and lenders always try to exact their full due. Tutuola's Palm-Wine Drinkard would have understood.

Trust is so important in Efuru's world because there is reason to mistrust. By its very nature, trade makes for rivals. It is taken for granted that everyone has enemies who will glory in one's misfortunes (9). A wealthy woman must also beware the jealousy of neighbours. Not only may debtors not repay, but "thieves could waylay traders and rob them of their money. The river could be rough and when that happened their canoe could capsize" (21). And markets are home to the trickster and the money-doubler (who cheats by appealing to the greed of the gullible).

The impersonal, generic character of money, whether cowries, gold or silver coins, or paper, facilitates not only trade but also theft.[16] Theft, which does not figure in the precolonial Umuofia of *Things Fall Apart* except in reports about the distant market of Umuike, is a prominent theme in *Efuru*. Once Efuru has bought goods in a distant market and paid for carriers to bring them to her canoe, she must sleep by the canoe to make sure they are not stolen. Onicha[17] market is "a terrible place" (113), where you can get anything at all at the best price, but there is always the risk of pickpockets (112) or of being sold articles – especially medicines and cosmetics – that are not genuine (113). Nwapa's characters regularly trade stories of how they were robbed or avoided being robbed (172). When word gets around that Efuru has lent ten pounds to neighbours, thieves come after dark looking for the money (178). Thieves, who keep their identities secret and work at night, constitute an unseen world of hostile forces that threaten the daylight world with ruin. They are as abhorred as murderers and for most people pose the greater danger, for if a thief comes to your house and you recognize him, he will not hesitate to kill you (178). When sympathizers come to commiserate with a near-victim of theft, she does not greet them because, for all she knows, the thieves may be among them (177). Instead she proclaims aloud, "Thieves! I am greater than you are, because you will for ever continue to steal. I am greater because you steal my things; I am greater than you are because you work in darkness and I work in light. Sons of darkness, rogues and vagabonds; our gods will visit you" (178).

In the treacherous world of Nwapa's novel a woman cannot trust any man of her own age, including her husband, nor can a husband trust his wives. Efuru's father explains that her mother was the best of his wives because to her alone could he confide his money:

> If I gave her one pound to buy things for me for my age-group, or things for my own use, she bought me things worth my money. If she was given any change, even if it was only threepence, she returned it to me. But others? the others? They nearly killed me. They cheated me each time I gave them money to buy things for me. One of them, I won't mention her name, I gave some ogbono to sell and she cheated me. Your mother was not at home then. The ogbono was worth some ten pounds, so your mother told me. My wife took it to the market and sold it. She brought back six pounds. I was furious. She swore by all the gods and goddesses of our people that that was what she sold the ogbono for. I left her. Days after I heard from a reliable source that she sold the ogbono for twelve pounds. (150)

Nathan Nunn and Leonard Wantchekon find high rates of mistrust in contemporary West Africa, which they blame on the trauma of the slave trade. They suggest that "individuals belonging to ethnic groups that were most exposed to the slave trade exhibit lower levels of trust in their relatives, neighbours, coethnics, and local government today"[18] because "the environment of ubiquitous insecurity caused individuals to turn on others – including friends and family members – and to kidnap, trick, and sell each other into slavery."[19] Nunn and Wantchekon blame the high levels of mistrust for the weakness of the state, contending that from the point of view of the modern state, mistrust is a pathology, the product of trauma and a measure of social breakdown. But it may also be that mistrust is so high *because* the state is weak and does not inspire confidence. Mistrust is not necessarily irrational. As we have argued with regard to Achebe's Umuofia, even if Igbo ways *have* been shaped by the experience of slavery, the practices depicted in Nwapa's novel feel coherent and satisfying to participants. A few in Nwapa's novel remember the precolonial past as a time when theft was not possible. One woman laments: "In my youth, there was no stealing. If you stole you were sold as a slave. If your property was stolen, you simply went to one of the idols and prayed him to visit the thief. Before two or three days, you recovered your property. But these Church-goers have spoilt everything. They tell us our gods have no power, so our people continue to steal" (176). In this version, as in Achebe's novel, colonialism represents a fall into a world of tricksters. However, the practical wisdom expressed here – thieves once feared the gods lest they be sold as slaves – implies that precolonial social control was more effective than the colonial state not because people were any different but because more fear was instilled of the consequences of transgression.

Trickster tales are found in village societies the world over, including where there was no slavery. Where relations are primarily face to face, trust is not, as it is in modern states, a function of institutions whose servants can be substituted for one another; rather, it arises from interpersonal relations, which need constant renewal and always involve a certain risk. The truth is that trader and thief both need the skills of the trickster, improvisatory tactics that in French Africa are called *la débrouille*.[20] Both are highly attuned to opportunity: thieves learn who has recently received money; traders know where goods are selling cheaper. It is not because traders are thieves that the two enemies resemble each other; it is because both live in a universe that does not allow for planning and that rewards improvisation.

In the cowrie zone, trade is a relation negotiated among individuals. The centralized state, by contrast, facilitates the development of the corporation, of large trading companies like the United Africa Company with its quasi-monopoly on the export of palm oil. By the end of *Things Fall Apart*, the "white man" has built "a trading store and for the first time palm-oil and kernel became things of great price" (128). Efuru does not deal in those cash crops, but they do figure in Nwapa's novel. Ajanapu tells the story of Omirima's daughter, who foolishly passed up a treasure put in her way by her *chi*. Omirima had just started trading in palm oil, and such was her "rapid progress" that she was able to pay off all her capital loans. However, when she sent her daughter to the trading company to cash in the voucher from the sale of her oil and the cashier overpaid by thirty pounds, the "foolish" girl gave the money back (213). The angry mother now must kill a white hen to placate the girl's *chi*, who will be angry that the good fortune cast before her had been spurned.

Nwapa's novel shows that face-to-face village societies are predicated as much on credit as modern capitalist societies. The difference is that in village societies credit is a function of interpersonal relations, while the trading company relies on impersonal institutions to secure credit for strangers. To take money attached to someone one knows, let alone a husband or wife, is theft, a blameworthy crime. As Pierce writes, "in Nigerian popular culture deception of individuals for personal enrichment is more morally dubious than the simple act of stealing from the state or of exerting influence on behalf of those with whom one has personal ties."[21] Conversely, to return money that has been lost is to establish a debt of gratitude: Kafo, a timber merchant in Munonye's *Bridge to a Wedding*, returns a wallet left behind by a customer, and the grateful owner repays that debt at every opportunity.[22] But money belonging to the company is impersonal and follows mysterious paths that astute traders can exploit. In other African contexts, money attached to people is called "hot money" and that belonging to companies or the state is "cold."[23]

READING THE MARKET OF THE WORLD

As the example of Omirima's daughter shows, if a person's *chi* is awake, it is frequently because another's (in this case the cashier's) is sleeping. What about Efuru? She is that remarkable combination, a good trader and a good person. Skilled at recognizing the opportunities in her path and seizing them, she also extends credit liberally and is herself absolutely trustworthy. Her goodness is recognized by all: a chaste and loving wife, a loyal friend, and a generous creditor, she is the rare woman who is loved and valued by her mother-in-law, and even (since she remarries) by two mothers-in-law. On every moral count, this virtuous woman deserves to be happy. Yet Efuru loses two husbands and is left childless.

Efuru's commercial success has behind it the favour of Uhamiri, the goddess of Lake Ugwuta. The goddess, whom elsewhere Nwapa herself describes as "beautiful, ageless, and partial to women,"[24] chooses whom she wills and blesses them with wealth: nearly all the "storey buildings" in Ugwuta have been built by women traders who are also worshippers of Uhamiri (153). But Uhamiri also withholds children from those she favours. Efuru's sorrows, no less than her wealth, are manifestations of the will of the goddess, who demands that women be wholly dedicated to her service. Since the Ugwuta community regards motherhood as the ideal of women's fulfillment, Efuru's divine election is as much curse as blessing. Her sorrows do not reflect what she deserves, but neither are they punishments for flouting the will of the goddess, nor or they merely the results of hazard. Efuru is less the agent she imagines herself to be than an unwitting handmaiden (and her philandering husbands are not agents either but doomed to leave her whom they love).

Efuru shares the same fate as Jagua Nana, the successful Lagos prostitute who is the title character of Cyprian Ekwensi's 1961 novel.[25] Two decades after Efuru, Jagua Nana contemplates joining the "Merchant Princesses" of Onitsha, women traders with their own shops, a lorry, and a driver.[26] Lucy Mair reports that at independence "some women dealers in the market of Onitsha may buy and sell a thousand pounds' worth of goods in a day and dispatch them by lorry all over the country."[27] Both women display a literal self-possession and pay the debts of the men who rely on them: just as Efuru pays her own bride price, Jagua has paid for her much younger lover to get a passport and to travel to England in order to study. Both women are skilled at reading others and making deals, yet their marriages break down and each loses her only child in infancy. Both women end without men of their own, back in the houses of their dead fathers. How are we to understand these women's fates?

Superficially, the trader's need to read the signs in order to discern whether her *chi* or the goddess is favourable has something in common with Max Weber's account of Protestant capitalism: success in the market is interpreted as a sign of divine grace. In the Protestant conception, the market is full of risk and ultimately inscrutable, but behind it lies a providential hidden hand that rewards the man on whom God bestows grace and who adheres to his true calling. Efuru operates on a smaller scale in a part of the world that does not figure in the business reports of newspapers, but she, too, risks her capital and has to be attuned to the flow of events: to droughts, floods, surplus, and scarcity. There is, however, a great difference between the trader in stateless societies and the capitalist in early modern Europe. Bernard Belasco explains that "uncertainty among the Yoruba is not fixed on the unpredictability of profit in market enterprise," as in Weber; "rather it is concerned with the possibility of existential reversals: consequences of encountering malignant spirits, loss of prestige, shortened life, drought or famine, death of children, abandonment of followers and so on."[28] There is less sense of election or reward of the individual, and more of an awareness of the fluidity and instability of life.

Susanna Adam, discussing contemporary West African traders, explains why, given the conditions of the markets in which they operate, planning would be counterproductive:

> There is no regularity in their obligations, no organized system imposed and maintained by the regular arrival of accounts due for services: bills from public utilities are not sent on a monthly or any other regular basis and the amounts to be paid often seemed equally arbitrary. Thus it was common to hear of small businesses with only a light bulb or very few electrical instruments suddenly billed for several years of industrial consumption ... Expenses of this type are in their nature utterly unpredictable. No rational plan could altogether prepare for such events and none of the small-scale tradesmen/women even attempted to develop such strategies.[29]

More congenial to such an economy would be pay-as-you-go plans, like those offered by mobile phone companies in Africa today, because they allow for planning in small, easily visible measures.

In Nwapa's novel, mistrust figures more centrally than it does in *Things Fall Apart*. Efuru's ability to read others and to win their trust in her own upstanding character – the very skills that stand her in good stead in trade – fail her when it comes to love: her too trusting nature lets her down not once but twice. She marries men whom she takes as her business partners and who benefit enormously as a result; then both of them betray her for reasons that remain as obscure to readers as to Efuru. Deception and betrayal are as common in marriage as in trade, and at stake in both cases is money. When Efuru's mother-in-law was married, her good-for-nothing husband told her he had sold all his yams and left the money under his pillow, but that "at night a thief came, lifted his head and took away all the money" (59). His doting wife defends him, but women with more experience scoff because they know the husband is lying (60). It is not just women who are fooled by love. Gossip has it that one woman was brazen enough to claim that thieves stole the fifty pounds her husband gave her to buy yams, and, just as scandalously, her besotted husband believed her (160-1). As these cases make clear, love is blind – indeed, it *prefers* to be.

Efuru's many sorrows are compounded by the false idea that happiness can be deserved. In nineteenth-century British fiction, virtue is often marked by the loss of money but the winning of love. The notions of poetic justice and recognition of merit are intimately tied to romantic love, a realm of fixed values where character is stable, desire fulfilled, and virtue rewarded. In *Efuru*, however, the real test of character is carefulness with money and romantic love proves foolish because it interferes with the protagonist's ability to judge creditworthiness. Efuru the astute trader is also a lover afraid to face facts. Her first husband is so lazy a farmer that she must pay for her own bride price from the profits of her trade, and she does not realize for the longest time how poor a deal she has made. Her second marriage breaks down as the first one did when the new husband proves another philanderer, and worse, a thief. Gilbert refuses to tell her why he was in jail in Onicha for three months, but assures her it was not for stealing, and Efuru is so "foolish" as to believe him (219). Efuru even keeps the news of Gilbert's imprisonment a secret from her co-wife and grows angry when the younger woman insists on knowing the truth. Efuru prefers to take what her lying husband says on trust rather than to acknowledge how deeply she has misread him. She tells herself that Gilbert cannot be a thief because there are no thieves in his family (309), as if theft were not the ever-present obverse side of trade in the great market town.

Like the people around Efuru, readers are likely to be shocked that her goodness, integral to her honour, is not rewarded with love. Readers who read the novel through the conventions of European genre are as likely as Efuru to make mistakes when it comes to romantic desire. The opening of the novel promises a love story – Efuru marries a poor man against her parents' wishes – so it comes as a surprise when the marriage breaks down for reasons that are not spelled out for a long time. Like Efuru, readers do not know what all others around her know: how lazy and worthless her husband is. If first-time readers of the novel sentimentally imagine that the subsequent love of the good and gentle Gilbert is a just reward for Efuru, now older and wiser, and compensation for the undeserved abuse she has endured, they will be undeceived. Like the dupe in trickster tales, Efuru's ignorance is not corrected but renews itself and invites further castigation in the next instalment.

Achebe wants to convince readers, his soon-to-be fellow citizens, of the readability of the world and of characters. Nwapa, by contrast, teaches readers the folly of trust without mistrust. Readers who think as lovers do and desire poetic justice and a happy ending will end up disillusioned and even perhaps, like Efuru herself, mystified by the course of the narrative. Readers who remain as careful and skeptical as traders need to be, and who remember that others' minds cannot be read because others deliberately conceal them, will not guess in advance what happens to Efuru but will at least be better prepared.

CENTRED AND DECENTRED KNOWLEDGE

Efuru, like *Things Fall Apart*, is focused on the end of the political scale furthest from the nation-state, but it is not a realist novel, meaning it does not rely on a consensual notion of the typical and does not understand the village group in terms of a larger identity, be that the state, the continent, or an abstract political ideal. As Andrade writes, women's fiction in West Africa focuses on the micro rather than the macro. Whereas, as we have seen, readers make sense of the fictive Umuofia in relation to the state, either as a model of a political alternative or as an allegory of colonization, Nwapa's interest is in the village group for its own sake, the village group that is not consolidated into the state.

Ugwuta has an existence outside the novel on maps and in books and is where Nwapa herself is from. (On maps it is usually written Oguta, reflecting an early Anglicized spelling.) In contrast to Umuofia, which we are repeatedly told consists of nine villages, we only learn that Efuru lives in Ugwuta because halfway through the novel a woman refers to "you Ugwuta women" (113). Three of Ugwuta's twenty-seven constituent villages, Umutogwuma (111), Umuenemanya (159), and Umuosuma (180), are mentioned by characters in passing, but the novel never tells us how many villages there are, how they came together, or how they are related. Somehow, the narrator of *Efuru* lacks an absolute outside perspective on the village group that would allow her to present its history in general terms to readers not from there. Achebe's narrator knows all there is to know about Umuofia because Umuofia is the author's invention. What Nwapa's narrator knows is limited *because* Ugwuta is a real place.

Achebe's narration presumes that the village group has been decentred, so that the story of Umuofia is now how it has been inserted to its disadvantage into a larger history made by others. Nwapa's Ugwuta, by contrast, is not contained by a larger history, and no larger history will help make sense of it. To be sure, Efuru's father is honoured as a warrior who once fought against the slave raiders of Aro, and there is a memory of the violent coming of the white man; there are schools, police, prisons, and pounds and shillings, but there is no mention of calendar dates, and the narrative only visits these institutions in the reported speech of characters. There is also mention of the powerful new medicine of the white people, but no white people are characters in the story. The medical clinic is run by a son of Ugwuta. The narration itself almost completely ignores the colonial state. The police and prisons are not so much associated with a foreign state imposed from above as they are considered part of the shame associated with theft. Only the mention of someone being conscripted to join the army points to the 1940s as the time frame (186). The narrator cannot present the kind of larger frame that a stranger needs to make sense of the story. As far as readers are concerned, Achebe's Umuofia is somewhere in Igboland, which in turn is in Nigeria; Nwapa's Ugwuta remains resolutely the centre of its own world.

It is a central irony of *Things Fall Apart* that it is the District Commissioner's proposed memoir, *The Pacification of the Primitive Tribes of the Lower Niger*, mentioned at the end of the novel, that supplies readers with crucial information about the location and even the historical period of the novel's setting. The novel, as a result, is explicitly located on the map and on the universal calendar, just as other events in history can be. A realist novel may include historical anachronisms, as *Things Fall Apart* and *Arrow of God* both do, but that we can even speak of anachronism is a function of realism's particular engagement with history. Anachronisms are impossible in, say, Tutuola's novels, which are set in story time and never claim historical consistency. The continuity of the realist novel with non-literary and non-fictional forms of writing means that the realist novel can be explicated by appealing to historical texts, as I have done in this book.

Things Fall Apart consistently introduces characters with a name, a description of the social role they perform, and then a description of their personality. The result is to emphasize their knowability. Okonkwo, the first word in the novel and the subject of the first sentence, is the protagonist. In the second sentence we are told that he defeated Amalinze the Cat in a wrestling bout. Who was Amalinze? "Amalinze was the great wrestler who for seven years was unbeaten, from Umuofia to Mbaino" (3). The next character introduced is Okonkwo's father, against whom the protagonist wrestles psychologically all his life. After we are told that "Unoka, for that was his father's name, had died ten years ago," the next sentence gives us the essence of his character: "he was lazy and improvident and was quite incapable of thinking about tomorrow" (4). Each time someone is introduced, the narrator pauses to classify him and then returns to the story by reminding us how he fits in: "It was this man that Okonkwo threw in a fight" (3); "It was for this man that Okonkwo worked to earn his first seed yams" (19). The narrator takes the unusual step of not just using a character's name but declaring his name: "The lad's name was Ikemefuna" (12); "His name was Nwakibie" (18).

The men in the novel are defined by the question "What are you?" The answer is phrased in terms of achievement and wealth as measured in terms of yams, wives and children, and titles earned. Before the end of the first chapter we learn that Okonkwo "was a wealthy farmer and had two barns full of yams, and had just married his third wife"; he has "also taken two titles" (8). The man who originally lent Okonkwo the seed yams with which he started as a farmer is "a wealthy man in Okonkwo's village who had three huge barns, nine wives and thirty children ... and he had taken the highest but one title which a man could take in the clan" (18–19). The implication is that the characters are fixed entities with an existence before and outside the story.

The answer to "What are you?" has to do with status and pretends to be absolute: how much do you have or have you achieved? Characters are presented in deliberate contrast to one another. Once Unoka has been introduced, the narrative provides a backstory, a few scenes illustrating his inveterate idleness. The next named character is "a neighbour called Okoye": "Okoye was also a musician," but "he was not a failure like Unoka" for he "had a large barn full of yams and he had three wives" (6). Once again the narrator supplies upfront all readers need to know. Achebe introduces Umuofia itself just as he does the people in it, with a description of its essential character: "Umuofia was feared by all its neighbours. It was powerful in war and in magic, and its priests and medicine-men were feared in all the surrounding country" (11).

Ikemefuna is introduced as "the doomed lad" (8). The ineluctability of the tragic story is a function of the characters' fixity. As Jane Bryce points out, Achebe's "characters (including the women) are possessed of certainties which direct them, even against the tide"[30]: their wills drive them forward, even against their better understanding. This is quite unlike the "open-ended questioning of Nwapa's women,"[31] where some impediment prevents the narrator from identifying a character by name until he or she has been named in the reported speech of another. Some characters the narration never names but identifies only as Efuru's mother-in-law or as "a woman she did not know" but whom "she had to pretend she knew otherwise she would be offended" (134). One result is that Nwapa's Ugwuta has room for more characters than Achebe's Umuofia. To compound the problem of names, no one in Nwapa's novel has just one name, and, when greeting others directly, especially members of the same age grade, people use honorifics.

Paradoxically, *Efuru* is also more densely populated with named people than Achebe's novel is, but most cannot be called characters since they do not figure in the narration proper. Reported speech in the novel is full of cautionary tales about characters absent from the events of the narration: Nwakaego's daughter, we are told, was not circumcised, and her son died; Nwanta's son was looked after by a maid and blinded himself in one eye in an accident (37); Nwanyuzo's daughter has a burnt face (37); Mgbokworo does not have a good reputation as a performer of female circumcisions (16); Omozere is a drunkard (93). We do not meet these characters, or, if we do, the narrative gives no indication that it is the same person. Is the Odikama who owes Efuru five pounds the same Odikama that Ajanapu suggests as a fitting trading companion (87) and the same Odikama that Efuru takes along as a cook on trade missions but does not trust with money (143)? Such a plethora of people who are known only as names not as characters is not typical of fiction.

Nwapa's narration thus creates a sense that, while characters exist in local stories outside the novel as Okonkwo does, these stories are not fixed and not everyone knows them. Characters are not classified in advance by a dominant personality trait and by social status; rather, they are the subject of gossip and rumour. Andrade writes of *Efuru* that "the feminine exchange of gossip and advice" is the epistemological equivalent of "the (equally feminine) exchange of goods and money."[32] We only learn about people when other people tell stories about them, and we cannot be sure whether we will meet these characters or if they are even significant. This is also how characters know about one another. Efuru learns what happened to her first husband when she overhears strangers in the market talking about their daughter, who has run away with an unnamed man (54). Ajanapu later overhears in Onicha market the news that Efuru's second husband, Gilbert, is in jail.

Robert Ellickson writes that "any close-knit group is likely to have procedural norms that ask members to help spread truthful information about the prior prosocial or antisocial behavior of other members": "the flow of reputational information encourages cooperative behaviour and deters uncooperative behaviour."[33] But information, as power, can be used for ill as well as for social control. As we have seen, when news gets out that Efuru has given ten pounds to Nwosu and his wife, thieves raid them in the night looking for the money. Gossip can also destroy reputations. Rumour is more likely than not to get events grievously wrong: an inveterate gossip like Omirima falsely charges Efuru with wanting to leave her second husband (165). The same woman misreports that Efuru gave Ogea's parents twenty pounds that were stolen (185).

By contrast, *Things Fall Apart* patiently explains Igboland to readers using the register of culture. While it is not the case that a common culture encompasses and explains all behaviour in Umuofia – people like Okonkwo unthinkingly break rules; a wise man like Obierika questions rules; and a common topic of discussion is that elsewhere people do different things – the narration certainly assumes that conventions exist, that everyone in Umuofia knows them, and that they can be explained to readers. We are told, for instance, that "the land of the living was not far removed from the domain of the ancestors. There was coming and going between them, especially at festivals and also when an old man died, because an old man was very close to the ancestors" (122). As mentioned above, this kind of cultural explanation appears to be addressed to outsiders, but is training Nigerian readers to regard their world as knowable, rational, and part of a larger world in which different peoples have different cultures but everyone has a culture that can be made sense of.

People have a culture in the sense of a shared repertoire of practices and meaningful explanations for those practices. But the meaning of culture alters as soon as it is expressed in terms of laws and definitions. At that point, what was a common language – meaningful acts and ways of making meaning of acts – acquires the extra charge of identity. And at that point it demands respect; it must be obeyed. A trickster like Tortoise finds other people's fixed, summarizable cultural principles always useful for winning acquiescence; his declarations that this is how people do things *here* cannot be questioned or doubted. He tells the birds, "When people are invited to a great feast like this, they take new names for the occasion" (97), and "The custom here is to serve the spokesman first and the others later" ((98), and the birds have no choice but to respect these "age-old" customs.

Nwapa's novel is as full of cultural wisdom as Achebe's – for example, how to take care of oneself when pregnant, how to care for a child, how to mourn and how not to. But this cultural knowledge is not already shared by all – it must be taught. Cultural knowledge depends on the authority of the one doing the imparting and is always subject to dispute. Ajanapu corrects her sister when she feeds a pregnant Efuru the wrong food (28). There are rival ways of doing things *within* Ugwuta, as well as different levels of knowledge. There is no single Ugwuta culture that can be summarized. There is no outside vantage from which readers are invited to understand Ugwuta and relate it to other places.

A conservative villager in Munonye's *Bridge to a Wedding* explains the distinction between the market and the village thus: "the homes from which we came to the market are bound by certain laws – laws which must be obeyed," but markets "belong to no one in particular and ... accommodate all sorts of persons and all sorts of things."[34] By that definition *Efuru* is a market novel and *Things Fall Apart* a village novel. Nwapa's characters are defined by their relations to one another instead of to the whole, and those relations are themselves not fixed but changing and so can never be finally known. Tellingly, in Achebe's novel, troubles in a marriage serve to illustrate the village group's justice system, whereas, in Nwapa's novel, women must decide themselves what to do when marriages break down: one woman remains tragically, perhaps stupidly loyal to the man who deserted her; another helps her husband take a second wife so that she can be free to pursue her trade; Efuru remarries but later gives up on men. The distinction I am making between market and village is a version of Andrade's distinction between micro and macro.

Things Fall Apart, about a village group that suffers a severe dislocation from the centre of its own universe, is centred on farming. The men of Umuofia, although they function as husbands, fathers, warriors, members of village council, and carriers of the *egwugwu* masquerade, are primarily self-sufficient farmers. *Efuru*, about a village group open to the world, is about trade. Trade explains the features of the narration enumerated above: in the market, knowledge is perforce incomplete and must be gleaned, guessed at, and learned from conversations with others.

Achebe imagines the village group as a self-contained unit that must work out its relations to outsiders. The action is set in motion when someone comes from outside: first young Ikemefuna from neighbouring Mbaino, then the missionaries, and finally the District Commissioner. One implication is that nothing would change if the outside were kept out. This is not to deny that the change, when it comes, unfolds according to the tensions already dividing Umuofia: young people reject fathers; the *osu* reject their inferior status. In *Efuru*, too, there are strangers from outside – for example, Efuru's husband's mistress in a distant town; a woman in European dress who only speaks English (95); and white people who swim in Lake Ugwuta – and they disturb the waters, but they do not bring substantial change. They therefore do not need to be named. This is not because Ugwuta is more self-contained than Umuofia. The opposite is true. As we have seen, Nwapa's characters travel far more than Achebe's do. Nwapa's Ugwuta is more open to a larger world than Achebe's Umuofia because, paradoxically, it has never been decentred. It is decidedly part of the cowrie zone and not even implicitly part of the state.

Achebe writes about the village group at the time of the colonial encounter for readers who are citizens of the prospective new nation-state. His novel teaches readers that character and creditworthiness can be known and judged according to principles that apply in the readers' world just as they do in the novel. This trust is needed for citizens of the new state. Nwapa, by contrast, is writing about the rules of the informal market that hold sway *despite* the new state. In *Efuru* trust is a question of epistemology: how far we can know, which is never far. Not only is the protagonist frequently mistaken in her judgments, but so too, inevitably, is the reader if she relies on the conventions of the novel genre in order to understand and judge. The mistake is to imagine that there are principles governing the world and other people. The only valid trust is what one works out with each person one meets in forging a new relationship.

6

The Law's Monopoly on Violence

Achebe's *Arrow of God*, set in the same area of Igboland as Umuofia, begins as *Things Fall Apart* does, with a call for war against a neighbouring village group, a war among "blood brothers" (131). Now, however, thirty or so years later, instead of a negotiated peace, war breaks out, and it threatens to be infinite in scope. Instead of emphasizing the traditional limits that reciprocity imposed on violence, the later novel appears to suggest that precolonial Igboland was prone to war and ill-equipped to limit it.

Five years before the present of the novel,[1] that is, in 1917, the village groups Umuaro and Okperi disputed a piece of land, and at stake were honour and perceived disrespect. When Umuaro presented Okperi with the choice of war or peace, the same choice that Okonkwo had once offered Mbaino in *Things Fall Apart*, so filled were the emissaries with the importance of their position that they rebuffed their hosts' hospitality. Rudeness inspired challenge. One young envoy lost his temper and broke an Okperi man's *ikenga*, an object imbued with the owner's own spirit, and everyone understood when that man in turn shot the offender: "How would the victim set about putting himself right again with his fathers unless he could say to them: Rest, for the man that did it has paid with his head?" (25). This is retaliatory violence such as we have met before: the offended party can only redeem his honour by killing the offender. Unlike in *Things Fall Apart*, however, such violence has no inherent limits. The clearing of one debt merely creates another. Ezeulu, the priest of Ulu and the protagonist, counselled against further reprisals, which would constitute a "war of blame" (27), but others continued to suspect an insult to Umuaro and joined Ezeulu's rival Nwaka in feeling that "three or four Okperi heads must fall to settle the matter" (27). In the ensuing war Umuaro killed six men and Okperi three, making the final score six to four, and Umuaro was proud that they had provided the dead emissary with "three men on whom to rest his head" (28). The war between Umuaro and Okperi was brought to a close only by the intervention of the British.

The reciprocal violence that maintained peace in *Things Fall Apart* was also fuelled by a masculine rivalry that threatened to destabilize the very equilibrium it had created. Okonkwo in a rage remembers a war against another village group, Isike, when "we killed twelve of their men and they killed only two of ours" (141). He himself has killed five men in battles (65). He keeps a human head he won in the "inter-tribal wars" against Umuofia's neighbours (6),[2] and the term "inter-tribal" carries derogatory connotations of endemic violence. Implicit is a phrase like "the dark days of inter-tribal wars."[3] Yet as we have seen, in *Things Fall Apart* village groups succeeded in converting reciprocal violence into gift exchange and so averted war. In the later setting of *Arrow of God*, however, violence is too contaminated by self-interest and false ideas of honour for any possibility of reciprocity. What has happened to explain the difference?

Whereas Umuofia a decade or more before 1900 was prepared to go to war over the murder of a daughter, Umuaro in 1917 fights over a piece of land. The shift in *casus belli* is possibly symptomatic of a shift in identity. In Igboland, as in most of Africa, wealth was measured in people – how many wives, children, and dependents a man had to work for him – rather than in land. The Igbo village group was defined by birth and interpersonal ties, and it was even possible for a village group to pick up and move to another place and still be the same group. Indeed, this is what Nwaka the warmonger argues Okperi has done in *Arrow of God*. Land was not an issue because it was still abundant. The young Okonkwo in *Things Fall Apart* could farm as much land as he had seed yams to plant. The best farmers in his father's time "cut down virgin forests" and were prepared to "cross seven rivers to make their farms" (17–18). When an older Okonkwo goes into exile in Mbanta, he is given "a plot of ground on which to build his compound, and two or three pieces of land on which to farm" (129–30).

Throughout its history, Africa has been underpopulated and land has been plentiful – by 1975, Africa had only reached the level of population density of Europe in 1500.[4] Igboland, though, has been a notable exception; there, land started to become scarce sometime in the nineteenth century.[5] Nicholas Brown has suggested that the dispute between the village groups of Umuaro and Okperi reflects a new, Malthusian scarcity of land: increased pressure on the land motivates an historically inevitable transition from self-sufficient farming to the new capitalist economy that colonialism has introduced.[6] In the process, the village group, based on membership, acquires a supplementary definition based on land. The titled men Ezeulu and Nwaka dispute whether their village group, Umuaro, came to live on Okperi's land or Okperi migrated to Umuaro's land, but both versions assume that a village group cannot simply expand into surrounding areas without encroaching on others. Robin Horton sees in such migration the possible origins of a different kind of society, one predicated on territory rather than genealogy: "Blocked groups pass through the territories of all their close genealogical relations and end up begging land from groups to which they acknowledge distant or nil genealogical ties."[7] The result is that, instead of segments of society (villages and village groups) being conceptually equal, "disjunctive migration has meant a division of lineages into 'landowners' and 'latecomers.'"[8] The competition for land is aggravated by what Achebe's novel *No Longer at Ease* calls "an unwilling and exhausted soil" (11), the problem of soil erosion that became manifest in Igboland by the 1950s.

Brown's argument, that the underlying motive for the violence at the beginning of *Arrow of God* is economic, has as its corollary that state formation and capitalism itself are inevitable historical processes independent of colonialism, which is but the form that capitalism took. Certainly, in many versions of European history, it is land scarcity and war that drove the development of the modern state.[9] I am arguing, however, that the dispute between the village groups in *Arrow of God* is primarily political and reflects Achebe's retrospective understanding of the role of violence in state formation. When in *Arrow of God* Achebe imagines a disastrous reciprocal violence without inherent limit, he is thematizing the coming of the law and adopting the law's point of view on violence in order to test it. I am attributing the difference between Achebe's two novels not to economic circumstances that emerged between the 1880s and 1917 but to the closing of political doors at independence in 1960. In *Things Fall Apart*, published in 1958, Achebe was interested in village democracy as an alternative political model; in 1964, in *Arrow of God*, reciprocity appeared outmoded as a principle regulating human affairs and came to be seen as a cycle of senseless retribution that needed to be ended.

When they invaded Igboland, the British regarded Africa as a field in which law and morality did not apply – only force did. They claimed legitimacy for their conquest on the basis of the establishment of a rule of law upholding a would-be transcendent morality. The colonial justice system, an "authority situated above the kinship system (and therefore above the network of matrimonial exchange) as well as above the authority generated by gift/countergift relationships,"[10] explicitly replaced retributive violence with an "arbitrational justice" administered by a judge.[11] Having subjugated all other political rivals within its territory, the modern state, of which the colonial state is a version, now regards any violence on the part of subject-citizens "as a danger undermining the legal system."[12] The state deplores all reciprocal violence between constitutive units as automatism, disproportion, and blindness that could allow violence to proliferate endlessly.[13]

As we have seen, the principle of reciprocity among precolonial village groups was based on balance and limits. Arguably, it is the state's "myth of the social contract" that "projects extrajudicial violence back into the prehistory of the state."[14] Raymond Verdier explains that the "conception of destructive vengeance without end does not describe an actual 'state of nature,' but proceeds from a modern vision that arises only after the establishment of the State makes of vengeance an entirely 'private' matter by arrogating to itself the monopoly on force and punishment."[15] The British-imposed rule of law did not rescue Umuofia from a Hobbesian state of nature, as it proclaimed it was doing; rather, it retrospectively created the vision of a natural state of war, which it then worked to prevent people from falling into.

RECIPROCITY AS NIGHTMARE

The violence with which *Arrow of God* opens is not a mere by-product of historical change but is itself the issue at stake. Harmful reciprocal violence percolates to every level, from the domestic to the world-historical, including the family, the council of elders, and even, in the end, the gods themselves. When the elders of Okperi meet to respond to the bellicose ultimatum from Umuaro, they are interrupted by a little girl who runs in calling for her father because her brother has slapped her (22), an ironic diversion that invites a comparison of the war between village groups to a squabble among children. The novel consistently pays as much attention to children's quarrels as to wars between village groups or between gods. In the opening pages, as Ezeulu waits for the new moon to appear and ponders the majesty of his priestly power, his young son and daughter begin an almost ritual exchange of taunts (2). Later, just before Ezeulu is summoned to appear before the District Officer, we are given a blow-by-blow account of the fight that erupts between young Oduche and his half-sister Ojiugo at the stream where they draw water, a fight that quickly spreads to neighbour women and, after the children return home, to their mothers (127–9). In the crisis at the climax of the novel, provoked when Ezeulu refuses to proclaim the New Yam Festival, we are told in some detail of the fight that the youngest Nwafo has in defence of his father with Obielue (210), the son of Ezeulu's best friend Akuebue (110), and then of a fight between Ezeulu's wife Matefi and another woman at the market (210–11).

Children's quarrels are put to an end by their mothers, who are, however, quick to defend their own children against the children of a co-wife. The mothers' disputes must in turn be silenced by their husband. As the proverb has it, the only way to escape from "the mouth of a leopard" is to find "something bigger than a leopard" (158). When a great uproar erupts in his compound, an exasperated Ezeulu refuses to listen to any of the combatants: "Let one of you open his mouth and make *fim* again and I will teach him that a man does not talk when masked spirits speak" (129). Women and children are to men as men are to masked spirits: subordinates who would quarrel endlessly were there not a superior authority to bring order. The converse is also true: men are like women and children, prone to limitless disputes that require the intervention of a superior party like the masked spirits. And the spirits themselves are not immune to contention: the god Ulu declares that he will fight the god Idemili "to the finish; and whoever throws the other down will strip him of his anklet" (192).

The risk of violence escalating from one level to the next until it overwhelms the whole is the theme of a children's song that tells the story of Nwaka Dimkpolo (whose name perhaps recalls that of Ezeulu's great rival[16]), who was killed by the falling of a big *ukwa* fruit. Even if it verges on comedy, a fatal accident demands retribution. That retribution in its turn will require further violence. The first verse asks who will punish the fruit, the next who will punish that avenger, and so on until the chain of retribution engulfs the earth:

> And who will punish this Water for me?
>   E-e Nwaka Dimkpolo
> Earth will dry up this water for me
>   E-e Nwaka Dimkpolo
> Who will punish this Earth for me? (65)

The children's hymn about the cycle of retribution is interrupted only when the singers quarrel over mistakes each has made in the song, that is, when the children have been infected by the violence they sing about. As young Obiageli complains to her playmates, the song really "has no end" (65).

THE VIOLENCE OF THE LAW

In *Things Fall Apart* the reciprocal exchange of gifts created between giver and receiver a relation that was a third entity transcending both. Barkun calls this "the invisible mediator."[17] In *Arrow of God*, however, warring parties require an external third party to adjudicate between them lest they destroy each other. "Vengeance is mine," saith the Lord, and the British act like the new God, putting an end to the cycles of violence and transferring judgment and punishment to a level beyond the possibility of recrimination. Rousseau wrote that

> in order to discover the rules of society best suited to nations, a superior intelligence beholding all the passions of men without experiencing any of them would be needed. This intelligence would have to be wholly unrelated to our nature, while knowing it through and through; its happiness would have to be independent of us, and yet ready to occupy itself with ours ... It would take gods to give men laws.[18]

When Captain T.K. Winterbottom imposed a peace on Umuaro and Okperi and confiscated their weapons, an event subsequently remembered as the Breaking of the Guns, he intended to impress people with the fairness of his judgment. Sally Falk Moore explains of the imposition of British colonial courts in Tanzania:

> The pivotal notion is that there should be a rule-governed judiciary that dispenses justice uniformly and a rule-minded citizenry that mobilizes that judiciary when it thinks it has a case "under the rules." This ideal of rule standardization goes hand in hand with the requirement of judicial impartiality. Such a model is also predicated on the existence of some kind of authoritative hierarchy that ultimately determines what the rules are and who the judges are – who commands, who obeys, what is obeyed.[19]

According to Moore, however, the model was flawed because

> the colonials did not picture these villages as they were, as social arenas seething with internal activity in which social credit was being accumulated and lost, reputations being made and broken, factions organized and loyalties mobilized.[20]

Such a village group is Umuaro.

Unable to ascertain the original owner of the land (and Achebe never does tell us who it was), Captain Winterbottom, like the Biblical Solomon, heeds the one person, Ezeulu, who did not plead his own self-interest and so rules in favour of the other side: Okperi. Finding a righteous man among the two sides allows the District Officer to feel vindicated in holding the contradictory beliefs "that British legal ideas are one of the great achievements of that civilization" and that "these ideas are actually no more than the embodiment of the universal principles of 'natural justice.'"[21] In any case, the facts do not matter to Winterbottom as much as the end of violence, which requires a law backed by overwhelming power *and* able to claim legitimacy on the basis of its manifest disinterestedness.

An early consensus even in Umuaro, the loser in Captain Winterbottom's judgment, is that "it was a good thing perhaps that the war was stopped. The death of Akukalia and his brother in one and the same dispute showed that [the god of war] Ekwensu's hand was in it" (28). Achebe, the citizen of a new state, is interested in the order promised by the rule of law. Much later, he recalls that when the British ran things, "driving alone, going all the way from Lagos to Asaba, crossing the River Niger, to visit my relatives in the east" was a much easier undertaking than it would later be: "That was how it was done in those days. One was not consumed by fear of abduction or armed robbery."[22] The colonial state's monopoly on violence secured colonial subjects from other violence: "There was a distinct order during this time."[23]

Steven Pinker and Jared Diamond quote statistical studies to argue that, in spite of the slaughter associated with twentieth-century war, modern states have suffered a smaller rate of war-related deaths measured over extended periods of time and as a percentage of the population than did small-scale traditional societies, where war caused few deaths at a time but was relatively continuous.[24] Even if one accepts their sources as reliable, one could still say, as Foucault does, that violence in modern states takes other forms. The discipline internalized in people's psyches is more effective than direct violence but is violence nonetheless.

"Colonial Africa, like eighteenth-century and nineteenth-century England, had only rudimentary policing ... Outside the towns and away from the main lines of communication, policing was very much a hit and miss affair where 'much was left to hazard'"[25]; yet it would seem that the mere idea of police served to discourage war among village groups and to rob reciprocal violence of its legitimacy. David Killingray attributes the relative absence of violence in colonial West Africa in part to successful "colonial bluff," in part to the traumatic memory of the original conquest, and in part to the desire on the part of the colonized for security,[26] which is not to discount Achille Mbembe's sardonic comment, citing Simone Weil, that "one can say of the colonial 'peace' that it differed from war only in that one of the camps was deprived of arms."[27] Remember: the imposition of the law is known in Umuaro as the Breaking of the Guns.

Arrow of God, however, is at pains to show that the British are not more peaceable and, in their relations with one another and with Africans, not more just. The British can force an end to a war among village groups, but their peace is itself based on their greater capacity for violence, which makes itself manifest in incidents like the whipping of Obika by Mr. Wright, the road overseer. A host of new "crimes," in particular offences against the colonial structure like Ezeulu's unwillingness to collaborate and accept the office of warrant officer, were more likely to be prosecuted than were incidents of personal violence.[28] John and Jean Comaroff characterize this new violence as "*lawfare*: the use of penal powers, administrative procedures, states of emergency, mandates and warrants to discipline its subjects by means of violence made actual by its own sovereign word."[29] The colonizers also created new sources of power that increased the potential for oppression. As we have seen, the new court messengers and warrant chiefs regularly abused their authority.

In *No Longer at Ease* a soldier returned from fighting in the Second World War "went regularly to a market in the neighbouring village and helped himself to whatever he liked. He went in full uniform, breaking the earth with his boots, and no one dared touch him. It was said that if you touched a soldier, Government would deal with you" (11). A soldier behaves as if he owns the market in Nwapa's *Efuru* as well, kicking over a basin of gari and threatening to hand people over to the police (47). In precolonial Igboland everyone recognizes that soldiers participate in the same violence that installed the law and thus represent a truth about the law even as they flout and undermine it.

Captain Winterbottom (the novel tends to refer to him by his title, just as it does Ezeulu[30]) imagines that, as District Officer, he stands to his new African subjects as a father to his children or as a "school prefect" to junior students (32). As one African policeman puts it, "the white man is the masked spirit of today" (154). The truth is, however, that childish quarrels characterize the entire world of the novel, including that of the British at Government Hill. Winterbottom resents having been passed over for a promotion, which was awarded to a man three years his junior (54), and he is bitter ever since he lost his wife to "some smart fellow" while he was away fighting the Germans in Cameroon (103). Even when he discusses colonial policy, the memory of that personal crisis can alter his voice and bring "a rush of blood to his face" (109). He compensates by asserting his authority over his subordinates, who believe his "personal loss during the war ... made him cling to this ridiculous Captain business" (103). He cannot fully control those under him, however, any more than he could his wife. Wright, the road-builder, casts aspersions on Winterbottom's masculinity in his absence and calls his superior "the Captain" in a "half-contemptuous manner" (102).

The British are not immune to quarrels, as they pretend to be, and are the cause of many of them. The law does not suppress conflict but foments it, for the external position that the law presumes for its authority is a function solely of power rather than of superior knowledge or wisdom. One young man observes of the dispute between Umuaro and Okperi, put a halt to by Winterbottom, that "it is all due to the white man who says, like an elder to two fighting children: You will not fight while I am around. And so the younger and weaker of the two begins to swell himself up and to boast" (20). Authority that comes entirely from above and is not negotiated face to face creates the potential for this kind of abuse. Superior force can put a temporary end to quarrels among subordinates, but does not thereby put an end to violence, which shifts upward and downward to different levels. So, too, within his own compound, where Ezeulu puts an end to quarrels among his wives and children, his absolute power contributes to feelings of resentment and the perpetuation of petty injustices that will fuel future conflicts. When, on the rare occasion of Ezeulu's absence, his eldest son acts as head of the household, he uses the opportunity to mistreat his younger brother and his father's current favourite (165).

Although Winterbottom believes that intercommunal war is a sign of African primitiveness and that the British monopoly on violence will bring a justice based on the law, he himself recognizes that the basis of British rule rests on a greater capacity for violence. He wishes the British could be as honest as the French, who say to those they have colonized: "This land has belonged to you because you have been strong enough to hold it. By the same token it now belongs to us. If you are not satisfied come out and fight us" (36). ("Come down and fight," "bolekaja" in Yoruba, is an expression used by touts of transport vehicles.) The same man who admires Ezeulu's disinterestedness prides himself on being a realist who understands that self-interest motivates everyone and that it is the prerogative of superior might to lay down the law.

The parity that Winterbottom recognizes between Britain and France had been until recently a rivalry like that between Umuaro and Okperi. For centuries the two imperial powers had waged wars in the Americas for control of territory and trade. In Africa in the nineteenth century the European powers expanded inland from ports along the coast. Before they could clash with each other's invading armies, however, they decided to fix borders between their imperial possessions at an international conference such as Europeans hold in a capital city after every great war. For a few decades following the Conference of Berlin in 1884, the European powers accepted limits to their expansion and respected the balance among themselves,[31] a détente made possible because, with the recent opening of the continent, there was enough territory for all. A major inspiration for European colonialism was a negative one: each country's fear of being left behind in the scramble for Africa; an international treaty was a way for them to reassure one another and thus avoid the worst-case scenario. The reciprocity among the European empires was not like that between Umuofia and Mbaino, which was based on gifts and countergifts; rather, it was based on a mutual self-interest in non-interference. Of course, war to the death broke out again among the European powers, and Nigerians were conscripted to fight for Britain against Germany in next-door Cameroon (where Winterbottom also fought) and later against Japan in Burma (mentioned in *No Longer at Ease*). *E-e Nwaka Dimkpolo*!

Looking inward, the state sees subjects whose violence it prohibits, but looking outward, it sees only enemies who must be defended against. In the international field, says Hobbes, "in all times, Kings, and persons of Soveraigne authority, because of their independency, are in continuall jealousies, and in the state and posture of Gladiators; having their weapons pointing, and their eyes fixed on one another."[32] Locke writes that the way we may know what a state of nature is like is by observing the "princes and rulers of independent governments all through the world" who "are in a state of nature," having made no social compact with one another and having no third-party authority to judge between them.[33]

Because each imperialist state justified itself according to a universal principle of morality, supposedly embodied in its law, inter-state violence could not acknowledge reciprocity as a value. Here lies the true threat of infinite violence – it is not in the cycles of reciprocity in a supposed state of nature but in the war between self-proclaimed universals, each feeling justified in its self-interest and refusing to acknowledge reciprocity. In *No Longer at Ease*, the young Obi Okonkwo, as a schoolboy in the 1940s, had so internalized the logic of the law that he believed its claims to transcendence and universality. He fondly imagined a single field of law, one that did not simply contain himself and Umuofia but also adjudicated among European nations and their empires. So he had written a personal letter to Hitler. For this crime he received six strokes of the cane as "a disgrace to the British Empire" (7). The colonial administration that has imposed the rule of law within the colony and the missionaries who have introduced the notion of a universal morality know that, in the larger field where empires operate and states are forged, there is neither law nor reciprocity, only an existential struggle among mortal enemies.

ACHEBE'S RIVAL

Achebe's contemporary Elechi Amadi, from an area just south of Igboland, but linguistically and culturally very similar, and a fellow student of Achebe's at Government College, Umuahia,[34] wrote a trilogy of novels set in the same historical period as *Things Fall Apart*, in a precolonial world without missionaries or colonizers. *The Great Ponds* (1969) imagines two villages that have not yet come together in a larger village group like Achebe's Umuofia or Umuaro, and tells the story of a dispute between them that escalates until the violence engulfs the entire region.

The villages of Chiolu and Aliakoro have long quarrelled over possession of the great pond of Walaga with its fish. A violent struggle thirty years earlier had ended with Chiolu's victory and effective claim to the pond. Possession is nine-tenths of the law: as the Eze of Chiolu now tells Aliakoro: "Might is not right but who can tell now who was right and who wrong? Time obscures many things, but time also establishes many things. That you have not challenged us for thirty years is proof enough that the Pond of Wagaba belongs to us" (20). Aliakoro, however, has decided once again to contest Chiolu's claim. Its members take up fishing in the great pond as an assertion of their rights, at the risk of provoking war. There are pitched battles, which Chiolu wins, but Aliakoro refuses to concede defeat. The right to the Great Pond is too close to its self-definition to be surrendered even at the cost of annihilation, because surrender would itself represent a kind of obliteration.

At first the violence is limited to reciprocity: the villages negotiate prisoner exchanges and ransoms that require determining relative worth and what each owes the other. The conflict escalates, however, when kidnapped women are sold into slavery in distant lands (though not across the sea; the transatlantic slave trade is over) and cannot be retrieved. Reciprocity then becomes no longer possible, and as a result, the killings become ever more gruesome until "Chiolu had achieved the ultimate in the horror game" and "Aliakoro had to show that they too could rig up horrors hitherto undreamed of" (82). The villages become beleaguered laagers, and the violence spills into the neighbouring villages, leaving no one in the forest safe.

Once retaliation has descended into attempts at mutual annihilation, outside forces try to intervene. There is, however, no larger entity capable of asserting a monopoly on violence. The *ezes* of the other villages in the Erekwi clan (which does not yet form a village group like Umuofia) summon the two sides to peace negotiations. In a Hobbesian social contract narrative this should be the moment when villages establish a sovereign that can maintain the peace and form a larger unit that can share resources. As the Eze of Chiolu predicts, "a time will come when there will be little or no fighting. Every generation, unless it meets fresh enemies, does less fighting than the one before" (101). Neither Chiolu nor Aliakoro is willing to budge, however. Sharing is out of the question, and so is dividing the rights to the pond. Adjudication is just as impossible: "Who really owned the Ponds of Wagaba? The answer was anybody's guess" (91).

Both villages continue to be prepared to die and to kill for the ponds. Sacrifice proves the absolute and sacred nature of their claims, but solves nothing because the rivals are equally willing to sacrifice. The only solution to the impasse is to force the gods to make a decision. The will of the gods is put to the test by giving them a deadline by which to signal their will, after which the absence of a sign will itself be taken as a sign: as Hobbes says, "it is not the Length of Time that maketh the Authority, but the Will of the Soveraign signified by his silence (for Silence is sometimes an argument of Consent)."[35] In order to compel the gods' decision one side must swear an oath that will commit it to win the gods' approval or die, and since a whole village cannot take an oath, a representative must: Olumba, the great warrior, swears on the god of the night that the pond belongs to Chiolu. Should the god disagree he will manifest his displeasure by killing Olumba within six months, but if Olumba survives the term, the pond will be Chiolu's.

The enforced mediation of the gods raises the existential stakes. On each side doubt enters as to the legitimacy of its own claims. Olumba wonders whether the gods also recognize the validity of thirty-year possession or whether they observe some other, metaphysical criterion (87). If so, his life is at risk. The six-month delay introduces a near intolerable weight for the human participants. The village of Chiolu tries to protect Olumba from accidental death; Aliakoro tries to harm him by sinister magic. The outcome has to do not just with the rightful owner or even the will of the god, but more with control of the sign that Olumba's potential death has become. Yet this cannot be acknowledged, for to do so would be to limit the god and make him irrelevant, thus robbing the sign of its meaning and, paradoxically, inviting the god's wrath.

In the end the god sends a great epidemic to punish both sides and their neighbours. The quarrel over the ponds expands to consume the entire world, for the final sentence of the novel reveals the epidemic to be the Great Influenza of 1918. If the gods are communicating by signs, they would appear to be unhappy with the greed displayed by the villages and want the violence to end. A *dibia* or priest reveals that the gods are displeased with the Erekwi clan as a whole, but since there is no frame for the clan to "get together for action" (151), nothing can be done in response: the god "Ogbunabali's action, killing off both parties to a dispute, was equally meaningless" (198). In the very end, Olumba survives, after coming perilously close to surrendering all hope and after many around him are felled. After a last-ditch attempt to kill him, Wagu, the Leopard Killer of Aliakoro, commits suicide in the great pond, which means that no one will ever be able to fish there again. The pond is lost to both sides. The man who desires that his own end will also be the end of the world is, like Okonkwo, a demonic parody of sacrifice.

The villagers' dispute brings on the death of millions around the world. The disproportion suggests that something larger than the villages and smaller than the world is required to mediate between the villages, something like the state, but the novel cannot see its way clear to this. Given the circumstances when the novel was written, on the eve of the Nigerian Civil War, we may suspect that the novel despairs of any mediation. During the Nigerian Civil War, Amadi himself fought on the side of the federal army against the breakaway state of Biafra, with which Achebe sided. Biafra promised a home to Igbos who had suffered pogroms in the north of the country, but Amadi, like many members of other ethnic groups in southeastern Nigeria, feared a state dominated by Igbos. One might expect, from someone who fought for a united Nigeria, a vision of a larger order established by social contract than can eliminate retributive violence, but *The Great Ponds* is about the inevitable disaster created by debts of blood, as if Amadi saw the approaching war not as a war of secession but as a civil war and an intertribal conflagration.

THE ORIGIN OF THE SOCIAL CONTRACT

In *Arrow of God*, the warring village groups of Umuaro and Okperi accept Winterbottom's enforced peace not because they acknowledge the justice of the outside arbiter's decree, but explicitly because, like Umuofia at the end of *Things Fall Apart*, they remember the massacre in nearby Abame, when the British took revenge for the death of a man on a bicycle by wiping out an entire village group.[36] Abame figures in both novels and unites their worlds. Twenty years later the story of what British "soldiers did in Abame is still told with fear" (28). The men of Umuaro feel complicit in Abame's fate because some of them had served as guides and porters on the punitive expedition.

Arrow of God also mentions, however, another entity called Abam, who do not figure in *Things Fall Apart*. Abam are "warriors" (28, 120, 134) or "hired soldiers" (202), whose "ravages" Umuaro had regularly to flee in the past (202). Unlike Abame, based on Ahiara in Mbaise, the Abam bear the name of an actual historical people: the Abam from the Cross River area, who provided soldiers to the Aro people, who in the early nineteenth century maintained a network of satellite towns throughout Igboland that allowed them to control the slave trade. The Aro did not themselves wage war, but relied on mercenary allies like the Abam. The Aro and the Abam are not mentioned in *Things Fall Apart*, which presents precolonial violence as if it were limited to the scale of village groups. The presence of the Abam in *Arrow of God* points to a violence among Igbo that is not governed by reciprocity. Indeed, some historians have seen in the historical Aro a proto-state emerging in stateless Igboland, "having a kingship (Eze Aro) and other institutions of government."[37] By the first half of the nineteenth century the Aro had "created what K. Onwuka Dike termed a regional 'pax' under which large-scale trade flourished in a multiethnic region, and their operations eased exchange and 'brought rapid impetus to economic expansion' in a region with a multitiered currency system."[38] They had set up an external arbitrator in the form of the Long Juju at Arochukwu, which the British later sent military expeditions to destroy. This indigenous proto-state is, however, regarded as a menace by Umuaro, and with good reason.

Before the events of the novel, the original six villages of Umuaro, pushed "beyond the end of things" by the slave raiders of Abam (134), had taken an almost existential leap of faith and come together in self-defence, creating a new social contract, including a new god and a priesthood to serve that god.[39] The need for communal self-defence is the origin of Ezeulu's priestly authority. Although the name Umuaro appears to mean "children of Aro," the villages are not a satellite of the Aro; their union is a response to the threat posed *by* the Aro. The social contract that created the village group of Umuaro arose from below and was a native development. When, in the narrative present, the villages are once again pushed beyond the end of things, this time by the British, and when one of their own demands sovereignty for the god Ulu, they will have to forge another social contract in self-defence.

The fictive Abame, the village group destroyed by the British in both of Achebe's novels, is strangely close in name to the non-fictive Abam, and Taiwo Osinubi has argued that Achebe invites a confusion of the two polities.[40] He reads Abam wherever Achebe has written Abame, even in *Things Fall Apart*, because his interest is in the disavowed connection between slavery, which divided Africans, and colonialism, which all alike suffered. But if the potential for confusion between the two entities needs explaining, so too does the consistent distinction maintained between them in *Arrow of God*, where Abame is always a victim and a warning, Abam always a violent external threat almost on the scale of the British themselves. Given the tonal nature of the Igbo language, a feature not captured in Roman orthography, we cannot be certain that the two names would be as close to an Igbo speaker as they appear to a reader of the English text.

According to Hannah Arendt, Europeans of the seventeenth century "clearly distinguished between two kinds of 'social contract.' One was concluded between individual persons and supposedly gave birth to society; the other was concluded between a people and its ruler and supposedly resulted in legitimate government."[41] The first, horizontal social contract involves individuals making promises to one another in public and "is based on reciprocity and presupposes equality." "Such an alliance gathers together the isolated strength of the allied partners and binds them into a new power structure by virtue of 'free and sincere promises.'"[42] Such would be the formation of Umuaro in the face of the threat by Abam. The second, vertical kind of social contract, by contrast, makes people into subjects, each of whom must surrender "his isolated strength and power to constitute a government; far from gaining a new power, and possibly more than he had before, he resigns his power such as it is, and far from binding himself through promises, he merely expresses his 'consent' to be ruled by the government."[43] The government "acquires a monopoly of power so that the governed are politically impotent so long as they do not decide to recover their original power in order to change the government and entrust another ruler with their power."[44] Such is the rule of law imposed by Winterbottom.

SOVEREIGNTY AND PATERNAL AUTHORITY

In *Arrow of God*, when Captain Winterbottom investigated the land dispute between Umuaro and Okperi, he found that "every witness who testified before me – from both sides without exception – perjured themselves" (38). Lauren Benton writes that British colonizers believed "that English law possessed a singular, rule-bound neutrality," but also "that the strengths of the legal system grew out of English subjects' special relationship to the truth."[45] How does the District Officer know what is a lie? He judges moral character and truth by whether a man's testimony contravenes self-interest, that is, by the manifest self-sacrifice of the witness. One man alone "witnessed against his people" and so won the District Officer's respect as an honest man (38). That man, of course, was Ezeulu.

We must imagine that when Ezeulu testifies to Okperi's rightful ownership of the land in question, he is indeed telling the truth as he knows it. His own understanding of the truth cannot be separated, however, from filial duty. In the war council of Umuaro, Ezeulu testifies:

> My father said this to me that when our village first came here to live the land belonged to Okperi. It was Okperi who gave us a piece of their land to live in. They also gave us their deities – their Udo and their Ogwugwu. But they said to our ancestors – mark my words – the people of Okperi said to our fathers: We give you our Udo and our Ogwugwu; but you must call the deity we give you not Udo but the son of Udo, and not Ogwugwu but the son of Ogwugwu. This is the story as I heard it from my father. (15)

Ezeulu seeks a stable and fixed truth beyond the need for interpretation and finds it in the father. For Ezeulu, morality requires subordinating self-interest and even the self to the authority of the father and of fathers in general. To be a moral man is to be a good son. Indeed, throughout the novel Ezeulu is known simply by his title, meaning "priest of Ulu," which he inherited from his father, and we never do learn what his name was before he assumed the role. To insist that the six villages and their gods stand in a junior, even filial relation to Okperi is, paradoxically, to uphold the authority both of Ulu, his god, and of his father. And the priest's own moral standing, derived from his explicit obedience to a higher principle, then allows him to put the filial obedience of the rest of Umuaro to the test.

Nwaka, Ezeulu's rival, replies that his own father told him "a different story": that Okperi people were wanderers who came to the area later than the people of Umuaro did (16). Nwaka claims to be faithful to his own father when he argues for self-interest, but he is not afraid to argue that in any case, fathers and memories of fathers cannot be fully trusted: "We know that a father does not speak falsely to his son. But we also know that the lore of the land is beyond the knowledge of many fathers" (16). In other words, the appeal to paternal authority does not close the argument but merely displaces it: fathers also disputed among themselves. The appeal to a stable authority is itself a form of rhetorical suasion that will be countered by the force of other arguments. Ezeulu, Nwaka argues, is not qualified to speak "about events that are older than Umuaro itself" (16). Ezeulu's argument for the singleness and supremacy of the truth as declared by the father appears to Nwaka to be a grandiose front. Moreover, Nwaka believes, parents are not just appealed to for partisan reasons; they are themselves the source of partisan feeling. Nwaka suggests that Ezeulu only sides with Okperi because his mother was from there. (As we shall see, Nwaka could not be more wrong here.)

Nwaka cannot imagine principles other than partisanship. Sally Falk Moore explains that in many small-scale African societies "evidence giving is more of a testimonial to the character and social place of the person on whose behalf the witness is testifying than it is an account of the 'facts.'" Moreover, the "structural requirement that there be partisanship and that it be given public demonstration necessarily has deep effects on community micropolitics."[46] Nwaka's opportunistic arguments persuade the council to go to war with Okperi, but they are likely to have the opposite effect on readers of the novel, who will, I venture, like Winterbottom, put more trust in Ezeulu's explicitly moral stance. Tejumola Olaniyan, for instance, writes: "The irony is that Ezeulu is always logically right. But to be right *logically* is not necessarily to be so *politically*."[47] But how does Olaniyan know Ezeulu is right about the facts in this case? Readers are likely to judge as Captain Winterbottom does: that Nwaka appeals to baser instincts such as greed and resentment and therefore must be wrong, while Ezeulu, that "magnificent man" as Achebe calls him in the preface, obeys a higher truth. The implied English-language readers of the novel, all of whom will be citizens of some state, will likely share what Michael Warner identifies as the ideal of republican ideology: "a neutral and rational ground of public representation, where citizens were called on to exercise civic virtue by placing the common good over personal interest."[48]

It would be wise to judge Ezeulu and Nwaka not in terms of truthfulness or even morality – which, I am arguing, are declared by the law – but in terms of the different models of society they represent. Ezeulu argues that the individual must be an arrow of god, subordinate to a higher ideal. His Umuaro makes itself manifest to its members in Durkheimian fashion, in rituals such as the Festival of the First Pumpkin

Leaves, when once a year all gather in one place and the priest of Ulu publicly re-enacts the First Coming of Ulu, the founding moment when the six villages became one and said to the first Ezeulu, "*You will carry this deity for us*" (189). The priest takes on himself all the guilt and misfortune of the previous year and tramples them underfoot so that the community can start anew. This ritual is an annual return to the origin, and the priest embodies the community as a whole. Umuaro, however, is also manifest to its members in the councils of citizens, where the issues of the day are debated and the fissures of the society make themselves felt. The council is a democratic forum in which power and authority are negotiated, competing interests need to be weighed, and rhetoric carries the day.

At the heart of Igbo rhetoric, the novel makes clear, is mastery of the proverb, and Nwaka has earned the designation of "Owner of words" (144). To undermine Ezeulu's patriarchal authority, Nwaka invokes a proverbial simile: "Wisdom is like a goatskin bag; every man carries his own" (16). Traditional proverbs do not imply a single truth to which all accede, not even the truth of relativism; they are instead rhetorical tools, the means of expressing and legitimizing conflicting opinions. Proverbs can serve both sides in a debate: to counter one proverb an orator must invoke another. Achebe himself says that "proverbs by themselves have little significance"; they are but "the dormant seeds lying in the dry-season earth, waiting for the rain."[49] Proverbs ask listeners to compare their own context to another: they say, in effect, "look at the current situation in terms of this other situation, already familiar to us all." Mamoussé Diagne writes that "the strategic goal is to establish that one cannot be right alone and that the truth is a truth-arrived-at-with-others."[50]

Nwaka the rhetorician presumes that it is always possible to speak on either side of a case. This will strike modern readers as perversely variable and inconsistent, but it expresses a world such as that of Renaissance humanism (before the arrival of the modern constitutionalism of Hobbes and Locke), where "the criteria for the application of moral and political concepts are so various and circumstantial, rather than essential and universal, that any case is always open to more than one description and evaluation, by means of comparisons and contrasts with other cases."[51] According to Falk Moore, British colonial authorities were frustrated that Africans did not understand that a case once tried could be appealed but could not be reopened and retried by the same authority. But among the Chagga people at least, changes in the balance of micropolitical power led to demands to revisit a closed case because they made an alternative judgment possible.[52] Stanley Fish argues that something similar is true even under Western law, although the law denies it:

> By definition the career of persuasion is unpredictable and theoretically interminable; there is no guarantee that either party will be victorious, although in some social structures – and the law is certainly one of them – victory is mandated in the form of an obligation to render a decision. But when victory occurs, whether by the surrender of one party to the party of which he now becomes a member or by jurisdictional fiat, it is always provisional; for, since it has emerged from argument, from the forceful urging of some partisan point of view, it is always possible, and indeed likely, that what has apparently been settled will become unsettled, and argument will begin again.[53]

The rhetorical nature of the law does not accord with the ideal of objectivity and transparency held by Captain Winterbottom, Ezeulu, or, I am arguing, the realist novel. Ezeulu believes the truth is not a matter of persuasion but is passed on by paternal authority. That makes patrilineal succession rather than persuasion the major question of legal and political authority. It is also, as we shall see in the next chapter, the major question in *Arrow of God.*

7

The Problem of Succession

J.M. Coetzee suggests that succession, the question of "how to ensure that power will be passed from one set of hands to the next without a contest of arms," is "the main problem in the life of the state."[1] That succession is a problem is obvious in postcolonial African states, where presidents have often refused to step down after the end of their term. Succession was especially fraught in the case of decolonization, when sovereignty passed from the colonizer to the colonized. The ceremonies of independence confirmed the rule of the law, which supposedly governed the transfer of sovereignty, but it was the colonizer's sovereignty that had established the law in the first place. Indeed, in former British colonies such as Ghana and Nigeria, independence at first involved retaining Queen Elizabeth II as head of state on the model of the Commonwealth dominions. In 1963 Nigeria became a republic, but the question of "Who would succeed the British?" retained its urgency.

INHERITING FROM THE COLONIZER

Having identified in Ezeulu the one man who respects the sanctity of the father's word, the District Commissioner orders that he be offered the warrant chieftaincy of Umuaro. A memorandum from the Lieutenant-Governor has called for "an effective system of 'indirect rule' based on native institutions" (55). Traditional social and cultural systems will be respected and preserved in order to reconcile colonial subjects to imperial rule. The policy of indirect rule, however, is deeply contradictory: the adaptation of imperial rule to local conditions is made into a universal principle to be applied everywhere without regard for context. Where there are no absolute rulers, as in Igboland, the British will create them. Such are the warrant chiefs.

Winterbottom wants to hand power to the man who has proven that he deserves it by his willingness to sacrifice self-interest. Nwaka speaks truer than he perhaps knows when he describes Ezeulu as the white man's friend (143): "Like every other thing Nwaka said from malice this one had its foundation in truth" (176). Ezeulu's junior wife Ugoye tells an uncannily relevant story (told in full only in the first edition of *Arrow of God*[2]) in which the two sons of two co-wives are each rewarded as they deserve. Because he is honest and courteous and follows instructions, the son of the younger wife receives riches from spirits who speak through their noses as white men do. He brings home "yellow metal, cloths and velvets, foods of all kinds, money, cows, goats and many other things of value."[3] The same spirits, however, punish the son of the older wife when he reveals himself to be greedy, dishonest, rude, and unable to obey commands. The older son brings home "leprosy, smallpox, yaws and worse diseases without names and every abomination."[4] The story addresses how a good son from a good parent can inherit what is not the parent's to give but also warns that the spirits' legacy can be as negative as it is positive. Ezeulu is like the obedient son, who deserves to inherit the Normative State and bring home all the bounty associated with a stable order.

A previous appointee to a warrant chieftaincy had proven hopelessly corrupt. James Ikedi inherited both the colonizer's capacity for violence and his propensity to exploit, without internalizing any of the colonizer's need for moral justification. A frustrated Captain Winterbottom can find no excuse for Ikedi's exploitation of his fellow Africans by "their own blood brother and chief" (58). But he is being disingenuous: Ikedi, appointed chief among a people that has never known chiefs, treats his new subjects with the same abuse with which Wright, the road-builder, treats Obika, the worker who comes late. The "offspring of a hawk cannot fail to devour chicks" (128).

There are two aspects to the colonizer's legacy: the Prerogative State, where laws serve the will of those who wield power, and the Normative State, in which rulers acknowledge they are themselves subject to the law. Winterbottom seeks someone worthy of inheriting the Normative State, the moral authority of the rule of law. Ezeulu, however, refuses the warrant chieftaincy for the very reason that Winterbottom offers it to him. Ezeulu's respect for the absolute authority of the absent father means he cannot accept the colonizer's authority. The "white man's friend" must oppose the white man. Ezeulu's moral stance reflects a larger problem faced by African nationalists, who sought to inherit the colonial state established by the British but could not inherit *from the British*. Valentin

Mudimbe, writing of French Africa, explains that part of the problem is that the colonized were not and could not be sons of the colonizer:

> What if the father to which you have subjected yourself is an imposter: a false father who wrongly usurped the position of authority? What happens then to the son? What about the status of memory: if I'm confronting a false father who imposed a false word on me, what sort of memory am I rejecting? This has long been the case in colonized Black Africa: Having been drilled from textbooks that speak of "our ancestors, the Gauls," what happens when you wake up and discover that your ancestors were not the Gauls? Do you remain silent – or shout yourself hoarse? What are the implications here for a practice and politics of patrimony and tradition?[5]

Mongo Beti, the Cameroonian novelist, writes repeatedly of the psychological contortions involved in taking the colonizer as a father. In *Le roi miraculé*, Père LeGuen regards his houseboy Gustave with the pride and tenderness of a father: "When he had taken him into the Mission House a few years back, the child had been a mere fetus or little better. LeGuen taught him French, with some success. The boy now spoke with LeGuen's accent and inflexions. He was even developing his teacher's private mannerisms."[6] To have a European missionary as a father is not, however, to inherit his power but to be infantilised. LeGuen speaks down to his "children," "prepared to go through that shameful subterfuge whereby parents pretend to place children on a common footing, when, in fact, they are making fools of them."[7]

One cannot inherit from another's father. Tutuola expresses the problem in a series of linked Yoruba proverbs:

> *The son of thief inherits "thieving"*
> *The son of poor man inherits "poverty"*
> *The son of lazy man inherits "laziness"*
> *The son of rich man inherits "wealth"*
> *The son of philosopher inherits "philosophy"*
> *The son of hunter inherits "gun, etc."*
> *so the "poverty", "misery", "wretchedness", and*
> "sorrow" shall never finish in the generation
> *that there is no "perseverance"*[8]

Ezeulu represents an admirable moral authority that is worth passing on, but it cannot be the sovereign authority the British have. *Arrow of*

God asks, in effect, "How can Nigerian readers inherit the colonial state and its law not from Winterbottom or James Ikedi but from Ezeulu?" To come to terms with this question, the novel breaks it down into several related questions, including these: "How exactly are the British able to pass on their authority from one generation to the next?," "Could one inherit from Ezeulu the same way?," and "Can the Normative State ever be separated from the Prerogative State?"

PATRILINEAL SUCCESSION AMONG THE BRITISH

Arrow of God devotes a surprising amount of attention to relations among the homosocial community of colonial administrators at Government Hill. The missionaries, Africans intent on converting Igbos by bringing schools, have arguably a greater impact on Umuaro than do the colonial administrators, but the novel shows us more of the latter precisely because of its concern with sovereignty and political succession. Although as divided among themselves and as mixed in their personal motives as the people of Umuaro, the British have solved the problem of succession that, as we shall see, besets Ezeulu.

The District Commissioner holds his position by virtue of a certificate of authority no less than a chief appointed by warrant does. "Nomination," writes Bourdieu, is "a very mysterious act": "Who certifies the validity of the certificate? It is the one who signs the credential giving license to certify. But who then certifies this?"[9] Certification is confirmed when it is handed on to and received by another. Soon after we meet Winterbottom, we are introduced to his assistant, Tony Clarke, newly arrived in Africa, who, in the course of the novel, will take over the Captain's duties when the latter suffers a collapse.

When we meet him, Clarke is busy looking at his gold watch, a gift from his father, and reading "The Call," an imperial manifesto that makes an appeal to his masculinity.[10] According to George Allen, as the author of "The Call" is identified in the novel, British sons must escape the feminizing influence of their mothers and leave childhood behind: "Our mothers do not draw us with nervous grip back to the fireside of boyhood, back into the home circle, back to the purposeless sports of middle life; it is our greatest pride that they do – albeit tearfully – send us fearless and erect, to lead the backward races into line" (33). The colonizers are explicitly interpellated by their own propaganda as sons. "The Call" presents a vision of "son after son" heading out to serve the Empire, "strong in the will of his parents today, stronger in the deeds of his fathers in the past" (33). Becoming an empire-builder, able "to deal with men as others deal with materials" (33), requires that the young man separate himself from his mother and follow, not his father, but the nation's fathers. In this imperial imaginary, Africans are perpetual children to be ruled by men who have left their own childhood behind.

The British on Government Hill constitute an ideal patriliny, a community of men entirely without women, indeed entirely without blood relations. The imperial bureaucracy requires its agents to speak and act as if they were without personal wills, interchangeable and replaceable. Their personal relations are presumed not to interfere with the running of the administration and the transition of power. Precisely because he has lost his wife and has no children, Winterbottom is able to pass his authority on to the next generation!

The people of Umuaro refer to Clarke as Winterbottom's "younger brother" (164). The Captain himself addresses his subordinate as "my boy" (148). Clarke is forcefully reminded on several occasions that as a junior officer, he counts for nothing (34). He feels "impotent anger" when Winterbottom will not let him finish a point he is making and "personal inadequacy" when he cannot make the point as beautifully to his superior as he had made it to himself (109). Winterbottom tells Clarke, with some condescension, "I see you are one of the progressive ones" (36). Superiors condescend because at some level they are threatened by their subordinates: Winterbottom observes of Clarke: "The fellow's cheek! He had been there barely a week and already he was talking as though he owned the district and Captain Winterbottom was the new boy, or some desk-ridden idiot at headquarters" (106–7).

Clarke, at first, identifies with Wade and the "boyish" Wright (102), men of a lower rank who are, to adapt Ezeulu's description of one of Obika's mates, not "fit friends for anyone who wanted to do anything with his life" (79). Clarke protects Wright by not investigating the report that he had whipped one of the "natives" and then by lying to the Captain about it (106). Wright's practice of sleeping with native women fascinates Clarke – he has been preoccupied by unfamiliar thoughts "since first seeing fully grown girls going about naked" (104) – but the Assistant District Commissioner will not act on his desires; he will instead integrate Winterbottom's prohibition into his own psyche. Clarke, unlike his friends, comes to identify with his superior. He feels guilty about talking about his superior behind his back with subordinates, "like one who had been caught back-biting one of his own group with an outsider" (104).

Clarke eventually comes to feel sorry for Winterbottom, who now seems merely "too tired and old" (107). The younger man will better appreciate the senior officer when Winterbottom suffers his breakdown and Clarke must take over his duties. He first tells the older man to go and see a doctor, "knowing that this was the kind of stuff expected of new boys" (148). Slowly, however, and "without making any conscious decision Clarke was preparing himself to assume the burden of the Administration in the event of Captain Winterbottom's death" (161). Like a latter-day Prince Hal, he separates himself from his worthless companions and now considers that Winterbottom represents the "*crystallization of civilization*" (108, italics in text), that is, the complete sublimation of the man into the role he must play.

Clarke integrates not Captain Winterbottom as such, but the moral responsibility for the colonizing mission. Clarke feels guilty when he detains Ezeulu at Government Hill without charge, until the older man provides a legal formula to assuage his conscience: "The moral of all this was that if older coasters like Winterbottom were no wiser than the younger ones they at least had finesse, and this was not to be dismissed lightly" (178). One week later, when he releases Ezeulu, "the first major decision Clarke had taken on his own," the younger man "had already developed considerable self-confidence. In letters he had written home to his father and his fiancée after the incident he had made fun of his earlier amateurishness – a certain sign of present self-assurance" (180).

Having succeeded to the burden of empire and the duties of the patriarch, Clarke "felt like a man who had just been initiated into an important secret society" (180). The phrase "secret society" suggests a parallel between the British and their African subjects. Another parallel is sacrifice. Clarke, newly empowered, and his subordinate Wade come across a traditional sacrifice on the road, which contains, in addition to the usual cocks, kolanut, and white chalk, an "English florin."[11] Wade feels uneasy seeing "the head of George the Fifth ... dragged into a disgusting juju" (161), and he removes the coin. Wade's action of respect for the king and disrespect for the sacrifice, in turn, shocks Clarke, who sees in it a "monstrous lack of feeling" (161). Clarke will rule over Wade and Wright, as well as over Okperi and Umuaro, because he understands the moral imperative that underwrites patriarchal authority. With patriarchal authority comes paternal responsibility: "It would fall on him to defend his natives if need be from the thoughtless acts of white people like Wade" (161–2).

When Wade locates the dignity and power of the king in the king's image, he is fetishizing the coin. I use the term ironically to emphasize that both the people who sacrifice the coin and the British administrator locate the king's power in his image.[12] Wade is also, however, disgusted by what he regards as primitive sacrifice, and he wants to keep the king free from African magic. By putting the king's head back where it belongs, he proves himself merely a loyal subject. Clarke, by contrast, who is willing to countenance the sacrifice of the king's head, will succeed to the imperial call and wield the king's authority in this part of the world. He has learned he must be prepared to sacrifice self-interest and his own desires in favour of a higher moral ideal. Wade takes the king as his Ego-Ideal, whereas Clarke is able to sacrifice the king and so also integrate him as his superego.

The sacrifice of the king-father re-enacts a much larger history. Carol Pateman summarizes the story of the social contract as it developed in Europe thus: "The father is (metaphorically) killed by his sons, who transform (the paternal dimension of) the father's patriarchal right into civil government. The sons alienate this aspect of political power into the hands of representatives, the state."[13] The colonizers' understanding of themselves is that Oedipal succession allows Europeans to integrate the father's command and thus achieve the "autonomy" required in order to rule others effectively, whereas Africans, who rely on direction from visible authority, that is, fetishes, suffer eternal "dependence."[14]

The modern state, as Captain Winterbottom knows and Clarke learns, involves a split in the citizen-subject such that what the citizen sacrifices in the way of self-interest is returned to him in the form of legitimized power. And in assuming moral responsibility, the modern citizen also sacrifices his personal relations with others. Clarke's readiness to enthrone a higher ideal in his conscience will put a distance between him and his companions, but that is the price to be paid for authority.

INHERITING FROM EZEULU

Ezeulu, dedicated to serving the truth of his father, is preoccupied with identifying the son best suited to succeed him as priest of Ulu. Should the next Ezeulu be his eldest, Edogo, an artist like Achebe and the carver of the Mask of Agaba, which "stood for the power and aggressiveness of youth" (199)? Or Oduche, the new Christian convert and the first literate person in the family, whose knowledge of Scripture so impresses the missionary John Goodcountry that he declares the boy will "be called Peter; on this rock will I build my church" (49)? Or Ezeulu's youngest son, Nwafo, who, some said, "was in every way an image of Ezeulu's father" (91) and who shows the most inclination for the task: "Although he was only a child it looked as though the deity had already marked him out as his future Chief Priest" (4)? "When the time came that Ezeulu was no longer found in his place Ulu might choose the least likely of his sons to succeed him," as indeed has "happened before" (4). Obika, the second son and the one who physically and temperamentally bears the closest resemblance to his father, dies at the end of the novel and so cannot inherit. Does he represent a succession that should have been?

At the sighting of the new moon that opens the novel, Ezeulu is joined by Nwafo, his youngest, who takes pride in emulating his father (4). Immediately after the idyllic opening scene of father and son, however, as if on cue, Ezeulu's eldest, Edogo, enters his father's *obi* or house and the father wastes no time in rebuking his woodcarver son for disobeying his express command not to carve a deity. Dealing with spirit forces is Ezeulu's preserve. The rebuke and the original prohibition remind us that, under patriarchy, even as the son takes to heart the precept to be *like* the father, he must also integrate the prohibition, "You *may not be* like your father," that is, "you may not do all that he does; some things are his prerogative."[15] To inherit from the father requires being subordinate to the father's authority, as we have seen from Ezeulu's own example in the debate over going to war with Okperi.

The dilemma of patriarchy is that the generation of Edogo and his brothers cannot appear as independent or as strong as their fathers because their elders will not allow them to. Clarke suffered a similar infantilization in the presence of Captain Winterbottom. All children in the novel, including the adult Edogo, who has embarked on a family of his own, remain distinctly subordinate to their elders. In Umuaro, young men live at home until they get married, after which their compounds continue to be attached to their father's. Key to Ezeulu's sense of himself is the image he has of the world in decline and of himself as the last bulwark of order, and this sentiment appears unrelated to the presence of the colonizers and the missionaries. On the first page we are told that Ezeulu felt himself "as good as any young man, or better because young men were no longer what they used to be." One game that "Ezeulu never tired of playing on them" was "whenever they shook hands with him he tensed his arm and put all his power into the grip, and being unprepared for it they winced and recoiled with pain" (1). Readers can hear in the priest's truculence the same contempt that Winterbottom bears for the younger generation.

Ezeulu is disappointed in all his adult sons. He is critical of the perceived complacency of Edogo, the eldest, and prefers Obika, who is less "quiet and brooding" (11). Obika, however, is hot-headed and keeps bad company, and his father must tell him, "It is praiseworthy to be brave and fearless, my son, but sometimes it is better to be a coward" (11). When Obika rushes to defend his father's honour from the perceived insults of a court messenger, Ezeulu roars at him to shut up: it is not the son's place to speak for the father in the father's presence (138). Ezeulu rebukes Edogo, on the other hand, for not defending his father's honour in the father's absence: "When I was your age I would have known what to do" (53). It is as though the two adult sons have inherited different halves of the balanced whole that should constitute an adult man.

On the one hand, the father's power over all, including his sons, pretends to be absolute, yet nothing is more certain than that the old man will die and the sons will inherit the power he had wielded against them and that they had grown to resent. Thinking about his father's unreasonable resentments, Edogo realizes that "the older his children grew," the more Ezeulu "seemed to dislike them":

> Edogo remembered how much his father had liked him when he was a boy and how with the passage of years he had transferred his affection first to Obika and then to Oduche and Nwafo. Thinking of it now Edogo could not actually remember that their father had ever shown much affection for Oduche. He seemed to have lingered too long on Obika (who of all his sons resembled him most in appearance) and then by-passed Oduche for Nwafo. What would happen if the old man had another son tomorrow? Would Nwafo then begin to lose favour in his eyes? (91)

Postcolonial African leaders would later operate this way, seeming always to fear potential successors as rivals and drawing them near only to push them away again. In Ahmadou Kourouma's *En attendant le vote des bêtes sauvages*, Tiékoroni, the dictator of the République des Ébènes (based on Houphouet-Boigny of the Ivory Coast), advises a younger dictator never to designate a successor: "a successor, whether one wishes it or not, is a rival, and the people cease their attachment to a guide once his demise no longer threatens to be a catastrophe."[16]

Edogo wonders "whether it was true," as his father said, "that a man never spoke a lie to his sons" (100). What if his own father is lying when he says fathers never lie? Does the truth of the father depend on which son he is speaking to? Mudimbe, writing of the filial relation of the colonized to the colonizer in terms that sound very much like Ezeulu's relation to his sons, says that the father's word

> is accorded a permanence that follows us from place to place and across the years. It becomes the memory of the world. Hence the burden of generations that is conveyed in the phrase "I am your

father." The child, crushed by such authority, withdraws into a position of weakness while, at the same time, the child would like to affirm a new authority and the voice of new ways to come. But a sovereign discourse, that of the father, clearly signifies a mortal refusal to the child's desire for power. "I am going to look elsewhere," the child thinks, and thus arouses suspicions that dictate a rereading of the familial memory. "And what if my father was wrong?"[17]

THE PRICE OF SACRIFICE

The problem of inheritance is complicated because at stake in the novel is not so much the priesthood of Ulu as the sovereignty of the British. As we noted, Nigerians must somehow inherit Winterbottom's authority *from Ezeulu*. One Igbo character in *Arrow of God* seems to grasp this necessity, and that is the man known simply as Nwodika's son, but called John by the District Officer. Nwodika's son is one of the new men who have taken to working for the white man, recognizing that "the race for the white man's money would not wait till tomorrow or till we were ready to join" (169). He serves Winterbottom as a cook but in the course of the novel transfers his allegiance to Ezeulu. He is from Umunneora, the village of Ezeulu's rival, Nwaka, but his long stay on Government Hill, away from Umuaro, has made it possible for him to escape the inter-village rivalry and to welcome Ezeulu as a countryman. From his perspective, Ezeulu and Winterbottom are on the same plane, and he is convinced that the priest's power is superior and has caused the white man's physical collapse. It is said of Ezeulu and this younger man that "their thoughts are brothers" (170), and a ritual of blood brotherhood with Ezeulu's son Edogo cements the relationship (169). Is Nwodika's son (whose personal Igbo name, Nwabueze, means "son is king"), rather than Oduche or any of the priest's other sons, the true heir of Ezeulu?

To move from blood lineage to adoptive filiation appears to solve the problem of inheritance, but it would be too easy. After all, as we have seen, succession requires sacrifice. *Arrow of God* begins by asking which of Ezeulu's sons will inherit the priesthood of Ulu, but concludes more sinisterly by asking this implicit question: what and *who* will have to be sacrificed for there to be an inheritance?

Ezeulu had originally sent Oduche, his least favourite son, to the mission school as a "sacrifice to the white man" (46). As Ezeulu tells Akuebue,

> A disease that has never been seen before cannot be cured with everyday herbs. When we want to make a charm we look for the animal whose blood can match its power; if a chicken cannot do it we look for a goat or a ram; if that is not sufficient we send for a bull. But sometimes even a bull does not suffice, then we must look for a human. Do you think it is the sound of the death-cry gurgling through blood that we want to hear? No, my friend, we do it because we have reached the very end of things and we know that neither a cock nor a goat nor even a bull will do. (133)

This is the obverse of Oedipal parricide, where sons sacrifice the father. The man who tells his son that fathers never lie to their sons is prepared to sacrifice a son.

Robert Wren and Olakunle George argue plausibly that Ulu's choice of a successor has fallen on Oduche, that the new Christian will inherit the colonizer's authority, and that Ulu the deity has, in effect, chosen self-immolation.[18] If the question, however, is not about Ulu's choice of an heir but about his choice of a victim, that choice falls not on Oduche but on Obika, Ezeulu's second son. The trigger for Ezeulu's final descent into madness is the death of his beloved adult son, who collapses after the strenuous exercise of carrying the *ogbazulobodo* masquerade through the villages while running a fever. It seems then to Ezeulu that the world has been turned upside down, contravening his prayer "*May children put their fathers into the earth and not fathers their children*" (6). This unmotivated and unbearable loss, and not the defection of his people, is what drives Ezeulu mad.

David Lee Miller establishes that patriliny in Western literature is frequently associated with the image of a father who witnesses the death of a son. Miller argues that the figure of the dead son brings home the cost of patriarchy: in submitting to the principle of fatherhood, a man gains patriarchal authority but in the process sacrifices personal relations, including all that he holds most dear.[19] To obey the father is to kill the son, both one's own son and the son within, a principle also illustrated by Okonkwo's killing of Ikemefuna.

The greatest sacrifice in the novel is, however, Ezeulu himself. Achebe tells us in his preface to the second edition that it is Ezeulu's "high historic destiny as victim" to consecrate and raise "to the stature of a ritual passage ... the defection of his people." According to this reading, Ezeulu's collapse into madness, an explicit parallel to Winterbottom's breakdown that allows Clarke to succeed him, constitutes the sacrifice necessary if the people of Umuaro in the novel and Nigerian readers of the novel are to reconceive of themselves and to embark upon a new social order on a larger scale than the village group.

To be effective, such a sacrificial regicide requires that Ezeulu, besides being worthy of being integrated into the psyche, be a tyrant who deserves to be overthrown. Ezeulu, resentful that Nwaka had persuaded Umuaro that he should heed the summons by Winterbottom and travel to Okperi, decides that the village group should face the consequences of their lack of respect for the god Ulu and his priest. His absence in Okperi means that Ezeulu does not eat two of the sacred yams associated with the lunar calendar. He perversely decides to punish Umuaro by imposing a literalist interpretation on the eating of the sacred yams and not giving permission to harvest the new yams when they are ready and need to be harvested because there are still sacred yams remaining. In order to resolve the existential crisis of the yams provoked by Ezeulu, the people of Umuaro take up the Reverend Goodcountry's invitation to join the Christian church and so harvest yams with immunity. Even Nwaka sends a son to missionaries ("the one who seemed least likely among his children to become a good farmer" [215]). The result: "Thereafter any yam harvested in his fields was harvested in the name of the son" (230). The people of Umuaro now harvest in the name of the Son sacrificed by a father, Jesus Christ.

Kant suggests that the prospects of "a universal history and a global cosmopolitanism ... depend on the planetary reproduction of a particular experience of the sublime," that of the French Revolution, which beheaded a king in the name of liberty, equality, and fraternity.[20] *Things Fall Apart* and *Arrow of God* are both tragedies in which a leader who asserts the absolute sovereignty of the village group is overthrown and abandoned, bringing to an end the old order and permitting people to join the new church in large numbers. If one thinks of Okonkwo and Ezeulu as proto-kings among a people without kings, then their fall resembles the regicide that, in modern republics, allowed sovereignty to pass from the king to the body of his subjects.

At the end of both of Achebe's novels of colonization the people leave behind their local god and join in the worship of the universal Christian God. As long as the village or the town is the experiential centre of the world, it can enjoy the protection of a local deity. But once the village group has been decentred and people have become colonial subjects, they will have to give their assent to a new, larger, and necessarily more abstract collective entity, the state, adapted to the scale on which the British operate. The state presumes a universal God, commensurate with a world divided into nation-states in which Nigeria will assume a place of its own.

It could even appear that the sacrifice of Achebe's fictional patriarchs was effective and readers have taken them into their psyches. Achebe, who did not write a bildungsroman or a memoir of childhood, but rather tragedies about patriarchs who lived before he himself was born and who were also much older than he was at the time he wrote, is now himself frequently recognized as the father of African literature. His descendants among writers and readers, like Abraham's, number as the stars in heaven.

Achebe says that "had he been spared," Ezeulu would "have come to see his fate as perfectly consistent" with the requirements of history. In other words, had he survived, Ezeulu would have seen why he had to perish. Achebe's convoluted logic in his preface signals, however, an ambivalence with regard to the new social contract that Ezeulu's fall ratifies. The logical conundrum, conflating life and death, imagines Ezeulu both dying and surviving to contemplate his death. The split in Ezeulu, between the victim who must die and the understanding that encompasses that death, creates the equivalent of the king's two bodies: the king is dead, long live the king.

When the six villages originally came together in self-defence against the raiders of Abam, they "sacrificed not a stranger but one of themselves and made the great medicine which they called Ulu" (134). Now the people without kings must sacrifice a man who would be king in order to create the great medicine called Nigeria. But Umuaro, although originally built on sacrifice, retains a deep mistrust of sacrifice. The town tells its own equivalent of Freud's story in *Totem and Taboo* of the original parricide. There was once a seventh village in Umuaro, called Umuama. Six brothers from Umuama killed the royal python, whom people addressed as "Father" (47), and cooked it to make yam pottage. Although each of the brothers brought a bowl of water for the pottage, once it was cooked there was only enough liquid for four bowls (48). The result: "The brothers began to quarrel violently, and then to fight. Very soon the fighting spread throughout Umuama, and so fierce was it that the village was almost wiped out" (48). The story of Umuama is an enactment of the story of Nwaka Dimkpolo's endless cycle of retribution, but in this case the fratricidal violence is not resolved by a sacrifice but *started* by a sacrifice and allowed to proceed to its logical conclusion. The original parricide did not unite the sons in a new union but resulted instead in social disintegration. For whatever reason, the brothers were not able to incorporate the dead father in their own psyches; their parricide merely removed the linchpin of the society without creating a new state or psychic realm to replace it.

The six brothers in the story appear foolish for not recognizing that some water boils away in the making of soup,[21] but the story stands as a warning not against foolishness but against the sacrifice of a father. Umuaro, built on an original sacrifice, is a whole much stronger than the six villages that make it up, but the seventh village of Umuama falls apart after its sacrifice of a father. One sacrifice is efficacious, the other disastrous. And what of Nigeria? In 1964 one might well have wondered whether something was gained or lost when a variety of ingredients were stirred together to make a single soup. When six bowls of water plus yam and python are reduced to four bowls of pottage, how is the result to be divided? Will there not be fights as everyone seeks a piece of the national cake, to invoke the common Nigerian metaphor?

PATRILINY AND MADNESS

The Dual State of the colonizers, based on both command and obedience to the law, corresponds to the division in the self that is implicit in patrilineal succession. According to collective memory, in "the first days of Umuaro," Ulu gave "only one son to his Chief Priests, for seven generations" (127), but that regular succession from father to son broke down at the time of Ezeulu's own father's death. Ezeulu's father had been that rare thing: a man "in whose body priesthood met with medicine and magic" (147), but when the great man died, his powers were divided between his two sons, the eldest succeeding to the priestly title and the youngest becoming a famous medicine man. In Mamdani's terms, the priest is the *subject* of a god, a mere arrow in the hands of a higher authority, while the man with the powers of medicine is a *citizen* with the sovereign power to harness the spirits for his own intentions.[22] A man may not tell his son a lie, but he may tell two sons different truths.

Ezeulu's half-brother, Okeke Onenyi, the medicine man, believes "that the cause of the coolness between him and the present Ezeulu ... was the latter's resentment at the splitting of the powers between them" (147). It is not clear, however, which of the brothers is the more resentful. Some people remember that "in their childhood their father led Okeke to think that he was going to succeed to the priesthood and that on the old man's death Okeke all but questioned the decision of the oracle" (148). What is clear is that Ezeulu's authority as father and his obedience as son both require constant reassertion because patrilineal succession is characterized by doubt and incompleteness.

The division of Ezeulu's father's two kinds of power, one merely representative and the other sovereign, results in Ezeulu's own self-division into subject and sovereign, son and father. The two aspects of the self can reinforce each other: as we have seen, the good son who serves the father is able to claim for himself the father's moral authority. But the two aspects can as easily come into conflict. The child that Ezeulu once was survives within, trembling before the arbitrary power of a father. On the tremendous occasion when Ezeulu obeys the summons from Government Hill and leaves Umuaro, he still can feel "like a child whose stern parent had gone on a journey" (160). His god later barks in his ear "as a spirit would in the ear of an impertinent human child" (191).

In the very first pages of the novel, the thought that he is but an arrow of god "intoxicated" Ezeulu, the good son and the loyal servant of the god, "like palm wine" (192). He thinks of his authority as coming from above rather than below, much as that of a warrant chief does. Even as he proclaims the new moon, however, Ezeulu wonders whether he has any power of his own not derived from the god's transcendent sphere. The new moon then calls forth the voice of an internal "enemy," who challenges him by saying he has no power in his own right, that he is but a "watchman" whose "power was no more than the power of a child over a goat that was said to be his" (3). The priest responds to the internal enemy's challenge, "Take away that word *dare*": "No man in all Umuaro can stand up and say that I dare not. The woman who will bear the man who will say it has not been born yet" (3). The priest now asserts his own sovereignty, issuing a mental challenge both to the voice of the elders who say he is no more than a child and to the voice of the sons whom he assumes want to supplant him. In other words, already at the beginning of the novel, Ezeulu is divided into the subject of the gods and the would-be sovereign.

At the beginning of the novel, as we have seen, readers are likely to side with Ezeulu the high-minded protagonist, who speaks truth come what may against Nwaka, his scheming and jealous rival, Like an arrow of god, Ezeulu subordinates personal interest to an overarching ideal, one that does not deign to compete, conspire, or negotiate because it claims simply to embody both the people and the truth. At the end of the novel, however, Ezeulu once again follows an ideal, the will of his god, even when it threatens to do great harm to the community. When Ezeulu insists that it is the will of his god that the people postpone the yam harvest and risk starvation, the same readers who sided with him against Nwaka are likely to judge him mad. The priest's fall then illustrates the maxim "that no man however great was greater than his people" (230). But this is what Nwaka had been saying when he accused Ezeulu of inheriting from his father not the true version of past events but the ambition "to be king, priest, diviner, all" (27). Umuaro once showed Ezeulu's father "that Igbo people knew no kings," says Nwaka, and it must teach the son the same lesson (27).

Ezeulu and Nwaka are each consistent throughout the novel: the former serves the will of his god and his father rather than the interests of the people; the latter denies that anything transcends self-interest. Yet between the beginning and the end of the novel readers change in their response to Ezeulu. In readers' contradictory responses, I read the novel's own ambivalence toward the social contract that would set up a higher moral good to which citizens can be sacrificed.

In the present of the novel, Ezeulu does not know which son will be chosen by Ulu to succeed him as priest, but one thing is certain: the succession will not fall to a daughter. Women must leave their father's house and join their husbands and so cannot inherit. It is said of Ezeulu's eldest daughter, Adeze, that "if she had been a man she would have resembled her father even more than Obika" (73), and she is addressed by Ugoye, one of her father's wives, as "*Mother of my Husband*," an acknowledgment that the first daughter is regarded as the reincarnation of her grandmother (73; italics in the original). That is precisely the problem.

The novel opens with Ezeulu on the lookout for the new moon, a sign from his god, but on the second page of the novel we are told that "the fear of the new moon which he felt as a little boy still hovered round him" (2). Only much later do we learn that that boyhood terror has its source in his mother's periodic fits of madness. The same moon whose regular reappearance confirms the priest's relationship with his god and therefore the authority he inherits from his priest-father used to awaken "severe but spasmodic attacks of madness" in his mother (176). As a child, Ezeulu had "lived in fear of those moments when his mother's feet were put in stocks, at the new moon" (223). And as an adult, he cannot see the new moon without recalling his mother's confinement. The "fear was often overpowered by the joy of his high office; but it was not killed" (2). The madness of Ezeulu's mother, a seemingly unmotivated detail in the novel, functions as an alternative aetiology for his behaviour at the end, when people "say the man has caught his mother's madness" (212).

A son only inherits half from his father and cannot even be sure of that half. Ezeulu is deeply concerned with the fates of the *other* halves, the half of his father that he did not inherit *and* the half he inherited from his mother. Patrilineal identity insists on the truthfulness of the father – "A man does not speak a lie to his son," Ezeulu tells his youngest: "Remember that always. To say *My father told me* is to swear the greatest oath" (93) – but, as Nancy Jay reminds us, knowing who one's father is actually depends on the truthfulness of the mother.[23] Ezeulu, however, does not tell his son Nwafo, "Remember, a son only knows his father because a mother never tells her son a lie." Instead, he is desperate to deny the relevance of anything the mother might say.

Ezeulu's father's priestly authority and his mother's madness are both recalled at every appearance of the new moon. Although this is not made explicit, it is easy to imagine that the father's possession of absolute truth is what makes the mother's word untrue, is what qualifies it as madness. If so, then women's madness would be not just the excuse used to justify patriarchy but itself the product of patriarchy. In his nightmares, Ezeulu associates his mother with Idemili and the python cult (222), that is, with the social organization "there at the beginning of things" (41), before the new social contract of Umuaro. In the contract that creates Umuaro, we may find unconscious traces of a move from cognate relations that involve both the paternal and maternal sides of the family to agnate relations involving patriliny alone. (Although Achebe presents the struggle between Ulu and Idemili as between two male gods, in reality Idemili is an Igbo goddess, an error corrected in the later novel *Anthills of the Savannah*.)

Ezeulu's final agony appears to offer readers, all citizens of a nation-state, the kind of psychic integration of the father that the British are able to achieve. The "ritual passage" from village and clan to nation is, however, far from straightforward. When Achebe says that Ezeulu is a "victim" who consecrates "by his agony ... the defection of his people," he employs the discourse of sacrifice, but we cannot describe what happens in the novel as an active parricide. Ezeulu does not go mad because the clan deserts him. The clan deserts him *after* he goes mad. And most readers will feel that the priest was already mad when he forced the ritual calendar apart from the natural cycle of the seasons and put the harvest and the community at risk, that is, when he listened to Ulu speak in his ear with "a dry, skeletal laugh" such as "only the insane could sometimes approach" (191). Ezeulu knows that laugh only too well from his childhood.

I am arguing that the priest of Ulu enacts in his own psyche the aporias of the modern citizen-subject that Achebe and his Nigerian readers would have felt in 1964: the son must kill the father in order to free himself and must integrate the father into his psyche, meaning he will never be free. Mamdani discusses how the African nation-state inherited a distinction made by the colonizers between citizen and subject that was also a distinction between modernity and tribalism. I take Mamdani's lesson but would note that everywhere citizenship in a modern representative democracy is a fraught status that divides the self. As Paul Downes writes of the nascent American Republic, democracy presumes that the subjects overthrow the king and become citizens, but citizens remain subject to the sovereignty of the state, whose own source of authority remains obscure: "The collapse of a distinction between lawmaking, sovereign power, and the subjectivity produced by subservience to that law, will form the paradoxical and apparently impossible ontology of the citizen-subject."[24] Coetzee asks, in a discussion of the conundrum of representative democracy, "Who serves whom? Who is the servant, who the master?" The citizen or the state?[25]

If I am right and Ezeulu's always incipient madness is a version of the psychic constitution of the citizen, then the atavistic return of the mother's madness at the end acquires a new meaning. Ezeulu, who throughout the novel has affirmed the supremacy of his father, in the end escapes the tyranny of the father, whom he has internalized, by joining his mother in her mania. Discussing Freud, Judith Butler writes that "the process of forming the subject is a process of rendering the terrorizing power of the state invisible – and effective – as the ideality of conscience."[26] Butler quotes Freud to the effect that conscience, the incorporation into the psyche of the will of the father, "often enough succeeds in driving the ego into death, if the latter does not *fend off its tyrant* in time by the change round into mania."[27] In mania, says Butler, "the tyrant is fended off, but not thrown off or overcome. Mania marks a temporary suspension or mastering of the tyrant by the ego,"[28] when the child for a moment is able to fend off the voice of the father.

The characters and the action in *Arrow of God* are hopelessly overdetermined. Ezeulu is at once subject to the father and a would-be sovereign who dictates to his people. I am arguing that his subject status and his sovereignty cannot be separated, that they are built into the nature of the modern state, whose citizens are always also subjects. The collapse into madness of Ezeulu authorizes the defection of his people: the king is gone, long live the people. But the madness of this man who would be king may be part of the very nature of sovereignty. The new Nigerian citizens should take note.

8

Modern Debt and the Civil Service

No Longer at Ease, the sequel to *Things Fall Apart*, was published in 1960, the year of Nigeria's independence.[1] For the characters in the novel, set in contemporary Lagos fifty or so years after Okonkwo's death, independence is ever on the horizon, approaching without ever arriving – "it was thought that Nigeria might become independent in 1956," but "in the event it did not happen" (96). Instead the novel opens and ends with a young man, a civil servant in the colonial administration, on trial for corruption. The first sentence of the novel is "For three or four weeks Obi Okonkwo had been steeling himself against this moment" (1). Dread not anticipation – is this any way to narrate the approach of independence? The last sentence of the novel, the sentence passed on Obi after the guilty verdict, is missing.

Just as *Things Fall Apart* retrospectively narrates how an Igbo man might have come to feature as a suicide in Arthur Glynn Leonard's ethnography – a colonial text that will be written after the end of the story but is the original impetus of the novel's writing – *No Longer at Ease* begins in 1958 with a tragic end, the trial of Okonkwo's grandson, then returns to 1956 in order to narrate how the promising young man, who had once styled himself part of a new generation defined by its refusal to take bribes, had come to this pass. Every narrative in the past tense implies a future from whose perspective the events are narrated. In *No Longer at Ease*, however, set on the eve of independence, the future implied by the past tense of the narration, the future that is the present of every reader, is not yet known to writer or character. Obi, a self-styled crusader against corruption, acts with an eye to an implied future, the Weberian ideal state that is also frequently the teleology of historical writing, but he senses that contemporary events may well be relegating that future to the past as a dream that failed to be realized.

In 1956, Obi returned from studies in London. The 1956 constitutional conference that was to have set a date for Nigeria's independence was postponed when the British struck the Foster-Sutton Commission of Inquiry to examine charges of corruption in the Eastern Region, which was ruled by Nnamdi Azikiwe's NCNC (National Council of Nigeria and the Cameroons).[2] After a series of commissions of inquiry, "many Nigerians regarded corruption as the main issue by which they and the outside world would judge the country's capacity for self rule."[3] The Foster-Sutton Commission was aimed, at least in part, at discrediting nationalist leaders like Azikiwe, whom the British disliked. Nationalist politicians themselves, however, were as eager to accuse one another of corruption: "Any group in opposition felt free to raise questions about venality not only to embarrass their opponents, but also to encourage the British to remove offending ministers and even whole governments from power."[4]

Behaviour labelled "corruption" *and* accusations of corruption together form what Steven Pierce calls a "corruption-complex."[5] As early as 1900 the word "corruption" had been used in Nigeria to designate "a failure to live by the mores of a particular kind of bureaucracy."[6] Some things labelled "corruption" were actually selected for by the colonial political system and Indirect Rule, which made traditional and so-called traditional rulers responsible not to those below but to those above them. Charges of "corruption" could be brought to bear against someone who was objectionable for other reasons.[7] And such accusations kept in the forefront of public consciousness the Weberian ideal of the impartial state, with its neutral bureaucracy and rule of law, however divorced that ideal was from the reality of the colonial state. Pierce suggests that, in order to understand corruption, we should not consider it as "something coherent and real, which states might be plagued by or not, naturalized in an ideological portrait of the noncorrupt state as a *European* state,"[8] but instead consider the entire complex of practices and moral judgments, as well as the context in which charges of corruption are made and the ideals such charges appeal to. Among the things we must consider in order to understand corruption are various forms of debt.

DEBT AND COMMUNITY

No Longer at Ease is, if anything, more obsessed with debt than *Things Fall Apart*. Obi's studies abroad were made possible by a student loan from the Umuofia Progressive Union of eight hundred pounds, which echoes the twice four hundred seed yams that roughly seventy years earlier Okonkwo at the same age had borrowed from Nwakibie in order to set up as a farmer and begin his progress up the ladder of *ozo* titles. Understanding that advancement in colonial society required a mastery of the law, the Umuofia Progressive Union sent a son of Umuofia to acquire this knowledge, much as Ezeulu sent his son Oduche to school to learn writing. The UPU investment went awry, however, when Obi in London studied English literature instead. Fortunately, in those days, university graduates in Nigeria numbered fewer than three thousand[9] and all could be assured positions in the rapidly Nigerianizing civil service. The UPU is still able to "have someone who is there."[10]

Obi is repaying his student loan from the UPU at the rate of twenty pounds a month (55), but he finds the moral debt to his sponsors is without term. The UPU counts on Obi's position in the civil service to advance the fortunes of others from Umuofia and the prestige of the whole. The first task the town union assigns him is to "look out for openings in his department and put in a word for" a lowly messenger fired from his last post for sleeping on the job (72). The town union's understanding of mutual obligations resembles the principles of gift exchange at the heart of *Things Fall Apart*. Alain Marie explains that

> the basic mechanism of solidarity and, more especially, of the communal bond is the "logic of debt," according to which every member, always already indebted to the community (to the ancestors, elders, parents, older brothers, from whom he receives his life, identity, education, life force, start in life and the original stake of capital – economic, social, cultural, symbolic – that will permit him to become one day a socially autonomous adult), must sooner or later, lest he incur the social death of exclusion, honour this manifold, multidirectional, and infinite debt, even as he begins to make debtors of others in turn, so that he can also hold people in his debt.[11]

Community, writes Roberto Esposito, is not, as often imagined, a group comfortable with one another or constituted by the exclusion of outsiders; it "is the totality of persons united not by a 'property' but precisely by an obligation or a debt; not by an 'addition' [*più*] but by a 'subtraction' [*meno*]."[12] At the etymological heart of *communitas* is the *munus* or gift. The gift, however, can be a burden: community is the wound that cannot be healed, the gift that cannot be repaid.

When such interpersonal ties of debt are extended to the modern state, the result is what Richard Joseph has called "prebendal politics," the use of office for the benefit of one's group. Offices of state are "allocated and then exploited as benefices by the office-holders," but the "practice is legitimated by a set of political norms according to which the appropriation of such offices is not just an act of individual greed or ambition but concurrently the satisfaction of the short-term objectives of a subset of the general population."[13] Olly Owen explains that "prebendalism is a two-way street": "it works reciprocally, both for the persons occupying office and for those who put them there. And the ability to further secure access to state payroll jobs, to reproduce being-in the state, is itself of value; this is also good for the occupier of that office as it can be brokered into personal status and prestige in the community that has sent them there."[14]

Obi, however, feels his manifold debt owed to the UPU as a moral burden. Something has changed in the meaning of debt since the days of Okonkwo. The system of mutual obligation that ties Obi to the men who invested in him feels to him like a betrayal of the modern aspirations he was able to acquire as a result of their investment. The opposite of *community*, says Esposito, is *immunity*, the goal of the modern individual who is no longer able to "bear the gratitude that the gift demands" and seeks exemption from the gift's obligations[15]:

> Modern individuals truly become that, the perfectly individual, the "absolute" individual, bordered in such a way that they are isolated and protected, but only if they are freed in advance from the "debt" that binds them one to the other; if they are released from, exonerated, or relieved of that contact, which threatens their identity, exposing them to possible conflict with their neighbor, exposing them to the contagion of the relation with others.[16]

"Modern liberty is essentially the absence of debt," writes Godbout.[17] Obi, who rejects his indebtedness to others, observes an ethics based on reason and the autonomous individual subject: "The Kantian moral subject is his own creditor and debtor, or at least acknowledges only one debt to reason."[18] He has this in common with characters in British Victorian novels, who also discover that "every debt of any kind conferred the obligation of relationship" and "restricted one's independence": "by making the individual dependent on others, credit and gifts made everyone's character … distended, displaced, a function of relationship, not an expression of a developmental self."[19]

The principles of gift exchange and mutual debt are no longer second nature to the young man returned from overseas. When Joseph asks Obi to think how his proposed marriage to an *osu*, a member of an outcast group, will offend "the poor men and women who collected the money" to send him overseas, Obi angrily retorts, "It was only a loan, remember. I shall pay it back to the last anini" (68). He seeks to escape his open-ended obligations to the community by assigning them monetary values and finite terms. Treating debt as a simple monetary transaction promises that one can clear one's debt and escape the risks it entails of interminable dependency.[20] The use of money, as Georg Simmel wrote, "is conducive to the removal of the personal element from human relationships through its indifferent and objective nature."[21]

The UPU originally sent Obi to study the law because its members understood that the law would be the key to power in the new dispensation and they wanted to be able to defend themselves against that power. But perhaps because Obi did not study law but literature instead, he has absorbed an idealized sense of the law's universality and impartiality. The loan that has allowed Obi to join the educated elite who administer the country has also removed him in class and self-understanding from the small traders and businessmen who are the bulk of the town union. Obi, now part of what Pierre van den Berghe calls the mandarinate,[22] has the sense that some things, notably state benefits, should not be within a person's power to give away or sell. Civil service jobs and overseas scholarships (he works for the Scholarship Board after his return) should, he feels, be disbursed impartially according to merit. Where the town union regards the law as a means, Obi regards it as an end, and he views as corruption the town union's demand that he use his position to benefit his people.

THE HOUSE AND THE STATE

Obi and the UPU judge differently, but the difference cannot be simply mapped onto modernity and tradition, as if corruption were a matter of different levels of modern sophistication. Both Obi and the members of the UPU live in Lagos. The Umuofia Progressive Union, as the name indicates, is a recent phenomenon, as modern as the colony itself. The town union is constituted by a social contract; it has elected officers and holds general meetings whose proceedings are recorded in minutes, and it taxes its members in order to accumulate capital that can be lent to members for purposes that advance the interests of all. Obi declares that his generation must be "pioneers" who will show their elders the way (68); similarly, the president of the UPU is proud that he and his peers are "pioneers building up our families and our town" (75). As the secretary of the UPU declares, Umuofia seeks to join "the comity of other towns in their march towards political irredentism, social equality and economic emancipation" (28), a long-winded rhetorical gesture to modernity. That is why it is so important for them to have "one of our sons in the vanguard of this march of progress" (28).

As a homesick student in London, Obi associated with fellow Nigerians of different ethnicities, wrote an insipid paean to Nigeria, and insisted on speaking Igbo rather than "a foreign language" when possible (45). When he returns to Lagos, his pride continues to inspire a preference for pounded yam over boiled potatoes (31). Benedict Anderson attributes the development of nationalism, a new psychic identification with the state, to the elites in the colonies, who, in forging careers in the colonial civil service, travelled from their provincial homes to the capital, where they met others who had made the same secular "pilgrimage" from other provinces.[23] These newly privileged citizens speak different mother tongues but have the colonizer's language in common.

Others, however, who have followed the same trajectory from the provinces to the capital, even from the same village group as Obi, are modern in a way that does not identify with the state. In the fifty or so years since the death of Okonkwo the sons of Umuofia have spread throughout the colonial territory in pursuit of trade. The state's monopoly on violence, which has made the roads safer and travel easier, the exaction of taxes, which has forced everyone, not just traders, into the cash economy, and increased access to foreign goods have together expanded the field for commercial activity far beyond the circuit of markets around Igboland. In *Arrow of God* we learn that within a decade or so after the death of Okonkwo, Umuofia had become one of the leaders in the new markets for cloth and tobacco (210). And everywhere the sojourners from Umuofia go in their search for profit or paid work, they organize branches of the UPU to advance the fortunes of their home "town."

The extension of trade throughout the territory is as much a by-product of colonialism as the civil service Obi joins. The members of the Lagos branch of the UPU differ from Anderson's nascent nationalists in that most do not have careers but are traders, labourers, messengers, and the like. Among the members of the UPU the journey to the state capital has reinforced not a national identity but an explicitly subnational one. Even the elite members do not view themselves as having come to the centre; rather, they consider themselves "sojourners" abroad (6). Wherever the sons and daughters of Umuofia find themselves in Nigeria, the centre of their personal world remains the homeland, to which they return annually on a pilgrimage that reverses Anderson's. Nigeria merely defines the field throughout which they disperse and in which they compete for resources with other subnational entities on the same scale as themselves. The members of the UPU are thus the spiritual heirs not of Okonkwo but of Efuru, who travelled up and down the Great River in the pursuit of trade.

The UPU is what anthropologists would call a House, a "mercantile household polity" defined between what C.A. Gregory calls the "homeland," to which members return typically once a year at Christmas and to which they retire, and "the tradeland," the field delineated by the frontiers of the colonial territory where they buy and sell commodities.[24] The members of the UPU win honour by sending home remittances and by converting the profits made in the tradeland into inalienable family goods in the homeland, such as "zinc" houses (with corrugated zinc roofs rather than thatch ones). Igbo town unions create a "diasporic public sphere,"[25] somewhat comparable to the "trade diaspora" of the Aro,[26] the network of dispersed communities established throughout Igboland in the eighteenth and nineteenth centuries from a base in Arochukwu.

The UPU is a "trust network," as defined by Charles Tilly: "Faithful participants in trust networks commonly get personal attention, help with personal difficulties, long-term reciprocity, and cushioning against possible disasters or disabilities – benefits they cannot ordinarily acquire elsewhere."[27] The town union's values "spring from reciprocally recognised relations of consanguinity, affinity, and contiguity,"[28] an endogamy that "includes not only the rules of marriage, which describe the innermost circle of territoriality, and the shared language, which describes the outer circle, but, most important of all, the principles governing the transmission of mercantile credit within these circles and over time."[29] David Pratten explains that "accountability is judged in terms of redistribution": "Wealth begets responsibilities and it is in these aspects that one's achievements are judged in terms of sending children to study overseas; educating poor people through sponsorship; donating in church; employing people in a company; entertaining visitors; holding the peace; and being truthful and steadfast."[30]

The House's "Tribal Brotherhood"[31] does not represent tradition threatened with dissolution by modern capitalism; on the contrary, the trust fostered by bonds of blood facilitates the extension of commercial credit to members and is the source of the House's economic success. Tilly writes that "where uncertain enforcement of contracts and high information costs prevail, naturally formed trust networks actually offer superior efficiency to reliance on impersonal economic transactions."[32] The insecurity of the colonial state fosters kin-based trust networks.

Every Igbo village group has such a town union, concerned with notions of progress, development, literacy, and education.[33] In Munonye's *Bridge to a Wedding*, also set on the eve of independence though written long after, the focus is not on the new state but on the establishment of a town union in Umudiobia, called the Mudi Enlightenment Committee or Mece for short. It is the creation of young people who want to launch a water project, university scholarships, and "a five-year development plan."[34] The proper constitution of a town union is a political question every bit as fraught as that of the new state:

> Doctor Daniel Koba, B.A., Ph.D., (alias Doc. or Don) was perhaps the most vocal, pronouncing from his knowledge of Political Science, as he claimed, that the Mece had been heading for a collapse all along. Indeed the new Executive, said he, was extremely immature and inarticulate, and the Mece itself terribly unwieldy. Had nobody heard what a representative of one of the world's big powers once said about the United Nations – that the organization had become too unwieldy? The same had become the fate of the Mece.[35]

If the town union and the soon-to-be-independent state are equally modern, why are they opposed, as they are in *No Longer at Ease*? If a town union is understood as a political organization along the lines of the UN, why are the civic virtues manifested by the members of that union not transferable to the state? Robert Putnam shows, using the example of Italy, that national feeling as manifested in participation in elections and in participatory citizenship is highest in those regions where people already have experience collaborating for shared interests in local collective endeavours such as trade unions, sports clubs, and social interest groups. He writes: "Generalized reciprocity (not 'I'll do this for you, because you are more powerful than I,' nor even 'I'll do this for you now, if you do that for me now,' but 'I'll do this for you now, knowing that somewhere down the road you'll do something for me') generates high social capital and underpins collaboration."[36] Why then is the UPU, which operates precisely according to such reciprocity, not a workshop where the values required of Nigerian citizens are developed?

The members of the UPU make decisions together in open discussion, much as their ancestors did on the *ilo*, the kind of activity that for Aristotle defined political freedom. As subjects of the British colony of Nigeria, however, they feel the precariousness of their ventures. Joseph attributes prebendalism to conditions of insecurity where "legal guarantees of physical security, status and wealth are weak or non-existent."[37] The House's central values, loyalty and trust among members, have as their corollary distrust of outsiders. The town union considers the colonial territory not as defining the larger society of which the town union is a part but as a more or less neutral field filled with strangers, where the Umuofians themselves but sojourn, *and* as a potentially hostile power: "the government was 'they.' It had nothing to do with you or me. It was an alien institution and people's business was to get as much from it as they could without getting into trouble" (27). Peter Ekeh expresses this division between homeland and tradeland in terms of two public realms created by colonialism: the one "a primordial reservoir of moral obligations, a public entity which one works to preserve and benefit," and the other "an amoral civic public from which one seeks to gain, if possible in order to benefit the moral primordial public."[38]

The secretary of the UPU argues that "every town and village struggles at this momentous epoch in our political evolution to possess that of which it can say: 'This is mine'" (29). The oldest member laments that "many towns have four or five or even ten of their sons in European posts in this city. Umuofia has only one. And now our enemies say that one is even too much for us" (6). The UPU would be in competition with the Mudi Enlightenment Committee in Munonye's novel or the Ipaja Descendants' Union in Aluko's *One Man, One Matchet*. "Let our enemies not glory in our misfortune" and "God see to it that our enemies are crushed" are common Igbo prayers in Nwapa's *Efuru* as well (34).

Tejumola Olaniyan finds the forthright competitiveness of the UPU "hilariously shameless" and a "crass moral cop-out,"[39] and so it is if one judges according to the transcendent moral ideal implied by the state and its law, which is how Obi and Achebe's novel also judge. By the measure of the prospective state, the unalloyed self-interest and paranoia of the town union are indeed contemptible. Citizens should put the greater good above self-interest and not wish destruction upon one another. We must recognize, however, that the UPU *does* require that its members put the greater good ahead of their personal interest. Everything depends on how one defines the "greater" in "greater good" and the self in "self-interest."

That "no man however great was greater than his people; that no one ever won judgment against his clan" (230), the final moral of *Arrow of God*, is often quoted by critics as if it expressed a simple truth. The parallel syntax suggests that a man's people *are* his clan, that is, the neighbors whom he knows personally and to whom he is related by kinship: Ezeulu therefore should not put himself above Umuaro. In *No Longer at Ease*, Obi, like Ezeulu, has integrated into his psyche a moral authority that is greater than both himself *and* his clan. Umuofia insists that no man should think himself greater than his "people" and that therefore Obi should heed his townsfolk's opinions about whom to marry; whereas Obi thinks of the clan as stupidly selfish and of the state as the source of morality. Readers, like Olaniyan, will side with Obi against the clan in this regard.

The president of the town union misunderstands Obi's flight from communal obligation as the selfish profligacy of youth. He explains that Umuofia's representatives in Lagos must sacrifice self-interest for the greater good: "Those who build must deny ourselves many pleasures. We must not drink because we see our neighbours drink or run after women because our thing stands up" (75). Ironically, Obi feels exactly the same way about the need to dedicate oneself to a higher ideal in order to build something: as a student in London, he gave a speech about "education for service, not for white-collar jobs and comfortable salaries" (29), worthy sentiments that are sincere even if they involve little risk on the part of a young man guaranteed to land a coveted white-collar job. Obi is not a prodigal like so many before him, young social climbers from the provinces who come to the metropolis like Balzac's Rastignac, Raphael de Valentin, or Lucien de Rubempré, or for that matter, Obi's fellow Igbo Freddie Namme in *Jagua Nana*. The immunity from obligations that Obi seeks is more ascetic than self-interested. Indeed, compared to his friends Joseph and Chris, he is a puritan in sexual matters.

The difference in outlook between Obi and the town union is not between morality and pleasure (both value asceticism and self-sacrifice), nor is it between tradition and modernity (both are modern), but between definitions of inside and outside and where one puts one's trust. Umuofia regards the field of the state as outside, whereas Obi feels himself inside the space of the nation-state and regards the many strangers within it as potential fellow citizens. He whom the town union sent to study the law so that he could "handle all their land cases against their neighbours" (6) now intends to represent the rule of law to his fellow Nigerians, explicitly including the townsfolk of Umuofia.

In the late nineteenth century, as we have seen, European nation-states that prided themselves on their advanced democracies raced one another to accumulate territory in Africa. As they competed for colonies, they acknowledged no morality greater than self-interest. Or, as Locke writes, "great robbers punish little ones, to keep them in their obedience; but the great ones are rewarded with laurels and triumphs."[40] Each state tried to project itself deeper into the interior of the continent and thus to frustrate the ambitions of the others. At stake was not just wealth – indeed, many of the new territories were considered economic encumbrances – but also prestige. Success in seizing distant territory was how states measured their status. Although Britain and the UPU operate on different scales – one operates in Africa as a whole, the other within Nigeria – they have in common the sense that the field on which they are operating is a moral vacuum where all that matters is success. British ambitions in Africa, like later American or Russian ambitions, could also be judged, in Olaniyan's words, as "hilariously shameless" and a "crass moral cop-out."

I do not mean that the UPU models its behaviour on the example of the colonial powers, but that the conquest territories, in which each colonial power asserted a monopoly on violence, were converted into tradelands not only by the colonial powers but also by some of their subjects, and such tradelands are best understood in terms not of morality and immorality but of inside and outside. When the British united Nigeria, traders from Igboland established themselves in the capital and in every town in the West and North.

Although their respective homelands exist on different scales and each saw their primary competitors on the same scale as themselves – Britain competed with France; Umuofia with Mbaino and later with other town unions – the conquest lands of the British and the tradeland of the Igbos are both, by definition, fields outside the homelands and populated by strangers, where young men and women can venture in pursuit of commercial advantage and, in the process, earn prestige for the homeland. As a trade diaspora, the UPU has much in common with Syrians and Lebanese in West Africa and with Asian traders (from the Indian subcontinent) who spread along the roads and railway lines in East Africa. Unlike these others, however, Umuofia's homeland falls within the same state borders as its tradeland, which explains in part why a son of Umuofia like Obi can transfer his identification to Nigeria more readily that most Asians in Kenya or Uganda could to those states. Within a few years, Igbos would be violently expelled from northern Nigeria, just as Asians later were from Uganda, and an identification with Nigeria would become more difficult for Achebe.

MODERN DEBT AND THE STATE

Even as Obi rejects his debt to the UPU, other financial responsibilities with a moral charge keep him awake: he takes on the duties of providing his younger brother's school fees (54), a monthly allowance to his parents (55), and his mother's treatment in a private hospital (89). Simmel writes that "a change in obligations is often experienced as freedom,"[41] but the converse is also true: freedom is often but a change in obligations. Hénaff explains that, even as the would-be modern individual denies the demands placed on him by the larger community, "'Family' takes over as 'kinship' fades away."[42] Obi's desire for immunity is not a desire to escape morality but a *different* morality, one that combines two mutually reinforcing values: the preservation of the self from compromising ties to others (except for immediate family), and fidelity to a larger, necessarily abstract vision of society identified with the state and its rule of law.

Obi, who, as we have seen, seeks to escape his debts to the town union by paying them off once and for all, finds himself immersed in a different kind of debt. Sarthou-Lajus points out that "the liberatory effects of capitalism represent less a cancellation pure and simple of debt than its displacement from the sphere of interpersonal relations to a more opaque financial realm."[43] Maurizio Lazzarato traces a modern "transition from 'finite debt' to 'infinite debt'" that produces "the indebted man, who will never finish paying his debts."[44] Debt is, if anything, more prevalent in Obi's Lagos than ever in precolonial Umuofia because in the modern city no one can get by without help: Obi has, ironically, more obligations than did his grandfather Okonkwo, that self-made man and self-sufficient farmer. As independence approached, the new Nigerian employees in the senior service were hired at the same salaries as the Europeans they replaced and given comfortable subsidized accommodation in the Government Reserved Areas formerly restricted to Europeans,[45] yet Obi finds he must pay for consumer goods that will satisfy both his own and his townsmen's expectations of a modern, educated man. He needs a car, which he buys with an advance that he must repay. A car requires a licence (£4 per quarter [91]), a driver (£4 pounds 10 shillings per month [62]), and regular maintenance. As a young professional Obi needs a steward and a garden boy (his share of the latter cost is 10 and sixpence a month [81]). Electricity costs another £5.7.3 every month (90). Then there is insurance: the bill comes to £42 (87). Just the named amounts, not including the initial cost of the car let alone his repayment of the debt to the town union, almost equal Obi's salary of £50 a month.[46] These expenses come as debts because the charges arrive at the end of the month, after the service has been received. The novel can be read most simply as the story of one who, unable to get by on his salary, is forced to resort to other means, but that reading underestimates Obi's dilemma.

One difference between Obi and his great-grandfather who recorded his debts in chalk on the wall is that, ironically, Unoka kept better written accounts. Obi's new debts are more impersonal than Unoka's were;

they are often for difficult-to-quantify items like education, electricity, and insurance; the bills arrive as letters in the mail; and they are payable to corporations rather than to individuals. At the same time, Obi's debts are very precise, measured to the pence. Unoka's debts were all multiples of two hundred cowries, two hundred being a "tropic number" that marks a kind of natural threshold around which sums of yams or cowries tend to gravitate because they are easily visualized.[47] The eight hundred pounds lent to Obi by the UPU illustrate the same principle, but Obi's modern debts, despite their eerie precision, cannot be visualized.

The last bill Obi receives in the course of the novel is a £32 charge from the Commissioner of Income Tax (144). The state (still a colonial state) imposes debts as onerous as the obligations to kin and more subject to rigorous accounting. The argument for taxes in modern states is that they pay for infrastructure, both human, like health services and education, and non-human, like roads, sewers, and electricity, that benefit all citizens. They also provide security in the form of the military and police, and the administration of justice in the form of courts and prisons. And they pay for the government and bureaucratic administration. In Aluko's *One Man, One Matchet*, the first black District Officer explains to the people of his district in 1949: "It is a sign of lack of civic sense for anyone to evade tax. People who want progress and amenities must pay for them. You cannot ask for progress and independence with one voice and at the same time refuse to accept the responsibilities."[48] He feels, as Michael Rubenstein does, that "the payment of taxes reveals itself not as *settling* a debt but as *instituting* one."[49]

The members of the UPU already observe the logic of taxes when they tax themselves in order to create a fund to further the interests of the whole. That tax is probably not enforceable except by honour, yet it is likely also seldom evaded. That tax is also progressive: those who earn more pay more. In meetings of the entire union, members decide directly where the money will go. It is from this fund that Obi's student loan came.

State taxes serve more purposes than providing goods and services: they also punish behaviour the government disapproves of and reward behaviour that it wants to encourage. In Africa, colonial states used taxes to force self-sufficient farmers into the cash economy and the labour market. However, in the colony, unlike in the town union, taxation is without representation and thus resembles a tribute exacted from subject peoples. Taxes were the means whereby the colonizers made the colony pay for its own occupation. Alain Caillé distinguishes taxes from gifts: "Instead of a gift between people which presumes a double initiative, the initiative of one person constrains all others in exchange for a global future service, farther away and less self-evident."[50]

The British first instituted direct personal taxation in Igboland in 1927, to be collected by the newly created warrant chiefs, and it was so resented that it sparked the Women's War against both taxes and chiefs in 1929.[51] Munonye's novel *Obi* recalls how the British originally instituted a head tax: "Many years back, an order had come from the District Commissioner, now called simple District Officer, through his barefoot court messengers, that every adult male should pay a hundred and eighty heads of cowrie, which was sixpence, each year."[52] When the chief objects to the head tax, the officials explain that "the monies so realized would be used in developing Umudioba and other towns around. Roads would be built, so also schools and hospitals. The money would not actually go into the white man's pocket but would be locked up in the Commissioner's safe at Ossa, and used as the need would arise, and accounted for in the end."[53] The grandiose promises made by the District Officer fail, however, to move the chief, who continues to raise objections. At that point "the officials reverted to type" and threatened the chief unless he complied.[54]

Jane Guyer notes that taxation in the colony was "viewed entirely as an imposition and its level bore no relationship to services to the population."[55] *No Longer at Ease* repeatedly draws attention to the poor condition of the roads, drainage system, electric grid, hospitals, and schools in the colony. The debt of taxes to the state feels abstract to those asked to pay; those taxes are not attached to any particular goods, and they establish no personal relationships. The sums appear arbitrary, and while in principle, such debts must be paid by everyone, one can never be sure that others are paying their fair share. Indeed, given the as yet rudimentary administration in the colony, it is probable that only employees of the state actually pay income tax. Obi's own salary comes from taxes he pays, a circularity quite unlike that of gifts because what leaves his pocket returns to him without passing through the hands of other named individuals. In the end Obi appears before a court and is sent to a prison that his taxes have helped pay for.

Obi is overwhelmed by the all too personalized mutual obligation represented by his debts to the town union and the impersonal debts imposed by his participation in modernity in the form of the state, utilities, banks, and the credit system. To escape, he turns to new personal relations forged in the city with like-minded people of his own age. Upset to see Obi mired in debt, Clara, his lover, makes him a gift of fifty pounds with which to clear an overdraft at the bank. She wants literally to redeem him, that is, to free him from the endless proliferation of debt, which she calls "digging a new pit to fill up an old one" (98), and calls him to a higher value: their transcendent love. Bruce Robbins shows that the disinterested intervention by female benefactors is key to the conception of the welfare state in Europe, where it functions as "a model of the ideal and necessary alienation and rediscovery of the self in the general will."[56] Yet Obi feels that Clara's redemptive gift of fifty pounds has imposed a new debt, like "digging two pits to fill up one" (99). The debt is further compounded when the money is stolen. The theft means that, instead of freeing Obi from debt, Clara's gift sinks him further, for his sense of guilt demands that he repay that which he never had the use of. Gone is the mutuality of loans, and like a demonic parody of the infinite debt to the state, all that is left is the obligation to repay.

Obi is also honour-bound to pay the thirty pounds for Clara's abortion, his first venture into breaking the law, and he borrows the money from their mutual friend Sam Okoli, the Minister of State. Although the novel does not emphasize this, readers may well wonder how the request of a loan of thirty pounds from a government minister of one's own ethnicity differs from the loan request for thirty shillings made to Obi by the messenger Charles Ibe. The messenger explains to Obi that he should be flattered to be asked for money: "There are many people in this department, but I did not go to them. I came to you"; "I take you as my special master" (88). The debt to a fellow Igbo, rather than to a kinsman or someone from the same village, will be the future of prebendal politics.

CIVIL SERVICE

Giorgio Agamben distinguishes between two kinds of power, the Kingdom and the Government, whose origins he traces to Christianity's distinction between the transcendent sphere in which God creates the world and the immanent sphere in which humans are free to act. In the secularized version inherited by modern European states (and their African colonies), the realm of God's providence, which laid down impartial and just rules by sovereign decision, corresponds to the foundation of the law. But once established, the law must be enforced. The immanent power that administers laws Agamben calls Government. It corresponds to the civil service, which is concerned with the "economic-managerial," the implementation of the rules made by others, rather than with the "politico-statal," that is, the power to make laws.[57] The Government, the bureaucratic civil service, mediates between the Kingdom and the governed. This is Obi's place in *No Longer at Ease.*

Realist novels in Europe and America have been uncomfortable with both the Kingdom and the Government but for different reasons. Unless they are set in the past or in foreign lands, realist novels seldom feature kings, prime ministers, or presidents as characters. Instead they train their focus on the ordinary citizen-subject, a level far below the rulers, who are represented solely by the state's agents, especially policemen and court officials. It is as though something in the mechanism of the novel as a genre blocks the elevation of the narrative focus above a certain political level. African novelists inherited the narrative focus on the middle level of society. This would change after 1966, the year of the coups, but at the time of independence African novels still averted their eyes from the Kingdom, the realm of state rulers.

Novelists around the world have considered bureaucracy a subject worthy of satire, focusing on delay, error, corruption, indifference, unresponsiveness, and self-importance. From Dickens's Circumlocution Office to Kafka's Castle and Kurosawa's *Ikiru*, novels and films routinely express contempt for the mediation of Government. Michael Herzfeld argues that jokes about inefficiency and illogic are inseparable from the understanding of bureaucracy in Western countries.[58] Not surprisingly, given the high level of mediation between the Kingdom and the governed in the colony – the distance from the imperial capital, the sheer foreignness of the laws, the confusing buffers between rulers and subjects created by Indirect Rule, and the cross-purposes of the interests of rulers and ruled – bureaucracy is a frequent target of satire in African novels as well: witness Sembène Ousmane's *Le mandat* or Ferdinand Oyono's *Le vieux nègre et la médaille*. The office-bound protagonist of Ayi Kwei Armah's *The Beautyful Ones Are Not Yet Born* discovers that a fellow clerk does almost no work but fills the day with an empty routine:

> the clerk had a meticulous system for stretching out his work, and he had done it so often and gotten so used to it that he had probably forgotten that most of it was merely a way to waste time. Alphabetical listings that would never serve any purpose; a search to try and find on the postmark the exact minute every letter was supposed to have been mailed; three transfers of all the lists to cleaner paper, each time in more careful, more beautiful lettering, with not a single smudge; periodic visits to the lavatory, from habit, from necessity.[59]

Precisely because Africans were subjects rather than citizens, however, the civil service did not just feel like the intermediary keeping subjects from the Kingdom, as it does in Dickens or Kafka; rather, it could feel like the Kingdom itself. No self-respecting social climbers in Balzac, Stendhal, or Dreiser would consider a job in the civil service such as the one Obi wins a desirable form of upward mobility. As Chabal writes of the colony in Africa, "the establishment of a bureaucracy, at once the symbol and the structure of the colonial state, largely defined the relationship between the individual and the state. To the individual, the bureaucracy in effect *was* the state. To be a colonial subject meant to enter into a relationship with the colonial bureaucracy."[60] In *Arrow of God*, Ezeulu is summoned before an Assistant District Officer, whom he finds busy writing: "The first thought that came to Ezeulu on seeing him was to wonder whether any black man could ever achieve the same mastery over book as to write it with the left hand" (173). The priest judges that the white officer has little sense: "But he had power; he could shout in my face; he could do what he liked. Why? Because he could write with his left hand" (189). Ezeulu does not understand Tony Clarke's capacity to record, store, and organize information about him but does appreciate that information's power. Ezeulu's misunderstanding is comic; readers know better. Yet the honest protagonist in Armah's *Beautyful Ones* sincerely appreciates the aesthetics of order and efficiency upheld by some levels of bureaucracy: "There really was a definite kind of beauty to the growth of the daily maze on the graph sheet, and a satisfaction in seeing the penciled lines crossing the time and station lines, red lines for passenger trains, lead pencil lines for goods trains, blue for manganese."[61]

Weber observes that

> bureaucratization offers above all the optimum possibility for carrying through the principle of specializing administrative functions according to purely objective considerations. Individual performances are allocated to functionaries who have specialized training and who by constant practice increase their expertise. "Objective" discharge of business primarily means a discharge of business according to *calculable* rules and 'without regard for persons.'[62]

The ideal of competent management is embodied in Udo Akpan, the hero of Aluko's *One Man, One Matchet*, the first black District Officer in the Ijapa region of Yorubaland. Akpan is devoted to the welfare of those he rules, which means he is concerned with collecting enough taxes to pay for infrastructure, educating people in the proper conservation of agricultural resources, and keeping the peace. In late colonial and early postcolonial Africa, the state was accepted by at least some writers as embodying universal values in which Africa was wanting.[63] The colonizers' administration, its laws and bureaucracy, could sometimes feel to the first educated generations of Africans like an "intangible revelation" of the ultimate order of things and appeared to promise access to the Kingdom.[64] As Étienne LeRoy explains, the state could appear as a transcendental principle in Africa because it came suddenly and in one piece instead of emerging there: "African politicians and lawyers became acquainted with the colonial institutional model very late on. Their knowledge, too, was superficial. Few had been in a position to assimilate that ideological aspect of their relationship with government which allows Europeans to eulogise about it while adopting practices which are partly or totally at odds with it."[65]

In Ekwensi's 1963 novel *Beautiful Feathers*, the new Nigerian Minister of Consolation explains without irony what his ministry does: it "looks after all the people ... women, men, children, who have no home, no father, no mother, no husband": "the Ministry was founded as a sympathetic gesture, a kind of Universal Aunt. It was felt that Nigerians – men, women, children – must have somewhere to run to in times of need."[66]

In his late memoir, Achebe offers this "piece of heresy":

> The British governed their colony of Nigeria with considerable care. There was a very highly competent cadre of government officials imbued with a high level of knowledge of how to run a country. This was not something that the British achieved only in Nigeria; they were able to manage this on a bigger scale in India and Australia. The British had the experience of governing and doing it competently. I am not justifying colonialism. But it is important to face the fact that British colonies, more or less, were expertly run.[67]

It is very doubtful that the colonizers could be said objectively to have provided better management than their postcolonial successors: they made no effort to extend education and health facilities very broadly, and the state had much less direct contact with subjects than the postcolonial state would have with citizens. But the colonizers were very successful at conveying the ideal of efficiency and incorruptibility. When Achebe says "there was a distinct order during this time,"[68] he is not so much nostalgic for colonialism – that is, rule by and for foreigners – as he is pointing to what is lacking in postcolonial Nigeria: "competent management," whose directives are effectively and impartially carried out, and security for citizens, made possible by an effective monopoly of violence by the state *and* subordination of citizens to the discipline of law. Weber's own account of bureaucracy is essentially heuristic and "cannot be found anywhere in reality."[69] When the ideal is invoked to denounce modern "corruption," it "implies a vision of a non-corrupt alternative, not degenerated, properly bureaucratic, fully modernized. It is a legitimating fiction, all the more powerful because it operates through its own denial."[70]

EMPIRE AND CIVIL SERVICE

The British in Nigeria may not actually have been better managers, but they were more successful presenting themselves as embodiments of the ideal of the state. In colonial Africa, the civil service could feel like the incarnation of the Kingdom not just to the colonized but to the colonizers themselves. William Green, Obi's racist boss at the Scholarship Board, conceives of his task not as the bourgeois *ordre du jour* that it would have been at home but as a form of potentially heroic self-sacrifice. Obi judges that Green, in an echo of Conrad's Marlow, "must have come originally with an ideal – to bring light to the heart of darkness, to tribal head-hunters performing weird ceremonies and unspeakable rites" (96). Not fog, dust, red tape, or mounds of paper – the usual associations of the civil service in Western literature – but light and civilization! The Weberian rationality of bureaucracy never looked as efficient or indeed as rational as when it set itself up against what it regarded as the forces of primitive magic in the colony. Kipling and Conrad both write of how "the work of empire" became "a substitute instrumental goal hypostatized to ultimate purpose."[71]

Mr. Green likes to imagine that his pushing of paper partakes of the heroism of those who had originally imposed the rule of law by violence. Katherine Baxter discusses a subgenre of imperial romance in the first half of the twentieth century that she calls District Commissioner fiction, in which the colonial administrator hero "represents the incorporation of the adventurer's spirit, the detective's acumen, and the soldier's loyalty into a figure of the law and the force of the law."[72] The Nigeria that Mr. Green came to was not, however, as dark as his desire for Promethean light-bearing required: "Africa played him false. Where was his beloved bush filled with human sacrifice?" (96). George Orwell found that by 1920, "the one-time empire-builders were reduced to the status of clerks, buried deeper and deeper under mounds of paper and red tape" (38). The tragedy of the Greens of the twentieth century, Obi decides, is that they were born too late. He judges that his boss would have been happiest fifty years earlier, at the dawn rather than the twilight of empire, that moment on the cusp when the law-bringers were not yet subject to their own law or even to morality. In 1958, Green is too late to be Lord Lugard, who established Nigeria, or George Basden, the missionary friend of Achebe's father, let alone Kurtz, who casts off the restraint of the law.

"With a flash of insight" derived from his reading of Conrad, Obi comes to understand that Mr. Green's motto could be thus: "By the simple exercise of our will we can exert a power for good practically unbounded." Those were the lines that Kurtz wrote "before the heart of darkness got him" (97). An older Achebe has famously denounced *Heart of Darkness* as a dangerous racist text, but we are not given reason to doubt Obi's assessment of Mr. Green and must presume that the author of *No Longer at Ease* appreciated Conrad's analysis of the imperialist in Africa. Conrad was suggesting that if the law were removed, the colonizer would sink into a lawless savagery – which stands as a comment on Mr. Green and his devotion to duty.

The allure of serving in the colonies was that it afforded, if not the opportunity to impose one's own will as the law, as in Edgar Wallace's Sanders novels, at least the chance to impose the law as one's own will. Bivona writes that "by demanding much personal sacrifice from would-be administrators, the theory of Indirect Rule evolved into a philosophy of government over the conquered masquerading as a philosophy of the self-government of the bureaucrat."[73] The colonial civil servant found compensation for his personal subordination to rules and protocols in lording it over native subordinates. By bending their wills to conform to the rules of the administration, colonial civil servants did not just serve "civilization"; they felt they represented "civilization."

Bivona writes that those who served the colonial administration discovered that "rule requires the successful management of the subject's own desires in the interest of the successful management of others."[74] Or, as Bourdieu says of bureaucracy, its "monopoly of the universal can only be obtained at the cost of a submission (if only in appearance) to the universal and of a universal recognition of the universalist representation of domination presented as legitimate and disinterested."[75] The Prerogative State had to bow to the Normative State. No longer, for instance, was it possible for a colonial officer to strike an African with impunity (58). Obi reasons that "in 1900 Mr. Green might have ranked among the great missionaries; in 1935 he would have made do with slapping headmasters in the presence of their pupils; but in 1957 he could only curse and swear" (96–7).[76]

Obi marvels at Green's devotion to the law without any corresponding faith in the state where that law holds sway: "Here was a man who did not believe in a country, and yet worked so hard for it. Did he simply believe in duty as a logical necessity?" (96). But the young Nigerian is just as prepared to devote himself to duty – indeed, has inherited Green's understanding of himself as the last link (but therefore also the foundation) on which the integrity of the law depends. Although the novel gives us little idea how he fills his days at his desk, Obi nonetheless has a sense of his overwhelming significance as the upholder of morality.

Nigeria, of course, is Obi's country as it is not Green's (but also not Umuofia's). The civil service was in many ways the repository of the very idea of Nigeria. Richard Joseph retells the story of how, at the time of the second coup in 1966, which ignited the pogroms of Igbos in the north and so the Nigerian Civil War,

> a group of Nigerian permanent secretaries and other civil servants made a pilgrimage to the army barracks at Ikeja in Lagos to argue the case that Nigeria should be kept together as one entity. In the rather telling words of [Allison A.] Ayida, when their driver was asked in Hausa by soldiers on guard to which tribe his passengers belonged, he answered, "They are civil servants." At that point, and throughout the years of crisis until January 1970, Nigeria's higher civil servants repeatedly demonstrated that they, more than any other corporate or social group in the country, could lay claim to being guardians of the splintered Nigerian nation.[77]

As the guardians of the nation, civil servants in the first years of independence also saw themselves as responsible for the state's moral health, which, as we shall see, was regarded as under threat from corruption.

9

Corruption

Criticism of *No Longer at Ease* consistently regards that novel as the story of a flawed young man who succumbs to corruption and takes bribes. By this reading, it is the moral lapse that needs explaining. The Africanist Colin Leys, however, expresses doubt as to how "typical" Obi is when he objects strenuously to bribes[1] and argues that corruption in Africa should be viewed in economic or cultural rather than moral terms. Corruption, in other words, should be in quotation marks: one man's corruption is another man's patrimonialism. I agree with Leys that we need to understand nepotism and bribery before we judge them, but that also means we should not judge Obi's moral stance against bribery as inherently false or inauthentic but as something that needs explaining as much as his fall into corruption.

Robert Tignor reports that, *pace* Leys, in Nigeria at the time it was only European colonial officers who excused corruption on the grounds that it represented "traditional gift-giving, a form of reciprocity between the powerful and the supplicants."[2] Pierce, too, reports that it was originally "a British political officer" who proposed "that corruption was the consequence of a clash between precolonial modes of political culture and new forms of the state that required a different mode of political comportment."[3] Igbos themselves, writes Tignor, blamed corruption among warrant chiefs not on a clash of cultural values but on the gulf between authority and people that had opened with colonialism.[4] As we have seen, in *Things Fall Apart* the court messengers, mediating between the British and the people of Umuofia, falsely declare that the fine imposed by the District Commissioner is 250 bags of cowries, not 200 – they intend, of course, to pocket the difference. In that novel, set in 1900, the victor in a land dispute that comes before the "white man's court" is the one who "had given much money to the white man's messengers and interpreter"

(176). Later, in *Arrow of God*, a warrant chief extorts payments from people by threatening to expropriate their houses to build a road. This is not a matter of those in power dispensing to clients in return for their loyalty, but rather the beginnings of a kleptocracy, where money flows upward, having been squeezed out of people by threats of violence.

Everyone everywhere recognizes and disapproves of something called corruption, even if they do not apply the name to the same things. Corruption usually has to do with something being for sale when it should not be. Umuofia would have considered it wrong had Obi won his student loan by bribing the president of the town union. It would have been illegitimate for the scholarship to go anywhere but where it is judged most likely to benefit Umuofia as a whole. Regarding Igbo town unions, Harneit-Sievers notes that "the accountability of town union executives can be assumed to be much greater than that of the executives of any organizations of comparable size that are not community-based – especially those created by the state as political-administrative units."[5] In Munonye's *Bridge to a Wedding*, it is a great scandal that one side in a land dispute has given money to the town union executive that is adjudicating the matter.[6]

What is morally unacceptable *within* Umuofia – offering money for personal consideration – may, however, be necessary and inevitable when it comes to relations with potentially hostile strangers in the new state. James Scott writes that "in approaching a civil servant, the peasant is not generally an informed citizen seeking a service to which he is entitled, but a subject seeking to appease a powerful man whose ways he cannot fathom."[7] What is commonly called corruption "is, in effect, a means of 'overcoming' the handicap of anonymity or compensating for it."[8] Bribery represents an effort to bind the stranger in a relationship of mutual self-interest. As Noonan explains, "relations with peaceful strangers are established by an exchange whose essential function is to oblige the offeree. The recipient is bound by receiving. If he does not accept what is offered he is hostile. If he does not respond after accepting he is hostile."[9]

A man who offers Obi a bribe asks him to accept this "small kola" (152), using the same language of gifts that Isaac Okonkwo used when he threw a great feast on the occasion of Obi's departure for England (8). The reference is to the ritual of breaking and sharing a kolanut with a guest:

> the "dash" (or bribe) draws its meaning from traditional social practices, according to which the transfer of material objects, and in

> particular food and drink, serves in sealing agreements and in marking relations and social events. In the bureaucratic universe, it fulfills two simultaneous functions: first, it acts as an institutional mechanism for establishing a personal link between the client and the bureaucrat if they are unknown to each other; and, second, giving the "dash" is an act of deference constituting the symbolic affirmation of the unequal status of the two partners.[10]

Alain Caillé notes that "the first question asked of humans, the political question that is but the other side of the issue of the gift, is knowing who are friends and who are enemies. In other words, in terms more Maussian than Schmittian, with whom does one make an alliance (and against whom)? To whom must one give and from whom can one receive?"[11] Those offering bribes, like those lending money, are making a wager on the character of another and whether he can be trusted. The man who repays that trust is a man of honour. In *No Longer at Ease*, "people would say that Mr So-and-so was a gentleman," because he "would take money, but he would do his stuff, which was a big advertisement" (153).

Vertical relations with strangers in power involve risk, which can be mitigated by establishing a relationship. The difference between the gift and the bribe, however, is that the latter is offered in secret. Briber and bribe recipient shun public recognition. That is why the preferred bribe is cash, which, as Simmel says, "more than any other form of value, makes possible the secrecy, invisibility and silence of exchange."[12] The impersonality of money makes bribes a form of commodity exchange rather than a gift. Unlike a gift, money bears no trace of the giver: "A bribe is not an expression of love. The briber seeks to move the bribee to serve the briber's interest. The more impersonal the medium, as Simmel observed, the better; if sex is used, it is as a commodity."[13]

The UPU observes a moral distinction between corruption and what Pierre-Joseph Laurent calls diversion (*détournement*).[14] The diversion of state resources is considered moral when it serves the interests of the town union and when it concerns "cold money," that is, money belonging to an impersonal entity like the state or international aid.[15] As in trickster tales, schemes hatched to gain from powerful others are admired as cunning; what comes in for censure is the greedy act of eating alone, the individual monopolization of collective or community resources. "Corruption" refers either to using collective goods for personal self-enrichment[16] or to an attack on property belonging to an individual – that is, to "hot money."[17]

EMPIRE AND CORRUPTION

As we have seen, Mr. Green needs to imagine that the rule of law introduced by the British is so precarious that it will collapse when Nigeria gains its independence, but that until then he is acting as its bulwark. In the face of the looming transition he behaves "like a man who had some great and supreme task that must be completed before a final catastrophe intervened" (96). His self-imposed burden as representative of civilization is itself a kind of sabotage: he wants Africans to fail in order to confirm how much he was needed. He imagines the threat that decolonization poses to white privilege in terms of moral degeneracy associated with the tropics. This understanding of corruption "in moralistic terms as a loss of virtue in the polity, a generalised condition afflicting political elites and citizens indiscriminately and contagiously," goes back to classical antiquity.[18] In the field of empire, the threat that corruption was thought to pose to moral health was combined with fears of imperial decline and pernicious ideas of racial hierarchy and of Africans' particular susceptibility to moral contamination.

In the eighteenth century in Britain, Adam Smith had argued that corruption was not a matter of the moral health of the body politic but rather "a problem largely created by archaic social forms and an over-intrusive, clique-ridden state."[19] Smith felt that "corruption did not arise from political apathy, hedonism, selfishness or an inattention to the public sphere as per classical accounts. Rather, it was a product of maladaptive political and economic arrangements: sluggish, paternalistic, particularistic, dependency-generating forms of governance and control."[20]

Pierce writes that in Northern Nigeria, "instances of bribe-seeking, extortion, and embezzlement on the part of government" were often regarded not as "corruption," meaning deviations from how things were supposed to work, but rather as "oppression," "acts that were wrong but that were nonetheless a common quality of people in government."[21] The term "oppression" better conveys that the problem is built into how the system functions, and any solution must therefore also be systemic. Corrupt behaviour is regarded as "antithetical to the functioning of government," whereas oppression "emerges directly from it."[22] Power derived entirely from above feels no responsibility to those below. Chabal explains that under Indirect Rule, "the patrimonial quality of chieftaincy no longer rested on the legitimacy conferred upon it by the ties of reciprocity that bound leaders and *followers*. It came increasingly to depend on the chiefs' capacity to distribute resources to *clients*."[23] And, argues Tignor, chiefs were primarily responsible for distributing hateful obligations, such as enforced labour duties, rather than largesse.[24] The sense of illegitimacy was exacerbated by the fact that the system was run on the cheap. The chiefs charged with the burden of colonial administration, including collecting taxes, recruiting labour, and dispensing justice, were chronically underpaid. To acquire the administrative and even coercive resources they needed to carry out their assigned duties, chiefs exacted "illegal" tributes from their subjects.[25]

Most of the corruption that Mr. Green identifies is generated by the colonial civil service's own inefficiency and inequities. Sluggish, paternalistic forms of governance actually suit Green. He is more comfortable than Obi with a hierarchy based on patronage and service: he loves "the Africa of Charles, the messenger, the Africa of his garden-boy and steward-boy," and he generously pays his steward's son's school fees (96). The man who believes that he is morally superior because he abides by British ideas of justice and impartiality is a member of a social club that, until recently, excluded Africans except as stewards (2). Green enjoys playing the beneficent master, while Obi wants only to escape the hierarchy of patrons and clients. It is the colonial civil service and not African corruption that represents an amalgam of traditional elements with modernity.

Obi recognizes that Mr. Green is a racist but shares his boss's sense of the vivid dangers that bribery poses to moral health. His duties as the secretary of the Scholarship Board include reviewing applicants for government scholarships to study overseas. He does not make the actual decisions; rather, he ministers to the board by making transparent and frictionless its access to information and the implementation of their decisions. He does not meet any of the candidates whose files he reviews and prefers to consider only their self-presentation on paper and in English. Those whom the board eventually selects to study abroad will not experience the intolerable irony that Obi himself has known – of owing everything, including his self-understanding as an autonomous citizen with a career and a wife he has chosen himself, to the sacrifices made by others (6). Future scholarship recipients will not be beholden to the equivalent of the UPU but will feel that their good fortune belongs to themselves alone, that they have received the beneficent attention of the impersonal forces associated with the state. By refusing to take bribes, Obi keeps himself and all those whom the board selects, the future leaders of the state, free of taint. He trusts that, because they have not had to bribe their way forward, the new generation of civil servants "can afford to be virtuous" and "that kind of virtue can become a habit" (18).

Obi refuses a bribe to advance an applicant's file even when he knows the file has already been approved for consideration by the board – when, in other words, the bribe would change nothing. As John Noonan writes, "the material harm done by ... bribery has often been slight, at times incalculable," but that is not what matters: "It is our desire to be rid of the pollution – not a demonstrated correlation between payment and action – that makes" bribery so unacceptable.[26] Bribes are wrong because they sully the soul. Obi's rejection of bribes is based on an almost physical revulsion that he associates with the decay of the flesh. Upon his return from England, he sees an emblem of Nigeria in the rotting carcass of a dog (15), a literalization of corruption. And when he encounters bribe-taking by the police, his comment is "What an Augean stable!" (40).[27] (The scatological will reach greater heights, literally, in Armah's *The Beautyful Ones Are Not Yet Born.*)

"Since the time of the Roman Republic," Noonan writes, "'to corrupt' has meant both to seduce a woman and to pay off an officeholder."[28] Both acts are immoral because they assign a price to a person. The ethics of both bribery and sexual sin "[lay] down the lines that separate a gift, understood as an identification of one person with another person, from the manipulative or exploitative use of one person by another person."[29] Obi by contrast, associates *turning down* a bribe with sexual triumph: the first time he refuses a bribe, he feels the same exhilaration as when he first had sex: "When the day arrived Obi was scared. He had heard that it was possible to disappoint a woman. But he did not disappoint her, and when it was over he felt strangely elated. She said she thought she had been attacked by a tiger" (80).

Of course, there is authorial irony at the expense of the young man who achieves satisfaction by proving his moral prowess to himself. Refusing bribes is after all less like having sex than like resisting temptation, and in Obi's case at least, it involves turning down sex. He who experiences a sexual thrill from his moral purity sounds like one of Nietzsche's despised Christians for whom "every 'no' which he is inclined to say to himself, to the nature, naturalness and reality of his being, he utters as 'yes,' as something existing, living, real, as God."[30] Derrida writes about the paradoxical relation of the upholder of the law to the law: "The inaccessible transcendence of the law before which and prior to which 'man' stands fast only appears infinitely transcendent and thus theological to the extent that, so near him, it depends only on him, on the performative act by which he institutes it."[31] When Obi turns down his first bribe, that momentous occasion creates the "man" whose "performative act," at once "violent and non-violent," fulfills a code of masculine honour and authorizes the law.[32] In his case, the "performance" that institutes the law he obeys is a negative act. Refusing bribes would not feel as satisfying if it did not set him apart so effectively.

Those who offer bribes to Obi are ordinary people, who appear deferential and tentative before him. The amounts offered are small. So are the favours asked for. Obi, however, feels that they are part of a much larger monster, which he wants to starve and thereby tame. Both Obi and Umuofia sense that a gulf has opened between authority and people, but they approach that gulf from opposite sides: Umuofia fears the inscrutability and arbitrariness of power wielded from above, Obi the contamination of gifts from below. The townsfolk of Umuofia are very conscious of the Prerogative State, distant and powerful, whereas Obi is determined to serve the Normative State.

The young man who regards his debt to the town union as a question of *mere* money, a burden from which he will be freed when it is repaid, also thinks of money as a taint infecting the older generation that he must keep clean of. Obi gives his heart freely to Clara and refuses to pay bride price out of a sense that money must not enter into marriage. Someone making a regular government salary can now expect to pay five hundred pounds for a bride (37), but Obi declares that he will not pay (38). As Simmel explains, a promise of marriage now "signifies not so much a value that we have but a value that we are. By surrendering all this for money, one exchanges one's being against one's possessing."[33] Hoping to be freed *by* money from communal obligations, the young man can even imagine himself free *from* money.

Everyone has a sense that some things, usually having to do with the sacred, should not be contaminated by money. In Munonye's *Bridge to a Wedding*, a masked spirit interrupts its performance at the Christmas festivities to turn on its human attendant, who is charged with collecting money from onlookers, and to denounce him as "a thief and a swindler."[34] Spirit and human differ "in their respective calculations of the total amount realized since the festivities began,"[35] but both are infected by greed. Modern masquerades display their wealth in the form of gaudy costumes and extort money from onlookers: "And when they receive the coin, they first examine it to make sure it's neither washed nor counterfeit, before they can croak their shallow thank-you."[36] In *Arrow of God*, Ezeulu and his family are critical of a diviner who takes a hen sacrificed to a god for his own use. According to Ezeulu, "there are more people with greedy, long throats in the pursuit of medicine than anywhere else" (121).

Armah's *The Beautyful Ones Are Not Yet Born* registers the corruption inherent in money even more strongly than does Obi. That novel opens with a bus conductor counting and smelling his day's take. There is a saying going at least as far back as the emperor Vespasian that "money has no odor," meaning that there is no such thing as clean or dirty, moral or immoral money.[37] The bus conductor's money is from fares, not from bribes, yet it stinks anyway. In Armah's postcolonial Ghana, money itself, because there are no legitimate ways of earning it, is an index of corruption. The corrupt deceive themselves that acquiring material goods will bring them closer to the "gleam" associated with modernity, whiteness, and Europe.

The one honest man in the postcolonial Ghana of Armah's novel feels "lonely in the way only a man condemned by all things around him can ever feel lonely."[38] A friend who shares his austere moral sense tells him that "loved ones are dead even when they walk around the earth like the living, and you know that all they want is that you throw away the thing in your mind that makes you think you are still alive, and their embrace will be a welcome unto death."[39] The "thing in your mind that makes you think you are still alive" is your soul, only kept alive by maintaining its immunity from corruption.

The satisfaction of maintaining one's purity requires, of course, that a bribe be offered. Obi's morality, like Green's, demands corruption in order to confirm its own virtue. Obi, however, has a romantic notion that love will grow where sex for favours is obliterated. He hopes that by rejecting the offer of sex from a young woman seeking a scholarship, he may have won her esteem. "Perhaps," he reasons, "she will remember that there was one man at least who did not take advantage of his position" (110). His friend Chris, a fellow Igbo of the same age, retorts that she probably thinks he is impotent.

In the eyes of his fellow townsfolk, Obi is to blame for not knowing how to take advantage of the opportunities for advancement afforded by his position in the civil service. His moral punctiliousness is also mocked by Chris,[40] educated at the London School of Economics, who represents an alternative modernity, one not based on Kantian morality but on utilitarian principles. Chris can imagine occasions when it is wrong to accept money bribes – "If you accept money from a man you make him poorer" – but he has no objection to accepting sexual favours: "But if you go to bed with a girl who asks for it, I don't see that you have done any harm" (111). Chris does not recognize honour as a real possession. He also does not believe that Obi's mother will kill herself – as she has declared she will – if her son marries an *osu*, and he advises Obi to deny that Clara's child is his (131).

Chris's pragmatic logic sees everything in terms of cost and benefit, of appearances rather than essences, and he doubts the sincerity of the moral standards that others invoke to justify themselves. He embodies liberal ideas of negative freedom premised on the principle that the pursuit of self-interest is the foundation of ethics. Chris regards Lagos and Nigeria much as the UPU does, as a morally neutral field where he must make his career; but unlike the town union, he does not locate the ultimate value in the village group but rather rejects the notion of absolute value.

Chris's hard-nosed approach to morality makes him an attractive libertine, and a novel based on him would more resemble a Balzac novel than the one we have. One can also imagine, however, another novel, one in which Obi was a stronger character and Chris, the educated man without moral scruples, would have played the role of a tempter and trickster. The young man on the make in Balzac or Stendhal can uncover the immoral foundations of bourgeois society and try to take advantage of them (though he is more likely to fail than to succeed), but the task accepted by Obi is the opposite: he wants to prove by his own example that the state about to become independent has moral foundations in the face of an absence of any consensus about the law and morality.

THE QUEUE

A metonym for the patience demanded of the citizen when dealing with the state is the queue. In the ideal rational state there is but one queue for all, not separate queues for white and black, rich and poor, citizen and subject. The queue renders everyone's dealings with the state readable: one can gauge how long the wait will be, and one's turn is a function of time of arrival, not of social status or personal relations. As each comes before the seat of judgment, her position is determined by the arbitrary but, if consistently applied, not unjust principle of first come, first served. The townsfolk of Umuofia, however, mistrust such arbitrariness when soliciting state services and want to establish a personal relationship with the one wielding power.

Of course, a queue is only tolerable because it is more impersonal than other ways of approaching authority. All too often, the wait is excruciatingly long or fault is found with one's papers. Those problems are frequently exacerbated in Africa because, as Scott points out, "demand for many government dispensations far outstrips their limited supply, and because the state makes no charge, or only a nominal one, the price for such services does not begin to reflect the supply-demand situation."[41] When there are not enough resources to satisfy everyone, there are major incentives to jump the queue. The dutiful person who obeys the rules (or, better said, who wants there to be rules so that he can obey them and be rewarded for his obedience) will feel like a chump mocked by the opportunism of others. The result, Scott argues, is either corruption – elites using their wealth to gain access – or violence – excluded masses insisting on access.

In Munonye's *Bridge to a Wedding*, a crowd gathers before the counter of a bank, where there is only one cashier; the others are "busy exchanging stories about ... parties and conquests, and predictably, about the politics of the nation."[42] More than twenty customers stand "pointing with their cheques at him and calling for attention," but the cashier affects not to notice "the humanity under his power." Instead, "he began a brief but pointed address on the need for good conduct, order and discipline on the part of bank customers, without which, in his own words, the black race would continue to have no future." The customers reply that "*he* had no future himself." From the back of the crowd the cashier then singles out Kafo, whom he calls Master of the Timber-Market and who regularly rewards him with beer or money. Kafo, an honest man, hesitates to jump the queue, but then holds out his cheque above others' heads. Where the people demanding services overwhelm the services offered, even the most dutiful will seek other ways of access. The rest of the customers "sighed and murmured, and even shouted out, in the interest of justice – so essential for the survival of their race! Such a thing, said they, would never happen in England, or America, much less China, not to talk of Russia, or even Ghana, or Guinea, or Israel."[43]

Well, maybe Ghana. In *The Beautyful Ones Are Not Yet Born*, another timber contractor is unable to secure the railway wagons he needs to transport his logs, which lie rotting in the forest. In appearance a cargo train resembles a queue – identical boxes all moving forward at the same rate – but the contractor sees wagons pass him filled with just stones or even empty. "Pleading with the words of millions and the voice of ages," he asks the man in the railway booking office, "what have I done to you? Why do you treat me this way?"[44] He does not believe that the treatment is the result of inefficiency or insufficient resources but is sure that someone in the office is hostile to him. And he is right: the allocations clerk *is* out to teach him "a lesson."[45] The timber contractor tries to offer a bribe to book the wagons he so desperately needs, but, unfortunately, he lights upon the one man in the office whose moral punctiliousness will not allow him to accept bribes or perform any service other than what he is supposed to – the novel's hero. How does an applicant attract the attention of an inhuman judge who is moved neither by favour nor by need? The novel reports with savage irony, "there was something miserable, something unspeakably dishonest about a man who refused to take and to give what everyone around was busy taking and giving: something unnatural, something very cruel."[46] It looks like the timber will have to rot in the forest.

THE GIFT OF GRACE

A *dibia* or priest in Obinkaram Echewa's novel *The Land's Lord* explains to a Catholic missionary that Igbo people "create [their] own gods to guide, rule and protect" them.[47] When the gods bless them, people respond with sacrifices: generosity repays generosity. The gods have a horizontal relationship with people, which the priest expresses in the proverbial idiom commonly used in Nigeria to justify bribes: "The right hand washes the left hand and the left hand washes the right hand, and both hands are happily washed."[48] As Noonan points out, "religion can be viewed as bribery on a grand scale, organized for the highest end, man's salvation, and practiced to persuade the Supreme Authority,"[49] but Ahamba prefers to think of human relations with the gods as gift exchange.

The Christian God, however, being on a different scale than humans, is not susceptible to offers of gifts or sacrifice. In Ndibe's novel *Foreign Gods Inc.*, the Anglican missionary Stanton is asked if his God owes money, for He likes to remain invisible and "around here, those who take to hiding are men who don't wish to pay their debts."[50] Stanton replies: "Tell them that our God can't owe anybody because he owns everything in heaven and on earth."[51] The Christians of Umuofia pray to a God so far above that hands cannot be washed by humans: "Oh God of Abraham, God of Isaac and God of Jacob ... the Beginning and the End. Without you we can do nothing. The great river is not big enough for you to wash your hands in. You have the yam and you have the knife; we cannot eat unless you cut us a piece" (*No Longer* 8). As Camille Tarot writes, the Christian "God who has need of nothing reaches out to humans who are in need of everything."[52]

The gulf opened between people and the divine – everything is owed to God, who owes nothing – is closed from God's end by the sacrifice of His Son, which requites what humankind owes and makes available God's grace. In *No Longer at Ease* the pastor regards the blood reprisals that once characterized Umuofia's relations with its neighbours, of which the exemplary case is the death of Ikemefuna, as "days of darkness" from which Igbos have been "delivered by the blood of the Lamb of God" (9). The sacrifice by God of his Son has put an end to the cycles of retribution and obligation and removed the need for future blood sacrifice. Tutuola registers this blanket clearance of debt and salvation from death as a blissful interlude, which the Palm-Wine Drinkard and his wife spend at the home of Faithful-Mother, where someone buys their death and another rents their fear, so that they are without both.[53] The one who "had bought" their death refuses to return it, "because he bought it from us and had paid for it already."[54]

The gift of God's grace, which cannot be earned or repaid, is closer to what Derrida or Levinas calls a "gift" than to the reciprocity analyzed by Mauss. A true gift, argues Derrida, is sublime and cannot be reciprocated. "For there to be a gift, there must be no reciprocity, return, exchange, countergift, or debt. If the other *gives* me *back* or *owes* me or has to give me back what I give him or her, there will not have been a gift."[55] In Maussian terms, however, it is the Derridean free gift that is not a true gift. Mary Douglas explains, "what is wrong with the so-called free gift is the donor's intention to be exempt from return gifts coming from the recipient. Refusing requital puts the act of giving outside any mutual ties ... A gift that does nothing to enhance solidarity is a contradiction."[56] Since "the primary purpose of this relationship is to institute *reciprocal recognition*,"[57] there can be no "pure" gift, that is, one independent of the web of reciprocal obligations encompassing a whole system of services.[58] Caillé writes: "If indeed a giver never envisaged the possibility of a return, then the gift, symbolizing a bottomless contempt for its supposed beneficiaries, would be truly a gift that kills, a poison gift."[59]

God's mercy, like a Derridean transcendent gift, erases people's debts but does so by rolling them into a single, infinite, unrepayable debt to Him. Nietzsche writes that "the appearance of the Christian God as the most powerful god ever conceived has for that very reason brought into the world the greatest feeling of indebtedness as well."[60] Noonan explains that "reciprocity is so regularly the norm of human relations that the conception of a transcendental figure, a Judge beyond the reach of ordinary reciprocities, was of enormous importance for the idea that certain reciprocities with earthly officials were intolerable."[61] "God's favor could not be bought" because "no human action could compel God's response ... Nothing man could do required God to reciprocate."[62] Tarot argues that universal monotheism developed in conjunction with the modern state, in which the usual distinctions observed by village groups between near and far, brothers and strangers, are forcibly derailed. So that the circulation of gifts may be extended to strangers, it is necessary to give more, in ways that are less and less visible and less and less attached to the expectation of remuneration.[63]

So unfathomably distant is God, writes Hobbes, that a personal covenant with the divine is impossible, for one can never be sure whether it has been accepted or not. One therefore needs the "Mediation of such as God speaketh to, or by his Lieutenants that govern under him, and in his Name."[64] In *Things Fall Apart*, the elder Akunna patiently explains to Mr. Brown the missionary why it is better to deal with intermediaries close to the human level, both in matters of religion and in matters of government: "Your queen sends her messenger, the District Commissioner. He finds that he cannot do the work alone and so he appoints kotma (court messengers) to help him. It is the same with God, or Chukwu. He appoints the smaller gods to help Him because His work is too great for one person" (132). The people of the Umuofia Progressive Union seek to reduce the distant impersonality of the state by forging personal relations with intermediaries.

Even after conversion to Christianity, the people of Umuofia remain suspicious of gifts from above that cannot be repaid and so escape control and intelligibility. As they try to explain to Obi, the gift that precludes return puts the recipient under an obligation that the latter will want to repay: "A man to whom you do a favour will not understand if you say nothing, make no noise, just walk away" (80). He "expects you to accept 'kola' from him for services rendered, and until you do, his mind is never at rest" (80). This is Hobbes's fourth law of nature: "That a man which receiveth Benefit from another of meer Grace, Endeavour that he which giveth it, have no reasonable cause to repent him of his good will."[65]

Obi, although he has absorbed a secular outlook from his literary education and betrays little interest in Christianity, nonetheless acknowledges a transcendent, unrepayable debt, in his case to the state. He recognizes that "there are many young men in this country today who would sacrifice themselves to get the opportunity" to study abroad that he himself has had (55), but the days of sacrifices to win the favour of the gods are over. There is no sacrifice one can make to put the Christian God or the modern state in one's debt. Successful scholarship candidates will be debt-free because their debt is actually infinite and therefore unrepayable. The ideal state Obi serves is, like God, outside the exchange of gifts. One can only acknowledge God's grace by serving His law. The only sign one can have of the sovereign's grace is that one feels a fidelity to the law written in one's heart. By the impartial way in which Obi carries out his duties on the Scholarship Board, he retrospectively proves his worthiness for his studies abroad.

Obi's modern sense that a transcendent sacrifice has made sacrifice by humans irrelevant also allows him to imagine marrying an *osu*, a member of a caste whose ancestors were ritual slaves dedicated to the service of a god. When his father, Isaac, disapproves of the marriage, Obi appeals to the rationalist in his father: "Our fathers in their darkness and ignorance called an innocent man *osu,* a thing given to idols, and thereafter he became an outcast, and his children, and his children's children for ever. But have we not seen the light of the Gospel?" (133). The light of the Gospel, here associated with literacy and Enlightenment, renders sacrifice mere superstition.

Obi is, however, unable to convince his father. Olakunle George has noted the paradox that Isaac's "deep Christian faith ... provides conceptual anchor for his perpetuation of a traditional pagan norm,"[66] but he does not specify why Isaac should perpetuate *this* norm, the ostracism of the *osu*, in particular. The answer has everything to do with his personal understanding of sacrifice. For Isaac the conflict between the first Christians and their pagan neighbours and family members was not between those who sacrificed to idols and those who adopted a rational attitude toward a disenchanted world; rather, it was between rival faiths, each prepared to sacrifice, but to different gods. The Christians call their pagan neighbours the "people of nothing" (58), meaning that their sacrifices are ineffective and their gods false. The falseness of those gods, however, is only in comparison to the true God. It is not the realm of the sacred, created by sacrifice, that is false. As a catechist, Isaac would not let his children eat at other people's houses if the food had been sacrificed to idols (Achebe's own father observed similar rules). Food sacrificed to idols is not *mere* food, for Isaac understands that sacrifice changes the nature of things. He says, in effect, that this food has been transformed and that to eat it is to partake in this new meaning. For the same reason, Isaac will not allow his son to marry an *osu*: the dedication of someone to the service of a god changes him and his descendants once and for all and cannot be undone. Isaac's church makes a point of accepting the *osu* to its communion, but the sacred nature of the slave's being (in the sense of a human that has been sacrificed) remains.

Obi argues that Christ's sacrifice has drawn a line across the past and rendered sacrifice obsolete. Isaac knows better. Christianity itself is about sacrifice, and sacrifice is about the ultimate existential stakes. Isaac tries to explain to his son "what it was in those days to become a Christian": "I left my father's house, and he placed a curse on me. I went through fire to become a Christian. Because I suffered I understand Christianity – more than you will ever do" (138). Munonye reports that the first generation of Christian converts "had made great sacrifices in joining the church. Some ... had dismissed their wives; some had burnt the family idols and household gods in public; some had willingly given up their land to the church. Naturally, they expected to be obeyed in everything."[67] Sacrifice, the willingness to give up something for the sake of something greater, is at the root of Christian authority. The lesson Isaac takes is not that the law has put an end to sacrifice, but that he who was the most prepared for sacrifice is now able to establish the law. Isaac feels that Obi has never given up anything and so does not understand sacrifice. And Isaac is right: Obi will lose Clara precisely because he thinks the law should be enough and has never appreciated the need for sacrifice. He will fail to take the kind of existential risk required by both sacrifice and love.

The three generations – Okonkwo, Nwoye/Isaac, and Obi – appear to illustrate the trajectory from tradition to Christianity to secularism, but each son is closer to his father than he is prepared to admit. Isaac, that bulwark of Christianity, objects to marriage to an *osu*, a caste whose abolition had been a pillar of Christian proselytizing. And Obi, that modern educated young man who thinks he can reason his father into accepting his marriage, serves the state and its law with the fidelity that a Christian owes to God.

THE ULTIMATE SACRIFICE

Obi is conscious of receiving a gift that cannot ever be repaid. Where did he get this sense of the overwhelming free gift? From his Christian upbringing to be sure, but why should Obi feel this sense of infinite indebtedness that others, more devout or at least more explicitly Christian, do not? As a child of ten, Obi experienced a transcendent gift, a parent prepared to bleed for his sake. He had a rusty razor blade that he used to sharpen pencils or cut up grasshoppers, and he left it in his shirt pocket one day, where it cut his mother's hand when she washed it. "She returned with the clothes unwashed and her hand dripping with blood" (68). Whenever Obi thinks of her, his mind goes "back to that shedding of her blood" (69). The blood Hannah Okonkwo shed is outside the circle of gifts and countergifts and does not demand reprisals. It is not possible to repay the debt any more than it is to bribe the transcendent judge. The only possible response to the mother's gift of herself is for the son to make himself worthy of that gift. Obi must not disappoint his mother and thereby wound her again.

It is the unrepayable gift of the mother's love that inspires the adult Obi's insistence on moral purity. The sight of her bleeding hand inspires Obi to keep his own hands clean. We know this because, after his mother dies, Obi, in his melancholy, starts to take bribes. He had felt that his mother, when alive, called him to transcend the circulation of debts among men, to occupy an Archimedean site beyond the earth from which to move the earth, but that space vanishes with her death, when Obi comes to feel that "beyond death there are no ideals and no humbug, only reality. The impatient idealist says: 'Give me a place to stand and I shall move the earth.' But such a place does not exist. We all have to stand on the earth itself and go with her at her pace" (151).

Why should Obi have conflated his unrepayable debt to his mother with a transcendent duty owed to the law? A mother's love is something that people felt long before there was a modern state, and in African literature, mothers, even when Christian, are commonly associated with the village and with tradition, while the idea of a primordial debt owed to the law is arguably a modern idea with its origins in the French Revolution and nineteenth-century European nationalism.[68] The thing to remember about the modern state, however, is that it is at once primitive and modern (using those terms as a modern might): like Christianity, the state demands sacrifice even as it makes sacrifice no longer something reciprocal but transcendent. Paul Kahn explains: "The historical narrative of sacrifice for the creation and maintenance of the modern nation-state invokes the same imaginative structure as the fictional tale of enduring love."[69] People are willing to sacrifice themselves for the sake of members of their family, and the state asks no less. "The sacrificial demand," writes Kahn, "is always the same: the parent must die for the child, Christ must die for man, and the citizen must die for the state."[70]

CAN THE SUBORNED SPEAK?

Any explanation of why Obi refuses to take bribes must also explain why, in the end, he takes them. When Obi internalizes his mother's example as the model of the unconditional sacrifice of the self that is required of the citizen, the unrequitable debt he owes strengthens his moral self. But, to Obi's horror, his beloved mother, on her sickbed, objects to his pure love for Clara, telling her son that if he marries an *osu*, "you will have my blood on your head, because I shall kill myself" (123). He already has her blood on his head (and in his head), but now the meaning of her shed blood has changed. Instead being a pure gift that lifts him out of the cycles of mutual obligation, it becomes a threat of reprisal. In effect, she is calling in the unrequitable debt and calling on Obi to sacrifice his love for Clara.

Obi, who has no trouble resisting his father and the men of the town union, is rendered helpless by his mother. He heeds her threat and does not marry Clara, but he also loses his sense of being the beneficiary of an absolute and unrequitable love. His mother threatens to die if he marries an *osu*; Clara will leave him if he does not resist the claims of custom. Obi fails to make a decision, and the result is that his mother dies anyway, Clara leaves him, and their child is aborted.

After his mother dies, Obi recovers, but "the picture of his poor mother returning from the stream, her washing undone and her palm bleeding where his rusty blade had cut into it, vanished. Or rather it took a secondary place. He now remembered her as the woman who got things done." Obi now feels he has misunderstood his mother's love all along. When Christians were still a minority, tolerated but not sponsored by the colonial administration, they and their God risked being caught up in the cycles of reciprocal violence to which God's grace and British law had supposedly put an end. At the start of his career as a catechist, Isaac worked in a town called Aninta, where he had to compete with the great god Udo, whose priest kept a sacred he-goat. The goat, allowed to roam free, was a menace at the mission, where it destroyed crops, and Isaac's complaints to the priest brought no relief. Once, when the goat entered Hannah Okonkwo's kitchen and ate the yam she was preparing, she took a matchet and hewed off its head. This is "the woman who got things done."

In another context, say, Sembène's *Les bouts de bois de Dieu*, such an act would have been a revolutionary event, signalling the overthrow of the old order and an end to all the old unjust debts. There the market woman Ramatoulaye slaughters a wealthy man's goat in order to feed hungry strikers.[71] Hannah Okonkwo's deed, however, threatens only to bring reprisals: the village elders utter threats, and the women in the market refuse to buy from her. Those reprisals, in turn, might have escalated and never have ended because there is no mechanism for equilibrium between Christianity and traditional religion as there was among village groups, whose gods were all of the same order. Finally, however, the colonial state intervened to end the potential for violence: "so successful had been the emasculation of the clan by the white man's religion and government that the matter soon died down" (151). When Obi's mother slew the great goat, she was not performing a heroic sacrificial killing that put an end to the endless cycles of retribution; she was merely giving another turn to those cycles. Christianity does not end the rivalries that threaten to break out in violence; it merely introduces new rivals.

When Obi takes his first bribe he does not succumb to temptation – he feels financial exigency but no desire – and neither does he make a choice between two rival codes. He simply transgresses against his own code. Obi never assumes the dignity Simmel locates in one who takes bribes, the "certain grandeur, a strictness and superiority of behaviour which seems to reduce the giver to the role of the receiver. Such external behaviour is supposed to present the person as someone who is unassailable and aware of his own value."[72] Obi cannot be said to *choose* bribes; he merely allows them to be left with him.

Obi fails the existential test created by his love across caste barriers and abandons the absolute position above the earth promised by both the rule of law and Christianity. Sacrifice is inevitable, but sacrifice that is not made when it is asked for is ineffectual. Obi is pitched into intolerable melancholy: it is now too late to repay his mother's love, just as it is too late to return to Clara. If, as I suggested, Obi's refusal to take bribes from those who want to study overseas had been a way of retrospectively proving himself worthy of his own opportunity to study, his eventual acceptance of a bribe is but the outward sign of his own sense of guilt. Sarthou-Lajus analyses the melancholia of guilt in terms applicable to Obi:

> In melancholia the haunting by the unrepayable debt is compounded by the obsession with the ideal of perfection and the feeling of always falling short. If the melancholic is haunted by contracting unrepayable debts, that is out of fear of being confronted by his impotence to give; the melancholic suffers from an impossible presence in the gift he makes of himself, his incapacity to love enough or well enough compounded with the sense of his own oblivion.[73]

The first time someone leaves a wad of notes for him on his table, Obi leaves it there overnight covered with a newspaper. This money is not the neutral impersonal medium of exchange described by Simmel; rather, it is filled with personal meaning. A later bribe, for twenty pounds, is more than Obi can bear, and he sits staring at it, paralyzed, unable to accept or return it. As it turns out, these are marked notes and will be used to prove Obi's guilt. The young moralist has accepted the logic of bribers and the bribed: "We all have to stand on the earth itself and go with her at her pace." Was he not "also a man of skin and fat, with a stomach and a throat which needed to be served"?[74] But the man who is but a stomach and a throat has lost his soul. After the loss of his moral centre, Obi knows himself damned.

For much of the novel, as Obi's debts mount, the future is a source of dread. Then, two pages from the end, he takes his first bribe and time suddenly collapses. We are told succinctly: "Others came." "In due course" the bribes allow Obi to pay off his debts: "The worst was now over" (153). But the worst is only over in the sense that it has occurred, not in the sense that it has ended. By abandoning the principles that had defined him, Obi has damned himself. He becomes numb and disconnected from his actions, and the narrative, too, pulls back from his point of view. But then he finds that he has not gotten used to the bribes after all and that "every incident had been a hundred times worse than the one before it" (154). Obi's story is over, and we do not need to await the sentence. He has passed it on himself.

In Armah's *The Beautyful Ones*, when a military coup overthrows Kwame Nkrumah, the corrupt politician Koomson falls from the heights to the depths: "The individual man of power now shivering, his head filled with the fear of the vengeance of those he had wronged. For him everything was going to change."[75] To attach oneself to the cycles of power and wealth that rise and fall like the tides is to end up in Hell. The incorruptible hero of that novel, by contrast, maintains his unflinching moral course, and in the end, even his long-suffering wife comes to appreciate the value of a virtue that steadfastly insists on its impermeability to the material world and that moves through Hell unscathed. In *No Longer at Ease*, by contrast, Obi's fall is from moral purity *into* corruption. The corresponding fall from respectability to criminal status merely underscores the loss of spiritual worth. The righteous young man who had so insisted on serving the law is in the end the law's prisoner. The young man who had refused the town union's plan for him to study law now requires them to hire a lawyer to defend him. Obi had thought that he was establishing the law by rejecting self-interest and refusing bribes. It turns out, however, that the law demands a different self-sacrifice. The trial for bribery, by punishing his transgression, establishes the foundations of the law not in love but in discipline.

10

Discipline

A key moment in *No Longer at Ease*, analyzed by all critics, is Obi's road trip by mammy wagon from Lagos to Umuofia, when he reverses the pilgrimage from the provinces to the capital that has been his career. Obi travels first class, meaning he sits in the cab with the driver, while in the back, Igbo-speaking traders sit crowded together, their knees pulled up in front of them. The educated English-speaker in front is a citizen, the traders in the back mere subjects. He is educated; they are not. He is alone; they are a group. He earns a government salary; they make a living from commodity exchange. He is travelling outward from the centre back to the provinces; they are returning home from the tradelands.

The traders sing bawdy songs to which the university graduate eagerly applies his exegetical skills, concluding that the "burden" of one song, about a man who kills an in-law and about a paddle that speaks English, was "the world turned upside down." So "pleased" is he with this reading that he "began to search in his mind for other songs that could be given the same treatment" (42). He imagines the social distance between himself and others as the distance between the critic and the text, and he takes pleasure in reading others.

As Olaniyan shows, there is irony at Obi's expense here: the young man returned from abroad does not appreciate how much his own distance from the traders is symptomatic of the upside-down world he diagnoses.[1] The irony is, however, unstable: the distance between critic and text is also Achebe's. Obi's outsiderhood puts him close to the novel's omniscient narration, which gives us access to his thoughts and leaves the traders nameless and without interiority. As Alex Woloch argues, the "asymmetric structure of realist characterization ... reflects actual structures of inequitable distribution."[2] The irony at Obi's expense is self-ironization on the novel's part.

Obi's objectivizing and would-be omniscient gaze "noticed" two policemen, who stop the lorry for no apparent reason. The driver's assistant is about to give one of them something until "Obi looked in their direction" (39), at which point the policeman becomes wary and sends the man away. Obi's critical eye here sees and judges all. His vigilance does not, however, spare the driver a bribe but costs him a larger "dash" after an unnecessary delay. "Why you look the man for face when we want give um two shillings?" the driver complains. "Because he has no right to take two shillings from you," Obi responds. The young civil servant applies the critical eye of the law and a knowledge of how things should be, but because he is not actually outside the situation, his observation has consequences for others and for his relations with others. The traders shift the target of their songs from career girls to "'too know' young men" (40). Even as he exercises his mastery over the traders' songs by interpreting them in terms the singers would not understand, they incorporate him and his ham-fisted response to bribes into their songs.

Is Obi wrong to denounce the demand for a bribe? In precolonial times, as we have seen, the security of travellers was based on a trust in known others with whom one established relations by gift exchange, marriage, and rituals and solemn oaths of alliance rather than on a confidence that strangers obeyed a rule of law enforced by a single authority.[3] Obi, however, feels that control of the roads should belong to the state, as Achebe himself and, I venture, all readers of the novel feel. Later, Obi will have money stolen from his car by street thugs when he does not heed their demand for money to watch his car. The thugs had really been asking for money *not* to break into the car. The police at the roadblock are doing the same, demanding money *not* to abuse their legally constituted authority. Obi makes a distinction between legitimate and illegitimate demands, but the lorry driver considers paying off the police part of the same game whereby he must pay state authorities taxes. Janet Roitman found that bandits on highways in Chad also saw their exactions as a form of redistribution comparable to taxes.[4] Conversely, Tilly compares the formation of states in Europe to organized crime and argues that government protection against local and external violence often amounted to a similar form of "racketeering": "Since governments themselves commonly simulate, stimulate, or even fabricate threats of external war and since the repressive and extractive activities of governments often constitute the largest current threats to the livelihoods of their own citizens, many governments operate in essentially the same ways as racketeers."[5]

The lorry driver and his assistant consider the law a convention that comes into play when dealing with those who wield power. The best they hope for is that the convention will limit the size and frequency of exactions. Obi's disciplinary gaze, however, represents a law that the police themselves seek to elude and angrily lash out at, the law of the Normative rather than the Prerogative State. This unreal gaze also features in Armah's *Beautyful Ones*, where a bus conductor counting his take at the end of his run suddenly imagines that a passenger, still seated in the bus, is watching him and silently saying, "I have seen you. You have been seen. We have seen all": "It was not the voice of the watcher. It could not be the voice of any human being the conductor knew. It was a large voice rolling down and everywhere covering empty spaces in the mind and really never stopping anywhere at all."[6] The conductor appears to have integrated into his psyche the interpellation by the police described by Althusser and the disciplinary gaze analyzed by Foucault. He calms down, however: "For, after all, how had he so frightened himself into thinking of the watcher as the bringer of his doom? Why had he placed the silent one above himself? Was it not likely, most probable, indeed, quite certain, that the watcher was himself also a man of skin and fat, with a stomach and a throat which needed to be served?"[7] Had the large voice he had imagined actually been that of a Ghanaian policeman, Armah implies, he would only have asked for a share of the take.

In Europe, argue Foucault and Althusser, the state's monopoly on violence wielded by the police has been integrated as a disciplinary function into the psyche of the citizen. Obi and Armah's protagonist have both integrated such a disciplinary gaze, and Obi wields it in his turn *against* the police. The disciplinary gaze has now a mimic aspect and an aspect of desire: the two honest men *wish* there were a state whose surveillance they could integrate. As it is, they must project such surveillance outward onto the state and its functionaries. The prison that Obi enters at the end of the story (and the beginning of the novel) is one he has already internalized. The early colonial administration considered that Nigerians did not tolerate prison and preferred flogging, though prison became increasingly favoured as a punishment

> The rehabilitative possibilities of the prison stemmed less from its capacity to punish (if anything, colonial logic implied that imprisonment punished Nigerians more than it did the British) than from its ability to force prisoners to internalize a set of governing constraints that would eventually propel them into law-abiding lives on the outside. Colonial sociologies identified the evolutionary standing of Nigerian societies with a "tribal communism" implying that specific

> Nigerians were not yet individuated – or subjectified, to use the terminology of Michel Foucault – in a manner that made them amenable to disciplinary practices like incarceration.[8]

On the eve of independence, however, Obi's example prove that *he* at least has been subjectified or disciplined in the way Foucault writes of. Pierce, discussing Foucault, could be speaking of Obi when he writes that "one's self-understanding as autonomous and rational is precisely what makes one most permeable to power."[9]

Weber writes: "What characterizes modern society is the inscription of a relation of obedience in the representation of the disciplinary order. Each one functions in relation to power as a person supposed already to know, by virtue of the impersonal authority of the law, how he should behave."[10] Obi, the great reader of novels, has picked up from bourgeois literature what D.A. Miller identifies as its disavowal of the police. The Victorian novel, writes Miller, took the state and the law so for granted that it could disavow the force needed to install and maintain them. It metonymically associated the police with those classes that need policing, for good citizens belonging to the middle classes pride themselves on having so integrated the law into their characters and behaviour that they do not need the police.[11] In his own eyes, Obi travels a moral high road, while the police belong to the world of lorry drivers and traders whose circulation they regulate, however irregularly.

In Achebe's and Armah's novels, the police represent the truth about the violence on which the state rests, but the violence is clearly distinguished from the law. The critical gaze on the world from a moral position outside it acknowledges an ideal of the state distinct from the tyranny of actual state actors. Obi knows how a citizen should behave with respect to the ideal state, but, unlike a character in a Victorian novel, he cannot pretend the police are not there. In his Nigeria the otherness of the police is not a middle-class fantasy: the police do not enforce the law, protect property, or safeguard people against violence; instead they extort from citizens and subjects alike.

Appiah argues that assigning policing and sentencing powers to particular people as a means of securing order always raises the question "*Quis custodiet ipsos custodes?* Who will guard the guards?"[12] This is not an academic question in Obi's Nigeria. Appiah further argues that a code of honour such as Obi upholds, if widely shared, is cheaper to maintain than are police. In effect, Appiah assumes, *contra* Foucault and Althusser, that the psychic integration of the law is a desirable thing. Simon Critchley writes about the disciplining of citizens that "the problem of politics is: how can those chains be made legitimate? Or, better, how can citizens wear legitimate chains?"[13]

How to instill in the masses the sense he himself has of the dishonour of bribery? Obi is skeptical: "It would take centuries." His comment on the police exacting bribes, "What an Augean stable!" (40), implies that it would require a Hercules. Obi favours "A handful of men at the top. Or even one man with vision – an enlightened dictator. People are scared of the word nowadays. But what kind of democracy can exist side by side with so much corruption and ignorance?" (40). Obi's dream of an enlightened dictator is an early version of the cry for discipline that would later motivate many military coups in Africa, which "never failed to cite corruption as a central reason for their seizure of power."[14] Paul Beckett contends that the educated elite who manned the Nigerian civil service served more comfortably under military rule than under civilian politicians, whom they blamed for corruption and for pandering to ethnic groups at a cost to the nation as a whole.[15] The military, by contrast, promised to give civil servants room to carry out their plans for centralization, regional balance, and enlightened rule. Udo Akpan in Aluko's *One Man, One Matchet* speaks for his author, himself a civil servant, when he complains that colonial civil servants are prohibited from discussing politics: "The best brains of the country are with a few exceptions all in the Civil Service. Can this country with its limited resources in educated man-power afford to have their mouths padlocked in the Civil Service while second-rate and sometimes semi-literate men are saddled with the very important duty of legislating and taking executive decisions for the State?"[16]

If the dictator whom Obi imagines were indeed successful in forging citizens who have absorbed a code of honour, all irony would disappear and the moral code would retrospectively justify the means with which it was implemented. Derrida explains that

> a "successful" revolution, the "successful" foundation of a State (in somewhat the same sense that one speaks of a "'felicitous' performative speech act") will produce *après coup* what it was destined in advance to produce, namely, proper interpretative models to read in return, to give sense, necessity and above all legitimacy to the violence that has produced, among others, the interpretative model in question, that is, the discourse of its self-legitimation.[17]

(The phrase *après coup* resonates more in the English translation than in the French original.) Of course, Derrida concedes, "there are cases in which it is not known for generations if the performative of the violent founding of a state is 'felicitous' or not."[18]

Obi does not imagine himself as the dictator he dreams of, but neither does he imagine himself under the dictator's rule. Because he alone recognizes and obeys the rule of law, he would be allied with the dictator and not subject to him. Obi's outside viewpoint is, as we have seen, an Archimedean stance outside the earth created by his consciousness of an absolute debt. Jens Bartelson could be describing Obi when he writes of "the citizen [anywhere] trying to account for his own existence within the state as the legitimate heir to royal and personalized sovereignty":

> As a rational subject, he participates in the subjective and indivisible will of the state, but at the same time he is estranged from it, looking into it and its conflict-filled prehistory from a point outside it, from the mytho-anarchic outside out of which he has himself emerged or escaped. This perspective invites dreams of transcendence or emancipation: the state is the result of crime organized on a huge scale, propelled by massive violence. But so is the citizen-spectator himself, since he is a modality of the same historically determined subjectivity; his estrangement is only partial, and he cannot be emancipated completely from this iron cage of modern sovereignty, without, as it were, simultaneously losing knowledge of himself.[19]

In 1958 Obi's idea of enlightened despotism is an idle daydream: we are told that, "not really in the mood for consecutive reasoning," his mind drifted from thoughts of dictators to more pleasant erotic daydreams, fuelled by the immediate presence beside him of a young nursing mother (40). Obi is outside the world of the lorry and able to interpret and judge it, but also inside. His two desires – he wants the rule of law, and he wants a sovereign who will assert it and make it stick – are mutually contradictory: the sovereign would be above the rule of law he asserts. The contradiction is that between the Normative and the Prerogative States. Obi imagines the State's sovereignty personified in one who, like the soldier in the Umuofia market, breaks "the earth with his boots, and no one dared touch him" (11), but who also rules with sufficient wisdom to shape subjects into responsible citizens, who would then in turn retrospectively accede to his sovereignty. It is therefore the most bitter irony that the novel ends with Obi arrested by a CID man who invokes "the name of the Queen, like a District Officer in the bush reading the Riot Act to an uncomprehending and delirious mob" (154).

The crucial difference between Obi and Mr. Green, his boss, is that Green saw himself as occupying a heroic state of exception – he is nostalgic for an original state before the law and foresees an imminent collapse into lawlessness – but his own career took place entirely in the in-between time of the colonial state, while Obi lives in what should be a state of exception, the moment before the new state is established, when the law must be decided upon and, just as important, decided *for*, yet he behaves as if the law has already been established. Obi refuses to contemplate the existential demands of sovereignty but is content to remain in the in-between time of the law.

We judge Obi as alienated and smug, hopelessly ineffectual, and wrong about the value of dictatorship. Our sense of that last irony owes a great deal, however, to a hindsight unavailable to the novel itself. Africa's experience since independence, like Europe's between the world wars, has shown that "'a 'protected democracy' is not a democracy at all, and that the paradigm of constitutional dictatorship functions instead as a transitional phase that leads inevitably to the establishment of a totalitarian regime."[20] In other words, the dictatorship that Obi dreams of is likely to put men with guns like the police whom he deplores in charge.

Obi's dream of military discipline echoes a discourse common in his time and even more common since, "in which Nigerians view their society as deeply corrupt and themselves as disorderly people in need of iron-handed leadership."[21] The observations Obi makes about the need for moral leadership are a variation of Achebe's own later arguments in *The Trouble with Nigeria*: that Nigeria's problems can be blamed on its poor leaders, who have failed to set an example. Twenty-five years later, Achebe still writes:

> A new patriotic consciousness has to be developed ... one based on an awareness of the responsibility of leaders to the led – on the sacredness of their anointment to lead – and disseminated by civil society, schools, and intellectuals. It is from this kind of environment that a leader, humbled by the trust placed upon him by the people, will emerge, willing to use the power given to him for the good of the people.[22]

Whereas Obi emphasizes the indiscipline of the people and Achebe the corruption of rulers, both presume the solution lies with moral leaders.

The contradiction that people must be treated as subjects in order to be formed into citizens is not an African idiosyncrasy but is built into the very notion of the state. There are three terms involved in state sovereignty – the citizenry, the ruler, and the law – none of which can act as the ground for the others. Sovereignty resides with the people but does not exist until ceded to leaders. It is a sacred function bestowed on leaders at the moment of their anointment. Obi believes that a sovereign dictator must impose the law on the people; Achebe believes that the leaders to whom the people have ceded their sovereignty must obey the law. The state, the people, and the law all somehow came into being together at some moment that is always in the past – except that, in the colony on the eve of independence, this coalescence has not yet come into being.

VIOLENCE AND THE NEW STATE

Although *No Longer at Ease* is set on the eve of independence, the only discussion of politics by any of the characters concerns a scandal of betrayal and a tragic fall from grace, in short, "the normal affairs of life": "The news of the day was about the Minister of Land who used to be one of the most popular politicians until he took it into his head to challenge the national hero" (148). The reference is to K.O. Mbadiwe, who was expelled from the NCNC in 1958 for trying to unseat Azikiwe as leader. In *No Longer at Ease* the rebel minister brings lorry loads of women supporters to Abame for a political rally, but there he is physically beaten and his supporters have their head-ties stripped from them (148). Recall that Abame was the site of the greatest violence in *Things Fall Apart* and *Arrow of God*, when the British exacted a disproportionate revenge for the killing of an Englishman on a bicycle. The violence meted to the minister and his supporters at Abame fifty or so years later is a direct challenge to the law established by the British in the aftermath of their conquest, but also a reminder of the violence on which the state rests.

Azikiwe had formed a militant youth organization called the Zikist National Vanguard, whose task was to protect his person and intimidate opponents like Mbadiwe.[23] The name suggests a dangerous identification of the man with the sovereign state. In response, Mbadiwe's breakaway party, the DPNC (Democratic Party of Nigeria and the Cameroons), formed its own brigades of uniformed young men, called the Demoguards.[24] In 1958 the Zikists paid a threatening visit to the young Achebe, then working at the Nigerian Broadcasting Corporation, to complain that he had allowed news of Mbadiwe to be broadcast.[25] Much later Achebe recalled Azikiwe as "basically a humane democrat," "surrounded at the critical transition phase by zealots reared under colonialism with little understanding of the willing restraint demanded of those who would practice the arts of democracy."[26] Mbembe calls such willing restraint the "politics of the gift," whereby "conditions are created such that partisan struggles, however severe they may be, do not have as their elemental goal the physical annihilation of the adversary. Nor do they have sedition or violent dissent as their only outlet. Instead, they draw legitimacy from their contribution to the making of a civic body that, by domesticating violence, gives birth to and consolidates the possibility of 'political coexistence.'"[27]

In *No Longer at Ease*, people denounce the rebel minister as a hubristic usurper and compare him to "the little bird *nza* who after a big meal so far forgot himself as to challenge his *chi* to single combat" (148). The people of Umuofia had once said the same thing of Okonkwo (31). In this case the proverbial analogy casts Azikiwe, the national hero, not just as the minister's *chi*, but as the *chi* of the people, the personal spirit who determines the people's destiny. The *chi* of the people is a suggestive way of conceptualizing the sovereign and the *vox populi*: when the people say yes their *chi* will say yes too, but if the sovereign says no, there is no possibility of proceeding against his will.

The violence in *No Longer at Ease* between the national hero and the Minister of Lands at Abame is not revolutionary anti-colonial violence but is for control of power already constituted. Moreover, it does not even assert sovereignty, for Azikiwe was premier of the Eastern Region, not Nigeria as a whole. Before Obi left for England, he and his friends used to talk politics, but no longer (37). Something has changed between 1952 and 1956. The new Lyttleton Constitution of 1954 assigned power to the regions, and it became clear that the Northern Region would dominate the new federation. Azikiwe, the leader of the NCNC, became premier of the Eastern Region instead of holding a federal position, and at the time it was not clear whether power would lie in the centre or in the regions. Douglas Rimmer explains that "the regional governments modeled their conduct on that of independent states. Each was concerned to cut what it could from the collective cake and to defend its own bakings from neighbouring depredations."[28]

On the last page of *No Longer at Ease*, the verdict having come down, the judicial sentence is about to be passed on Obi, and readers closing the book must make their own judgment. That judgment will be not just on Obi but, by extension, on his generation as well, those prospective citizens who have come of age just as the nation-to-be receives its independence. The significance of the novel is that, at the original cusp of transition, it diagnoses not a future distinct from the past but rather the moment of transition itself. Endless transition would turn out to be the new nation's future.

Conclusion

Where did Obi originally get his ideas of the morality of service to the state? In the course of his interview for a job with the Public Service Commission, he discussed with the chair of the committee for "the greater part of half an hour" poetry and fiction, including Graham Greene, W.H. Auden, Evelyn Waugh, Amos Tutuola, and the nature of modern tragedy. In looking back on his interview, Obi feels he said "a lot of nonsense, but it was a learned and impressive kind of nonsense" (35). As far as we are given to judge, Obi did speak a lot of nonsense at the interview – he argued that suicide constitutes a happy ending that spoils a tragedy – but it is the kind of nonsense that generates cultural capital that, in the late colony, can be converted into a job with a salary. We may disagree with Obi's opinions on tragedy and even decide that they are proven wrong by *Things Fall Apart*, which would appear two years later in 1958, but Obi's fluency with such cultural nonsense allows other people – in 1956 in Nigeria mostly white Englishmen – to assess his suitability for a position in the civil service. This kind of nonsense is not so easily faked. Obi belongs.

Obi's examiners are impressed when he disagrees with them and expresses his own opinion of the character of Scobie in Greene's *The Heart of the Matter*, because such original self-expression comes in the context of a larger consensus: about the value of literature, the need for ethics, and one's personal responsibility for leading a meaningful life. The training Obi received at university made literature "assume the role of a repository of ethical experiences, and thereby absorb the key functions of moral training."[1] Ian Hunter argues that English developed as a school discipline because it fostered a soul "insensibly acquired in the instituted space between self-expression and social normativity."[2] Hunter would say Obi has internalized "the function of moral surveillance itself: finding in himself the onerous ethical antinomies and thereby beginning to shape a 'balanced' self as the condition of shaping the selves of others."[3]

The exchange of literary references at his job interview creates a climate of trust, as if, surely, someone who has read Eliot, Greene, and Tutuola would not take bribes. Of course, historically readers of literature have not proven morally stronger or more discerning than other people – as Obi himself recalls, Conrad's Kurtz is a well-read man who scrawls "Exterminate all the brutes!" at the bottom of a peroration on the value of colonialism – but they are likely to consider bribes shameful. His study of British literature would have taught Obi that money bears a taint. Whereas in eighteenth-century England, economics and English literature had shared a common understanding, Mary Poovey explains that a great divide opened between them in the nineteenth century. Literature then defined itself as an alternative to the values championed by economics, regarded as materialist and amoral; the anti-market model favoured by literature "defined *value* in terms of subjective qualities that defied quantification, were immune to exchange, and were sometimes difficult to grasp or convey. Writers used words like *imagination*, *genius*, and *originality* to characterize the qualities by which this value could be recognized."[4]

Those without Obi's education speak of studying abroad in a grandiose way that gestures toward both self-improvement *and* financial gain. The Secretary of the Town Union, for instance, welcomes Obi back from his "quest of the Golden Fleece" (28) and hopes that more sons of Umuofia will drink "deep at the Pierian Spring of Knowledge" (29). As long ago as 1925, Nnamdi Azikiwe's father had told him to bring home the "golden fleece of knowledge" from America.[5] Obi speaks in much less inflated terms but places as much or more emphasis on his deep personal engagement with the texts he studied.

Philip Rogers and Tejumola Olaniyan diagnose that Obi's too-great admiration for English literature itself has led him to abandon his African roots and become culturally hollow. Simon Gikandi judges that Obi is quixotic in the sense that his understanding, derived from books, is hopelessly distant from reality.[6] The irony the novel directs at Obi's readiness to quote from literature is, however, mild and inconsistent. Rogers scoffs at Obi's love of English literature but never mentions Obi's preparedness to marry an *osu* or his righteous refusal to take bribes, moral stances that readers of novels, *because* they have read novels, will approve of. The realist novel may not inculcate morals but it does teach a framework for judging characters. The novel considers Obi's fall from his moral high ground regrettable, almost tragic in the deliberately banal sense of modern tragedy evinced by the alienated protagonists of Graham Greene.

Rogers and Olaniyan can dismiss Obi's love of literature, which was also Achebe's, because we no longer think of literature the way university-educated people did in the British Empire and Commonwealth in the 1950s. Gone is the understanding of literature as an inalienable non-material good that builds the soul by providing it with moral exercise and that must be kept from contact with the world of money, the understanding that dominated English departments at the time, including in Ibadan, where Achebe transferred from the study of medicine to that of literature.

Obi's education made him think of literary texts as inalienable gifts circulating in an exchange that accrues cultural capital. He behaves to Conrad or Greene, whose texts he receives and values, much as Charles Ibe, the messenger in the office, behaves to him: being in the debt of such luminaries constitutes a claim on his own part to be part of their circle or at least part of the circle of those who have read them. Like gifts, texts carry something of their giver. This cultural capital accrues to Achebe, who borrowed the title of *Things Fall Apart* from Yeats and that of *No Longer at Ease* from Eliot (also the source of the title *A Handful of Dust*, Waugh's novel, which Obi discusses at his interview). The patronage of an older generation of writers wins credit for his own literary works among readers.

Of course, there are other ways of relating to texts, especially foreign texts if one has been colonized. Instead of seeing texts as gifts, one could regard them as crippling debts that must be repaid or as blows that must be reciprocated. This is how elsewhere Achebe has responded to *Heart of Darkness* or Joyce Cary's *Mister Johnson*, which he regards as as dangerous as Leonard's *The Tribes of the Lower Niger*. Their false representations of Africa must be responded to and corrected. In 2000, Achebe looked back upon the African literary response to European writing about Africa and characterized it in terms of a cycle of reciprocal violence:

> When the African response began, I think there was an immediate pause on the European side, as if they were saying, Okay, we'll stop telling this story, because we see there's another story. But after a while there's a certain beginning again, not quite a return but something like a reaction to the African story that cannot, of course, ever go as far as the original tradition that the Africans are responding to. There's a reaction to a reaction, and there will be a further reaction

> to that. And I think that's the way it will go, until what I call a balance of stories is secured.[7]

He foresees the cycle of blow and counterblow exchanged among texts eventually reaching equilibrium. Achebe sees not a World Republic of Letters, where texts from the provinces compete to make it in the centre, but a stateless field where Literary Peers establish relations with each other observing the principle of reciprocity: the blows they exchange now may eventually lead to equilibrium and be replaced by the exchange of gifts.

More recently, academic readers have tended to regard literary texts not as gifts and not even as blows but as commodities circulating in a market and authors as brands with market share. Even to consider literature's value as a kind of cultural capital, however, is to collapse the moral distinction between literature and the world of money upon which literature's cultural status once depended and thus, paradoxically, to accelerate the loss of literature's cultural capital. The capital that literature represented now risks becoming like cowrie shells, which can no longer be converted into coins or notes and so can only serve as ornamentation or be crushed to make lime. Not surprisingly, literature degrees like Obi's today carry less status everywhere, not least in Africa.

AFRICAN LITERATURE AFTER ACHEBE

In 1966, military coups overthrew the First Republic in Nigeria (January), Kwame Nkrumah in Ghana (February), and the Kabaka of Buganda (May).[8] The coup against Nkrumah, says John Dramani Mahama, whose father lost his ministerial post and had to flee, "serves as the line of demarcation, separating the certainty of what was from the uncertainty of what lies ahead. It is a moment in which you suddenly become aware of who you are; you become aware of the fragility and unpredictability of the world in which you live."[9] Achebe's novel *A Man of the People* (1966) ends with a military coup (the Nigerian coup had not yet taken place when Achebe wrote), and the coup against Nkrumah is the climax of *The Beautyful Ones Are Not Yet Born*, published in 1968.

The military coups of 1966 changed the world, but not because they introduced violence and tyranny and dispelled whatever optimism may have lingered. As Armah vividly shows, Ghanaians had been under no illusions about Nkrumah's regime. Indeed, the coups in Nigeria and Ghana were greeted with optimism at first as potentially *ending* violence and tyranny. *A Man of the People* predicts a coup that will bring an end to the corruption and violence of party politics. Nor was the significance of the 1966 coups that they threw out constitutions and relegated the states' foundations to the dustbin. The independence constitutions had already been amended – Ghana and Nigeria, for instance, became republics in 1960 and 1963 respectively – and had never had the sacrosanct nature of the documents produced by the American Revolution. Young writes that "they reflected bargains struck with the colonizer rather than a negotiated compact between state and society."[10] In the last fifteen years of colonial rule Nigeria had four different constitutions.[11] Between 1963 and 1989 Nigeria had another five. Such a cavalier dismissal of foundations would be unimaginable in the United States, where the constitution is at the origin of all law, or in Great Britain, where the constitution is the accumulation of every law. (In France, of course, there is more of a tradition of throwing out constitutions and beginning over again.) Okoth Ogendo describes the African political situation as "constitutions without constitutionalism; that is, constitutions have been used just as any other instrument to achieve narrow political ends."[12]

The significance of the military coups is that they turned back the clock and instituted a kind of eternal return to the moment of transition that was decolonization. Like late colonialism, military rule relied upon what Paul Beckett and Crawford Young call "Permanent Transition": each regime "legitimated by a sense of *progress* toward creating its own alternative: civil democratic government."[13] The military rulers, like the colonizers, justified their persistence by declaring that they were laying the foundations for their own obsolescence. Oyeleye Oyediran calls the last colonial decade in Nigeria the "Mother of Transitions,"[14] and the label is apt, for independence proved the model for a repeated return to that moment when the Prerogative State prepares to give way to democracy.

Of course, a second or third return to foundations feels different from the first. I have been arguing that the generation of independence understood the state in terms of its founding, related it to other political models such as the village group, and considered the law the legacy of colonial sovereignty. For the generation of the coups and after, however, origins and legacies scarcely mattered. The future no longer explained the present. No more thought was given to a historical progression from village to king, or from colony to democracy. Nor was there any longer any point in seeking sources of authority in the village or the colony, for these had been swept aside.

The coups that overthrew the First Republic in Nigeria and Kwame Nkrumah in Ghana also divide the history of African literature in two: the period just before and just after independence, and the period from

1966 to at least 2006, the year of publication of Ngũgĩ's *Wizard of the Crow*. On or about February 1966, African literature changed when the military coups forced a reconsideration of what the state meant. I have already quoted Appiah who argues that the novels of "the generation of Achebe's *Things Fall Apart* and Laye's *L'enfant noir*" were "realist legitimations of nationalism," but a later generation of writers, including Yambo Ouologuem, author of *Le devoir de violence*, sought "to delegitimate the forms of the realist African novel, in part, surely, because what it sought to naturalize was a nationalism that, by 1968, had plainly failed."[15] *Things Fall Apart* (1958) and *Le devoir de violence* (1968) do indeed belong to distinct moments in literary history that can legitimately be termed two generations (though only ten years separate the authors' birthdates and the novels' publication dates), but Appiah's characterization of the two moments in terms of nationalism and anti-nationalism is incomplete. The new violence-soaked and more fiercely satirical literature written after the military coups of 1966 was often written by the same writers whom Appiah characterizes as belonging to the first generation. The break observable in African literature as a whole was also a change in direction in the literary careers of the fathers of African literature: Achebe stopped writing novels for two decades, but Soyinka wrote *Season of Anomy*, Ngũgĩ wrote *Petals of Blood*, and Sembène wrote *Xala*. The break is not strictly speaking generational.

Appiah celebrates the clear-sighted disillusionment of the second wave of anti-nationalist fiction because he rejects nationalism as closed and inward-looking; he prefers cosmopolitanism. Indeed much postcolonial criticism, taking its cue from Homi Bhabha, has been concerned with critiquing nationalism, the ideology that summons citizens to identify with states. Scholars commonly show how, as an identity, the nation is always raced and gendered: nationalism relies on an invented tradition of origins, blood relations, history, and the body; it creates harmful and artificial distinctions based on indigeneity and alterity; and it narrates the past teleologically, as a history leading to the nation. But if, *pace* Appiah, we recognize that African literature is obsessed with the state rather than the nation, then the distinction between literary generations looks different. The first generation, examined in this book, approached the state with curiosity and ambivalence, seeking to understand it by contrasting it to political alternatives on different scales, notably the village group. The later, post-coup generation could not even imagine an alternative to the state and, in great satirical allegories, depicted the state, detached from any nation, expanding to occupy the continent. There is no reality but the state in the novels *A*

Man of the People, *Devil on the Cross*, *Season of Anomy*, *La vie et demie*, and *Le dernier de l'empire*.

The difference in literature after 1966 is one of literary form. *No Longer at Ease*, published in 1960, is a realist novel set in a particular state, Nigeria in its case. After 1966, however, it became a straightforward matter to set an African novel in a fictive state, a state in every significant way like the author's own but not found on any extratextual map. Ouologuem's *Le devoir de violence* is set in a fictive Sahelian empire and its colonial and postcolonial successor state, Nakem-Ziuko. Other examples of fictive states are in Kourouma's *Les soleils des indépendances* and *En attendant le vote des bêtes sauvages*, Soyinka's *Season of Anomy*, Achebe's *A Man of the People* and *Anthills of the Savannah*, Beti's *Remember Ruben*, Sony Labou Tansi's *La vie et demie*, Ben Okri's *The Famished Road*, and *Matigari* by Ngũgĩ wa Thiong'o. Not all African novels written after 1966 are political allegories about the workings of power, but after 1966, it became easy to imagine another African republic called Kangan, Songhai, Katamalanasie, the Ebony Coast, Congheria, or Kanem, or not called anything at all.[16] The fictive state, the state that resembles the author's own but has a different name or is unnamed, is an African literary innovation.[17] As a thought experiment, try to imagine an English writer setting a novel in a state in every way like present-day or historical England but not called England.

The prevalence of fictive states in African literature poses a direct challenge to the nationalist ideology that claims for each nation-state a uniqueness in the sight of God making it worthy of a seat at the table of history. In his article "On Politics as a Form of Expenditure," Mbembe develops a comprehensive typology of the African state without naming a single one. He does, however, cite Kourouma and Labou Tansi as authorities. An entire branch of African political thought indulges in imagining the redrawing of state borders into a continent-wide federation of alternative states, from five to fifteen in number, that would have the advantage of being larger and therefore more viable than the continent's existing fifty-odd states. Guy Martin lists six such projects, including one of his own invention,[18] and such counter-geographies are also a regularly recurring feature of African journalism. Martin and his partner Muena wa Muiu argue for just five states called Mali, Kimit, Kush, Kongo, and Zimbabwe in an African federation with a single capital called Napata newly constructed in the centre. Their model is premised on an overarching African culture, which makes it possible to ignore the history of colonialism, and at the same time on something generic about statehood that allows borders to be fixed at a desk with pencils and coloured markers, which is not unlike how the actual African states were originally determined. These counter-geographies also presume, however, that states should reflect economic logic (none of these new inventions is landlocked, as so many actual African states are) as well as the consent of citizens, the ideal of the social contract. In other words, these new inventions seek to be less "fictional" than the existing states are and to correspond more to nations that citizens can identify with. All of these models deliberately ignore that African states, like states everywhere except in Europe after the First World War and after the Cold War, were originally defined by conquest.

The counter-geographical models of political scientists and journalists are literally utopian – they imagine states that do not exist – but they also present the optimal political organization. African novels set in generic fictive states, by contrast, are overwhelmingly dystopian. They do not redraw borders in order to create fewer and better states for Africa, but they do presume that African states constitute an unbounded series with room for more. Kourouma's *En attendant le vote des bêtes sauvages*, the supreme African example of the dictator novel, recklessly mixes fictive and non-fictive states. The novel is a series of praise songs performed for Koyaga, the president dictator of the Republic of the Gulf, who has learned important lessons from his fellow dictators from the Republic of the Hills, the Ebony Republic, the Republic of the Great River, the Country of Two Rivers, and the Country of the Djebels and the Sand, all of which have obvious models outside the novel. But in the novel these fictive states exist alongside non-fictive states, including the countries they are modelled on: the Ivory Coast, Zaire, Oubangui-Chari (the Central African Republic), and Morocco. Koyaga and his peers are fictional (though it is easy to recognize their models), but the novel also mentions by name Hamani Dioré, Seyni Kountché, Kadhafi, Boumedienne, Nkrumah, and Mengistu Hailé Mariam. The pseudonymous states are explicitly like the states that already exist because, it is implied, there is something generalizable about the African state.

Achebe's *Anthills of the Savannah*, Soyinka's *Season of Anomy*, and Labou Tansi's *La vie et demie* are parables that invite generalization to the continent as a whole. The fictive states in which these novels are set might well be called "pan-African nations," and the setting of Peter Abrahams's *A Wreath for Udomo*, a state that resembles the Gold Coast/Ghana, is even called Panafrica. Fictiveness suggests that what matters about African states is the terrible ways they are all alike, the interchangeability of neocolonial arrangements in a multi-national order that withholds from some the possibility of change and making history.

The same fearful shared conditions that make it possible for the World Bank and the IMF to assume that "the state and its institutions remain strangely ahistorical entities, a set of functional imperatives of regulation arising from society but devoid of distinct characters and different historical trajectories,"[19] also make it possible to imagine a generic substitute that epitomizes the whole series.

But the novel set in a fictive state is never indifferent to the *idea* of the state. The characters in such novels are more thoroughly defined by their citizenship than are characters in realist novels, European or African. In Western European literature the boundary between levels at which fictiveness is possible (the street, the school, the village all invite pseudonyms) and levels where it is not (one's own state cannot be given a pseudonym) is the boundary between the private and the public. The nation is a public stage and cannot have a fictive substitute, but below that level, autobiographical elements often must be rendered fictive in order to allow the private sphere to be represented in public. The familiar modern splitting of the subject into public and private depends on the fixed and shared identity of nationality. This is Hegel's point when he says that "the principle of modern states has prodigious strength and depth because it allows the principle of subjectivity to progress to its culmination in the extreme of self-subsistent personal particularity, and yet at the same time brings it back to the substantive unity and so maintains this unity in the principle of subjectivity itself."[20] The European realist novel, even when apparently concerned with the psychology of the individual, presumes the public identity of nationality: fictional characters can be private citizens because they *are* citizens.

In the fictive African state, by contrast, there is, paradoxically, only public life. In the African fictive state citizenship is of such burning concern because the state is not a guarantor of identity. Where there is no secure public realm there can be no self-contained private realm. If Fredric Jameson's thesis that in Third World literature the private is an allegory for the public retains any validity as a description of African literature, it is precisely because the state is in such doubt.

The fictive states in *A Man of the People*, *Anthills of the Savannah*, *Season of Anomy*, and *La vie et demie* are inhabited by resolutely political animals. These would-be citizens need a public and political stage in order to work out the redemption of the collective, and only the state provides such a stage. The citizens in Soyinka's, Achebe's, and Labou Tansi's fictive states are willing to die or even to kill for states that have no existence outside the novel. This runs contrary to most thinking about nationalism: Paul Kahn explains that no one is willing to sacrifice their life for universal law or the United Nations; citizens are only willing to die for the state imagined as unique and particular: "The state embodies the universal character of law within the borders of a very particular historical project. It understands itself as sovereign not by measuring itself against an abstract, universal standard but by standing within a particular history and at a particular place. Sovereignty literally creates a rent within the universal that is beyond repair."[21]

The sacrifice of citizens is precisely what makes borders sacred. But the sacrifice of characters for fictive states is not to assert borders – in the fictive state these never matter – but rather to resist those who wield state power. This reflects an important truth about the African state: its enemies are not neighbour states; it carries its enemies within.

As we have seen, realist novels, whether in Europe or Africa, train their narrative focus on the level of the ordinary citizen-subject, several levels below the rulers who are represented only by the state's agents: civil servants, policemen, and court judges. The second generation of African novels, however, increasingly raised their focus to include the sphere of political rulers, who had not until then figured in fiction. The narrative in *Le devoir de violence* moves freely upwards to include the level of those directly wielding power, including African emperors and French governors, the rulers who rarely feature in European fiction and perhaps cannot. Soon government ministers themselves came to have stories, as in Aluko's *Chief the Honourable Minister*, Sembène's *Xala* and *Le dernier de l'empire*, and Achebe's *Anthills of the Savannah*. Soyinka's drama became more and more concerned with presidents: *From Zia with Love*, *A Play of Giants*, and *King Baabu*. French African literature produced a new mode without European precedent (but with Latin American precursors[22]), the dictator novel: Ouologuem's *Le devoir de violence*, Cheikh Alou Ndao's *Mbaam dictateur*, Sony Labou Tansi's *La vie et demie*, and Amadou Kourouma's *En attendant le vote des bêtes sauvages*. Ngũgĩ's *Wizard of the Crow* is a late example from Kenya.

African political allegories are set in a state of exception, before or outside the law, in a way that Western novels are not. They are thus also able to consider an aspect of power that Western novels tend to ignore: the way that a person inhabits power and is in turn inhabited by power. Charisma, rivalry, contentious succession, and the violence of power are all known in Western societies, of course, but they cannot be treated easily in the novel, which by and large presumes that the social centre is restrained by the law.

The possibility after 1966 of the fictive state in African literature is not just a change in literary convention but a change in what it is possible to think. This book, however, has insisted that the change to a more allegorical mode in African literature retrospectively reveals how much the earlier generation of novels, those written around the time of independence, had already been obsessed with the state and political first principles. In hindsight, with the example of later African fiction in mind, we can see that *Things Fall Apart* was already a political parable about the original or minimum conditions of state organization. If the radical novelty of African novels after 1966 is the state that resembles in every significant way the author's own but is called something else, I note that, already in *Things Fall Apart*, the basic unit of political organization, the village group of Umuofia, is fictive.

In the last decade of the twentieth century and the first of the twenty-first, many African states, reeling after dictatorships, coups, and civil wars, have instituted sovereign national assemblies to determine new foundations. These may feel like merely the latest example of the eternal transition from Prerogative State to Normative State whose first iteration was decolonization, but it is also possible that something has changed. In literature it certainly has. Many, perhaps most of the novels produced by Nigerians today are realist in mode: most famously those by Ngozi Chimamanda Adichie, but also those by Sefi Atta, Adaobi Tricia Nwaubani, Ayobami Adebayo, Jowhor Ile, Chika Unigwe, Abubakar Adam Ibrahim, Jude Dibia, Unoma Azuah, and Chinelo Okparanta.

The most recent generation of Nigerian novelists, although (or perhaps because) they have been educated and often live overseas, emphasize not just that they are Achebe's heirs, but that they share his realist idealism about the readability of characters. A common trope makes the experience of reading *Things Fall Apart*, most often as a set text in school, an event in the lives of countless characters in novels, films, and memoirs from across Africa.[23] In the later literary and cinematic imagination, Nigeria was not just shaped by but always *includes* Achebe's novel. Adichie's *Purple Hibiscus* begins, "Things started to fall apart at home"; and her short story "The Headstrong Historian" is an explicit rewriting of Achebe's novel from the perspective of a granddaughter of one of the characters. The implication is that Adichie and her fellow Nigerian novelists recognize the world they live in as the same one Achebe wrote about at an earlier moment. They too are invested in the ideal of the state.

One explanation for the resurgence of realism has surely to do with the number of African writers who have studied or lived in Britain or America, but it may also have to do with a new consensus regarding the inevitability of the state and of the desirability of a state ideal. It may be not that the Nigerian state is more secure or accepted by its citizens, but rather that the state ideal is more taken for granted by writers. The new wave of realist writers, led by Adichie, who comes closest to the reputation and status of Achebe and Soyinka, write with an apparent faith that, if only the world can be described in would-be impartial and objective terms, then, just possibly, the ideal state will be affirmed among citizen-readers, even if the corruption complex remains as, well, complex as ever. There remains something utopian about realism.

Achebe felt that, in contributing to a literary tradition, he was fulfilling a great duty, needed by the state, and he wrote in the first instance for his fellow citizens. Contemporary Nigerian literature is more extroverted than the first generation was and is now often published in the United States. Nigerian realism was always cosmopolitan, but there are new cosmopolitanisms with which the nation-state is in competition. Nevertheless, the state is not only still with us; it is impossible to imagine it disappearing. For that reason, we can expect realist novels to continue to be written and to be read. This book is written in the faith that authors wrestling with genre and tradition are capable of generating insights into the world that are worth the closest of attention. The founders of the Nigerian literary tradition are still worth reading for what they can teach citizen-subjects of states everywhere.

Notes

INTRODUCTION

1 Gikandi, "Chinua Achebe."
2 Appiah, *In My Father's House*, 150.
3 Appiah, "Cosmopolitan Patriots," 27–8.
4 Ofeimun, "Taking Nigeria Seriously (II)."
5 See Ermarth, *Realism and Consensus*.
6 Korang, "Making a Post-Eurocentric Humanity," 8.
7 My discussion of realism is in line with Ato Quayson's in "Realism, Criticism, and the Disguises of Both" when he critiques realism's supposed capacity for mimesis and emphasizes instead its production of a world through rhetorical processes of metonymy and metaphor, and its inherent self-subversion.
8 Gallagher, "The Rise of Fictionality."
9 Li, *Dear Friend*, 107.
10 Benedict Anderson in *Imagined Communities* emphasizes the imagined community the novel creates among readers whose careers follow a similar trajectory defined by a state capital and state borders. He, however, is discussing the nation, a shared identity, whereas I emphasize the state: a collection of institutions and a shared ideology.
11 "Extroversion" is Eileen Julien's term: see *African Novels and the Question of Orality*.
12 Newell, *West African Literatures*; Huggan, *The Postcolonial Exotic*.
13 Culler, "Anderson and the Novel," 29–30.
14 Hansen and Stepputat, "Introduction," 10.
15 Ibid., 17.
16 Abélès, *Anthropologie de l'État*, 82. My translation.

17 Abrams, "Notes on the Difficulty of Studying the State," 58.
18 Bourdieu, "Rethinking the State," 53.
19 Baucom, *Specters of the Atlantic*, 93.
20 Andrade, *The Nation Writ Small.*
21 Morrison, *Chinua Achebe*, 92.
22 Gikandi, *Reading Chinua Achebe.*
23 The one exception is Ethiopia, a feudal empire that avoided colonization through force of arms but also by mirroring the trappings of modern statehood – written law, central administration – which meant that the European powers were unable to justify an invasion. Ethiopia was invaded by Fascists in the 1930s, as were many nations in Europe soon after, but that invasion was short-lived. Until the nineteenth century, there were only two African colonies: the Cape Colony and Sierra Leone. Britain and Portugal had had imperial possessions in Africa since the sixteenth century, but these were trading posts rather than colonies organized as states.
24 In North Africa, Egypt became independent in 1922, Libya in 1951, and Morocco, Tunisia, and Sudan in 1956. The rapid dismantling of the European empires in West Africa began with Ghana's independence in 1957 and reached a precipitous apogee in 1960.
25 Benedict Anderson uses the examples of Spanish America and the Philippines to argue that nationalism, the ideology that calls upon individuals to identify with the state, originated in colonial territories.
26 The handful of new states that corresponded in some measure to precolonial kingdoms – Lesotho, Botswana, Swaziland, Rwanda, Burundi – are the smallest of the African states and landlocked. Also, they had been colonies or colonial protectorates – the indispensable condition for being awarded independence.
27 Chabal, *Power in Africa*, 76.
28 Cooper, *Africa in the World*; Wilder, *Freedom Time*.
29 Young, *Postcolonial State in Africa*, 301.
30 Liberation wars were fought in the Portuguese colonies, including Guinea-Bissau in West Africa, and in the white settler colonies of Kenya, Rhodesia, and South Africa.
31 Azikiwe, *Meditations: A Collection of Poems*.
32 Conrad, *Heart of Darkness*, 10.
33 Mamdani, *Define and Rule*, 20.
34 Qtd. in Baxter, *Imagined States*, 4.
35 Tutuola, *The Witch-Herbalist of the Remote Town*, 12.
36 Oppenheimer, *The State*, 8.
37 Foucault, "*Society Must Be Defended*," 124.

38 Nietzsche, *Genealogy of Morals*, 72.
39 See Thornton, *Africa and Africans*.
40 Manning, *Slavery and African Life*, 132.
41 Horton, "Stateless Societies," 78.
42 Hawthorne qtd. by Klein, "The Slave Trade and Decentralized Societies," 52.
43 Horton, 87.
44 McIntosh, "Pathways to Complexity," 7.
45 Manning, 132.
46 Lonsdale, "States and Social Processes in Africa," 139.
47 Horton, 80.
48 The great exception is the Dutch Republic.
49 Downes, *Democracy, Revolution, and Monarchism*.
50 See David Brion Davis, *Inhuman Bondage*.
51 In Britain's case, also in Canada and Australia.
52 Arendt, *Origins of Totalitarianism*, 126.
53 Ibid., 153.
54 Lefort, *The Political Forms of Modern Society*, 254.
55 Arendt, 230.
56 Santner, *Royal Remains*, 36.
57 Qtd. in Warner, *Letters of the Republic*, 73. Italics in the original.
58 Ibid., 101.
59 Fraenkel, *The Dual State*, xiii.
60 Qtd. in Meierhenrich, *The Legacies of Law*, 76.
61 Warner, 112.
62 Sitze, *The Impossible Machine*, 5.
63 Ibid., 68.
64 Chatterjee, *Lineages of Political Society*, 337.
65 Sitze, 92.
66 Qtd. in Young, 327.
67 Thompson, *Whigs and Hunters*, 263.
68 Dyzenhaus, *Hard Cases*, 289.
69 Ibid., 289.
70 Ibid., 249.
71 Dyzenhaus, "'The Organic Law,'" 55.
72 Tilly, *Coercion, Capital, and the European State*.
73 Herbst, *States and Power in Africa*, 113.
74 Ibid., 113.
75 Qtd. in ibid., 114.
76 Ibid., 96.

77 Chabal, *Power in Africa*, 102.

78 Ibid., 108.

79 The great exception among weak African states is, of course, South Africa. But see Breckenridge, *The Biometric State*.

80 A common distinction has it that the British ruled by Indirect Rule whereas the French favoured assimilation, creating an elite of évolués with a French education. The French, however, were no stronger than the British and required their own policy of indirect rule, which they called "*association*."

81 Ekeh, "Concept of Second Liberation," 91.

82 Guyer, "Representation without Taxation."

83 Ekeh, "Colonialism and the Two Publics in Africa," 102.

84 The term "mistake of 1914" was coined by Ahmadu Bello, the Sardauna of Sokoto (Ajayi, "The Anti-Colonial Struggle in Nigeria," 97).

85 E. Weber, *Peasants into Frenchmen*.

86 Fanon, *Wretched of the Earth*, 74.

87 Ibid., 73.

88 Herbst, 110.

89 Ibid., 98.

90 Kelly and Kaplan, "Nation and Decolonization," 183.

91 Herbst, 106.

92 Owomoyela, *The Columbia Guide to West African Literature*, 33.

93 Nwakanma, "Metonymic Eruptions."

94 Occupying the position of founder in East African literature in English that Achebe does in West Africa is Ngũgĩ wa Thiong'o, whose people, the Gikuyu, were also a stateless people.

CHAPTER ONE

1 Ezenwa-Ohaeto, *Chinua Achebe*, 63.

2 Ochiagha, *A Short History*, 51.

3 Newell, *West African Literatures*, 98.

4 I am speaking of the Liberian Joseph Jeffrey Walters, who wrote *Guanya Pau* in 1897; and of J.E. Casely Hayford, who wrote *Ethiopia Unbound* in 1911, and R.E. Obeng, who wrote *Eighteenpence* in 1943. Both the latter were from what was then called the Gold Coast.

5 Bernhard Siegert argues that literature itself is an epoch of the postal system, meaning that both are institutions presuming equality of access and that both are based on trust in the system's neutral workings.

6 The publisher James Currey discusses the "mythology" of *Things Fall Apart* in *Africa Writes Back*, 28–30.
7 Isin, "Theorizing Acts of Citizenship."
8 Graeber, *Debt*, 324.
9 There is no satisfactory synonym for the term "village group": Umuofia, made up of nine villages, is sometimes called a "clan" (122, a translation of *Umunna*) and sometimes an *obodo* (121, usually translated as "town"), but each of those terms can mean something quite different: a "clan" is the descendants of a common ancestor; a "town" inappropriately suggests something urban.
10 Mauss, *The Gift*.
11 Gregory, *Gifts and Commodities*, 12.
12 Hénaff, *The Price of Truth*, 144.
13 Gillespie, "On Debt," 63.
14 Qtd. in Hyden, *African Politics*, 48.
15 Godbout, *Ce qui circule*, ch. 3.
16 In Munonye's *Bridge to a Wedding* a character explains that generosity in lending money only "brings the donor into the recipient's power, for he needs to keep up his prestige as a good samaritan, failing which he might become unpopular – in fact more unpopular than he perhaps would have been had he not embarked upon the kindly act" (116).
17 Nietzsche, *Genealogy of Morals*, 55.
18 Ibid., 45.
19 Ibid., 43.
20 Ibid., 45.
21 Flannery and Marcus, *The Creation of Inequality*.
22 Ibid., 121.
23 Ibid., 121.
24 Gikandi, "African Literature," 3.
25 Guyer, *Marginal Gains*, 16.
26 In his monograph on Achebe, Gikandi does note that "wealth is not only the mark of dominance and presence in this culture, it is a precondition for self-engenderment and subjectivity" (*Reading Achebe*, 36).
27 Falola, "Money and Informal Credit Institutions," 166.
28 Ibid., 166.
29 Barber, "Money, Self-Realization and the Person," 207.
30 Ibid., 207.
31 Ibid., 207.
32 Ibid., 208.

33 Guyer, *Marginal Gains*, 78.
34 Ibid., 74.
35 Ibid., 69.
36 All quotations from this novel are from the second edition unless explicitly identified as from the first.
37 A key incident in *Things Fall Apart*, the killing of an Englishman on a bicycle, is based on a historical event that took place in Mbaise in 1905. However, at the end of the novel it is made explicit that Britain is ruled by a queen, something that would not have been true after 1901.
38 Igboland was one corner of Africa where population was abundant and land was not (Nwokeji, *The Slave Trade and Culture*, 24), but in *Things Fall Apart*, there appears to be still enough land that anyone who wants to can farm.
39 Guyer, 70.
40 Barber, 213.
41 Sahlins, *Stone Age Economics*, 85.
42 Ibid., 122.
43 Qtd. in Blumberg, *Victorian Sacrifice*, 181–2.
44 Godbout, *World of the Gift*, 137.
45 Guyer, 70.
46 Chabal, *Power in Africa*, 104.
47 Ibid., 105.
48 Wehrs, *Pre-Colonial Africa*, 138.
49 Ogo Nwokeji writes that Nri-Awka, the area of Achebe's home Ogidi, was organized around a "'personality cult,' a phenomenon that combined strong character, drive, entrepreneurship and big ego in a 'big man'" (*The Slave Trade and Culture*, 190).
50 Flannery and Marcus, 95.
51 Guyer, "Wealth in People," 256.
52 Ibid., 256.
53 Sahlins, 106.
54 Falola, "Money," 166.
55 Ibid., 166.
56 Parry, "*The Gift*," 465–6.
57 N.A. Fadipe quoted by Falola, "My Friend," 407.
58 Guyer, "Wealth in People," 253.
59 Amadi, *The Slave*, 82.
60 Ibid., 82.
61 Bataille, *Accursed Share*, 87.

62 Most critics of Achebe argue that he is rewriting Conrad's *Heart of Darkness* and Joyce Cary's *Mister Johnson*. While that is true, the rewriting of Leonard is far more explicit.
63 Leonard, *The Lower Niger*, 260.
64 Ibid., 259–60.
65 Ibid., 260.
66 Ibid., 261.
67 Kwaku Larbi Korang makes the argument that Achebe turns to realism in order to counter the misrepresentation of Africa in Conrad's *Heart of Darkness*. Achebe suggests that cultural differences can "address themselves intelligibly to each other" through "a humanist 'interlanguage,'" which is realism ("Making a Post-Eurocentric Humanity," 7).
68 Gallagher, "The Rise of Fictionality," 342.
69 Ibid., 342.
70 Smith, Brown, and Okonkwo are more ordinary than monikers in fiction usually are and thus lean more toward the typical than the individual. Names such as Obierika or Ikemefuna, ordinary but not *too* ordinary, are more usual for fictional characters.
71 Poovey, *Genres of the Credit Economy*, 116.
72 Ibid., 116.
73 Armstrong, *How Novels Think*, 8.
74 Ibid., 4.
75 Ibid., 8. Armstrong is speaking of Victorian novels but explicitly suggests that they set the pattern that all novels everywhere follow.
76 M.M. Bakhtin. "The *Bildungsroman* and Its Significance."
77 Lukács, *Studies in European Realism*, 55.
78 Poovey, "Demonizing," 41.
79 Lewinnek, "'I Consider It Un-American," 27.
80 Poovey, "Demonizing," 39–40.
81 Poovey, *Genres of the Credit Economy*, 91.
82 Ibid., 113.
83 The first five chapters of Franklin's autobiography were written in 1771, to which he added others in 1784–5 and 1788.
84 Baker, *Securing the Commonwealth*, 70.
85 Moodie, ch. 5.
86 Rider Haggard's *Nada the Lily* and Sol Plaatje's *Mhudi* concern Zulu and Tswana chieftaincies and their subjects in the nineteenth century, before Achebe's Okonkwo.

CHAPTER TWO

1 Godbout, *World of the Gift*, 15.
2 Graeber, *Debt*, 133.
3 Meek, *Law and Authority*, 233.
4 Sahlins, *Stone Age Economics*, 205.
5 Nwokolo, *Diaries of a Dead African*, "Meme's Diary: 5th June 2000."
6 Godbout, 104.
7 Achebe, *Arrow of God*, 265.
8 Obeng, *Eighteenpence*, 54.
9 Nwapa, *Efuru*, 191. Efuru's own dowry, for her second marriage, is twelve pounds ten shillings (135).
10 Ekwensi, *Jagua Nana*, 167.
11 Piot, "Of Persons and Things," 406.
12 Chabal, *Power in Africa*, 106.
13 Meek, 242–3.
14 David Borman, in "Playful Ethnography," shows that Achebe takes Meek as a model for his own ethnography in the novel.
15 Carroll, *Chinua Achebe*, 41.
16 Ibid., 41.
17 Anspach, À charge de revanche, 9–11.
18 Hénaff, *The Price of Truth*, 225.
19 Anspach, 12.
20 Barkun, *Law without Sanctions*, 16.
21 Ibid., 109.
22 Sahlins, 156.
23 Ibid., 159.
24 Anspach, 19.
25 Rospabé, *La dette de vie*, 34.
26 Ibid., 31.
27 Abélès, *Anthropologie de l'État*, 44, my translation.
28 Qtd. in Sahlins, *Stone Age Economics*, 166.
29 Meek, 242.
30 Ibid., 242.
31 Barkun, 21.
32 Isichei, *History of the Igbo People*, 79.
33 Meek, 234.
34 Sahlins, 162.
35 Ibid., 153.
36 Ibid., 156.

37 Ibid., 154.
38 Ibid., 154.
39 Abélès, 44, my translation.
40 Qtd. in Godbout, *Ce qui circule,* ch. 10; my translation.
41 Abélès, 30.
42 Ibid., 45, my translation.
43 Wise, "Excavating the New Republic."
44 Rowell, "An Interview with Chinua Achebe," 76–7.
45 Arendt, *On Revolution*, 33.
46 Ibid., 31.
47 J. Dunn, *Democracy: A History*, 63.
48 Munonye, *Bridge to a Wedding*, 93.
49 Arendt, 255.
50 Dunn, 178.
51 Ryan, *On Politics*, 108.
52 This makes Umuofia considerably larger than the average Igbo village group, which, when Achebe was writing, numbered up to ten thousand people (not just adult men) (Harneit-Sievers, *Constructions of Belonging*, 30).
53 Arendt, 30.
54 Ibid., 31.
55 Lévi-Strauss, *Elementary Structures*, 496.
56 Graeber, 158.
57 Ibid., 133.
58 Patterson, *Slavery and Social Death.*
59 Graeber, 168.
60 Nwokeji, *The Slave Trade and Culture*, 118.
61 Ibid., 196–7, Ohadike, "The Decline of Slavery," 443.
62 Nwokeji, 119.
63 Rospabé, 107.
64 Munonye, *Bridge to a Wedding*, 28.
65 Rospabé, 107.
66 Nietzsche, *Genealogy of Morals*, 56.
67 Isichei, 113. In *Things Fall Apart* the massacre of Abame occurs in the second year of Okonkwo's seven-year exile in Mbanta, which means it is several years before Okonkwo's death, itself sometime around 1900.
68 Falola, *Colonialism and Violence*, 26.
69 Ibid., 31.
70 Mahmood Mamdani argues that only a thirst for revenge can explain the disproportionate violence of Kitchener's conquest of Mahdist Sudan (*Define and Rule*, 70).

71 The 1901–2 expedition against the Arochukwu included seventy-four Europeans and 3,464 African carriers and soldiers (Falola, *Colonialism and Violence*, 21). Jago Morrison argues that by eliding this large military campaign, Achebe misleadingly suggests the untouched nature of Umuofia, given that Igbos and Europeans had been interacting for centuries (*Chinua Achebe*, 77–8).
72 Robert Wren shows that "the white man could not rule these independent stateless societies save by terror" (*Achebe's World*, 28).
73 Cooper, *Colonialism in Question*, 157.
74 Hussain, *The Jurisprudence of Emergency*, 129. Italics in the original.
75 The number of Europeans who died in the conquest of Nigeria has been put at around twenty (Falola, *Colonialism and Violence*, 21).
76 Nietzsche, 61.
77 Sifton, *Violence All Around*, 255.
78 Locke, *Two Treatises*, 19.
79 Ibid., 19.
80 Ibid., 118.
81 Cover, *Narrative, Violence, and the Law*, 155.
82 Balibar, *Violence and Civility*, 32.
83 Adéẹ̀kọ́, "Okonkwo, Textual Closure, Colonial Conquest," 82.
84 Derrida, "Force de Loi," 941, 943.
85 Ibid., 991.
86 Ibid., 991.
87 Foucault, "*Society Must be Defended*," 100.
88 Ibid., 96.
89 Hobbes, *Leviathan*, 205.
90 Foucault, 95.
91 Abélès, 52; my translation.

CHAPTER THREE

1 Wren, *Achebe's World*, 16.
2 Johnson, *History of the Yorubas*, 29.
3 Žižek, *Enjoy Your Symptom!*, 56 (italics in original).
4 Caillé, *Anthropologie du don*, 175.
5 Hobbes, *Leviathan*, 176.
6 Kahn, *Sacred Violence*, 132.
7 Nzegwu, *Family Matters*, 12.
8 Ibid., 17. Ifi Amadiume makes the same argument about Igbo society in her influential study *Male Daughters, Female Husbands*.

9 Nzegwu, 17.
10 Ibid., 100.
11 Ibid., 100.
12 Kahn, 132.
13 Jay, *Throughout Your Generations*, 150.
14 Meillassoux, *Maidens, Meal and Money*, 41–2.
15 Ibid., 47.
16 Ibid., 17.
17 Ibid., 48.
18 Ibid., 48.
19 Abélès, *Anthropologie de l'État*, 75; my translation.
20 Hobbes, *Leviathan*, 175.
21 Harneit-Sievers, *Constructions of Belonging*, 40.
22 Cott, "Chinua Achebe," 77–8.
23 Abélès, 52; my translation.
24 Munonye, *Bridge*, 93.
25 Ibid., 102.
26 Hobbes, 196.
27 Chabal, *Africa*, 95.
28 Harneit-Sievers, 89.
29 Ibid., 173.
30 Ibid., 173.
31 Ibid., 174.
32 Ibid., 181. The great historian of the warrant chief system, A.E. Afigbo, was chair of a committee that in 1976 recommended the restoration of a system of traditional rulers in Igboland (ibid., 175)!
33 Franklin, *Autobiography*, 60.
34 Balzac, *César Birotteau*, 5226, my translation.
35 Ibid., 5121.
36 Ibid., 5340.
37 Graeber, *Debt*, 69.
38 Obeng, *Eighteenpence*. All citations are from this edition.
39 Newell, *Literary Culture in Colonial Ghana*, 185. The previous Gold Coast novels are *Marita, or the Folly of Love* by A. Native, serialized in a Gold Coast newspaper starting in 1886, and J.E. Casely Hayford's *Ethiopia Unbound* in 1911.
40 S.K. Okleme notes that the rags-to-riches theme found in *Eighteenpence* "usually occurs whenever the novel appears for the first time," for example, Defoe's *Moll Flanders* ("R.E. Obeng's *Eighteenpence*," 106).
41 Newell, 190.

42 Equiano, *Interesting Narrative*, 136.
43 Austin, "Human Pawning in Asante," 189.
44 Ohadike, "The Decline of Slavery," 446.
45 Qtd. in ibid., 447.
46 For instance, the practice of *sati* or wife-burning failed the repugnancy test in India.
47 Phillips, *The Enigma of Colonialism*, 29.
48 Ibid., 43.
49 Ohadike, 448.
50 This paradox that colonialism opposed slavery yet resembled slavery is the subject of Taiwo Adetunji Osinubi's "Chinua Achebe and the Uptakes of African Slaveries."
51 Kirk-Greene, "'Le roi est mort!,'" 23.
52 Ekeh, "Concept of Second Liberation," 90.
53 Phillips, *The Enigma of Colonialism*, 50.
54 Ibid., 72.
55 Ibid., 2.
56 Coleman, *Nigeria*, 436n10.
57 Ibid., 68.
58 Hyden, *African Politics*, 142.
59 When the Asantehene of Ashanti was deposed by the British in 1883 he buried his gold, which was recovered by his lieutenants (McCaskie, "Wealth and Belief," 6).
60 Two hundred cowries, Unoka's debt, was a standard unit of currency, called a "bunch" – five strings of forty cowries each (Hogendorn and Johnson, *Shell Money*, 121). Around 1900 in Igboland, two hundred cowries would have been worth less than two pence (ibid., 140). We can appreciate the small size of this sum if we consider that the dowry paid for an eligible bride in *Things Fall Apart* is twenty bags of cowries, with each bag containing 20,000 shells (ibid., 115) – that is, a hundred times Unoka's debt. There are indications that devaluation has halved the value of the cowrie by the Palm-Wine Drinkard's time so that £1 would have been 240 times Unoka's debt.
61 Achebe, "Work and Play," 73.
62 Ibid., 73.
63 Ibid., 75.
64 Ibid., 68.
65 Ibid., 73.
66 Ibid., 68.

67 Korang writes that Achebe the realist solicits "his readership to be humanist critics, passing negative judgment against the 'quality of persons' whose ideology, belief, and practice – as characterological indices of a certain 'quality of life' – fall short of an affirmation of human community and communality" ("Making a Post-Eurocentric Humanity," 10).
68 Bryce, "Evading Canonical Constraints," 393.
69 Ekechi, "Igbo Response," 178.
70 Ibid., 178.
71 Ofonagoro, "From Traditional to British Currency," 626. Meek explains that "if an unmarried man pledges himself in return for a sum of money or even for a wife, he must live with and work for his creditor-master every day in the week, the master providing him with food" (*Law and Authority*, 205). He can "redeem himself by repaying the loan, plus 50 per cent" (205).
72 Ekechi, "Igbo Response," 171.
73 Ibid., 169.
74 Ibid., 172.
75 Graeber, 82.
76 Hobbes, 141.

CHAPTER FOUR

1 Unoka's flute-playing is something he has in common with Tortoise, the hero of folk tales, and with the eponymous trickster hero of Nkem Nwankwo's novel *Danda*.
2 Nwakanma, "Metonymic Eruptions," 6.
3 Qtd. in Poovey, *Genres of the Credit Economy*, 189.
4 See Stratton, Andrade, and Morrison, among many others.
5 Chabal, *Power in Africa*, 100.
6 Ibid., 113.
7 Onwueme, "Shifting Paradigms," 292.
8 Barber, "Money, Self-Realization, and the Person," 207.
9 Gikandi, "African Literature and Modernity," 3.
10 Graeber, *Debt*, 29–33.
11 Ofonagoro, "From Traditional to British Currency," 637. Barter is more likely to be a contemporary phenomenon than a historical one, as Third World states, lacking dollars with which to trade abroad, exchange commodities. Nigeria, for instance, has sent oil to Brazil in exchange for manufactured goods (Hart, "Heads or Tails?" 641).

12 Manning, *Slavery and African Life*, 101.
13 Naanen, "Economy within an Economy," 426–7.
14 Manillas feature in Amadi's precolonial trilogy: *The Concubine*, *The Great Ponds*, and *The Slave*, set in an area to the south of Umuofia.
15 Manning, 101.
16 Ibid., 101.
17 Ekejiuba, "Currency Instability," 142. As late as 1944 the Nigerian Legislative Council was concerned that British coinage was not circulating in the country in spite of the efforts of the banks and the West African Currency Board (Ofonagoro, "From Traditional to British Currency," 624), and cowries were still occasionally being used for the smallest transactions in Lagos in 1950 (ibid., 650).
18 Ibid., 634.
19 Northrup, *Trade without Rulers*, 152.
20 Ibid., 152.
21 Ibid., 155.
22 Harneit-Sievers, *Constructions of Belonging*, 70.
23 Northrup, 97–8.
24 Hogendorn and Johnson, *Shell Money of the Slave Trade*, 150.
25 Ibid., 140. R.E. Obeng confirms that the rate in the Gold Coast at the turn of the century was also 35 cowries to the farthing (1/4 pence), or 1,680 cowries to the shilling (xxiii). By the time of Tutuola's Palm-Wine Drinkard, however, devaluation has halved the value, and two thousand cowries are equivalent to 6 pence (86).
26 Because the value of cowries is in direct proportion to their weight, in certain circumstances and for limited terms, when dealing with large values, cowries must themselves be represented. In *Things Fall Apart*, when negotiating his daughter's bride price, Obierika gives the suitors thirty short broomsticks and they return fifteen to him. At the end of these negotiations, the value of the bride price is established at twenty bags of cowries, which are later brought to Obierika on the heads of twenty young men (73). A "bag" of cowries weighed about 50 pounds depending on the kind of cowrie (Hogendorn and Johnson, 117). Unlike cowries, however, broomsticks are not negotiable and can only be redeemed for cowries by the one person to whom they are assigned and in the appropriate context.
27 Hogendorn and Johnson, 128.
28 Herbst, *States and Power in Africa*, 53.
29 Hogendorn and Johnson, *Shell Money of the Slave Trade*, 147.

30 Naanen, "Economy within an Economy," 427.
31 France used its own franc in its African colonies until after the Second World War.
32 Hopkins, "Creation of a Colonial Monetary System," 128.
33 Munonye, *Bridge to a Wedding*, 58.
34 Coleman, *Nigeria,* 85.
35 Chabal, *Power in Africa*, 136.
36 To understand the difference consider the following point made by Jane Guyer: in the 1990s, Western currencies circulated at such a rate that "the equivalent of the entire U.S. money issue passes through financial monitoring and transaction every day," whereas in Nigeria, by contrast, "at least 60 percent of the currency, once issued, *never goes back through the banking system again*" (*Marginal Gains*, 3; her italics).
37 Chabal, *Africa*, 112.
38 Carroll, *Chinua Achebe*, 42.
39 Godbout, *Ce qui circule*, ch. 14; my translation.
40 Hyde, *Trickster Makes This World*, 268.
41 In Okey Ndibe's novel *Foreign Gods Inc.*, a corrupt chief is called "*onu na elili ora*, 'the mouth that eats for the community'" (235).
42 Abélès, *Anthropologie de l'État*, 101; my translation.
43 For a discussion of the Andersen story that draws exactly opposite conclusions about sovereignty to mine see Paul Downes's *Hobbes, Sovereignty, and Early American Literature*.
44 Thomas Jay Lynn points out the parallels between Tortoise in the story of the birds and the District Commissioner (*Chinua Achebe*, 49). He does not, however, comment on the strangeness of the fact that a traditional story should foreshadow the behaviour of the British. Others have also read Ekwefi's story allegorically: e.g. Priebe, Nnolim, and Harlow.
45 Pierce, *State Formation*, 3–4n5.
46 Newell, *The Power to Name.*
47 Azikiwe, *My Odyssey*, 272.
48 Ibid., 372.
49 Ibid., 328.
50 Ibid., 333.
51 Agamben, *Kingdom and the Glory.*
52 Aluko, *One Man, One Matchet*, 187.
53 Ibid., 159.
54 Ibid., 187–8.

CHAPTER FIVE

1 Andrade, *The Nation Writ Small*, 59.
2 Nwapa, *Efuru*. All citations are from this edition.
3 Mair, *New Nations*, 57.
4 Gikandi, "African Literature and Modernity," 4.
5 Mair, 33.
6 Gregory, *Gifts and Commodities*, 12.
7 Godbout, *Ce qui circule*, ch. 7; my translation.
8 Guyer, "Wealth in People," 259.
9 Nietzsche, *Genealogy of Morals*, 55.
10 Munonye, *Obi*, 64–5.
11 Roitman, "Unsanctioned Wealth," 222.
12 Ibid., 215n5.
13 C.K. Meek writes of Igbos around 1930 that "the normal interest chargeable on a loan was 100 per cent. per annum, at compound interest, and loans at this annual rate were known as *omunruwa afọ*. But loans (for trading purposes) might be arranged for short periods, e.g. one week (8 days), three weeks (24 days), or on the basis of a commission for each market attended by the borrower. This system was known as *omunruwa ego-ezoahia*" (*Law and Authority*, 234).
14 Andrade, 60.
15 Johnson, *History of the Yorubas*, 131.
16 Graeber, *Debt*, 213.
17 The novel's spelling of Onitsha.
18 Nunn and Wantchekon. "The Slave Trade," 3222.
19 Ibid., 3221.
20 E.g., Bilakila, "The Kinshasa Bargain."
21 Pierce, *State Formation*, 4.
22 Munonye, *Bridge to a Wedding*, 19.
23 Blundo, "La corruption," 16.
24 Nwapa, "Priestesses and Power," 415
25 Andrade draws attention to the parallels between Nwapa's and Ekwensi's novels: *The Nation Writ Small*, 56.
26 Ekwensi, *Jagua Nana*, 192.
27 Mair, *New Nations*, 33.
28 Belasco, *Entrepreneur as Culture-Hero*, 32.
29 Qtd. in Guyer, *Marginal Gains*, 96–8.
30 Bryce, "Evading Canonical Constraints," 405.
31 Ibid., 405.

32 Andrade, 60.
33 Ellickson, *Order without Law*, 232.
34 Munonye, *Bridge to a Wedding*, 85.

CHAPTER SIX

1 The present of the narration is two years after 1919 (109), but it is mid-February, so it could be either 1921 or 1922.
2 Meek reports of the Igbo that "Every warrior endeavoured to obtain the head of an enemy" (*Law and Authority*, 243).
3 Aluko, *One Man, One Matchet*, 112.
4 Herbst, *States and Power in Africa*, 15.
5 Nwokeji, *The Slave Trade and Culture*, 189.
6 Brown, *Utopian Generations*, 114.
7 Horton, "Stateless Societies," 94.
8 Ibid., 94.
9 See Tilly, *Coercion*. Franz Oppenheimer, however, argues that land scarcity even in Europe has never been such as to force people off the land and that to use land scarcity to explain class differentiation is a "fairy tale" (*The State*, 5).
10 Hénaff, *The Price of Truth*, 221.
11 Ibid., 225.
12 Benjamin, "Critique of Violence," 59.
13 Verdier, "Le système vindicatoire," 24.
14 Kahn, *Sacred Violence*, 149.
15 Verdier, 14; my translation.
16 Without diacritical marks indicating tone it is unclear how close the two names are.
17 Barkun, *Law without Sanctions*.
18 Rousseau, *The Social Contract*, 68.
19 Moore, "Treating Law as Knowledge," 22.
20 Ibid., 15.
21 Ibid., 40.
22 Achebe, *There Was a Country*, 44.
23 Ibid., 43.
24 Pinker, *The Better Angels*; Diamond, *The World until Yesterday*.
25 Killingray, "The Maintenance of Law and Order," 415.
26 Ibid., 422.
27 Mbembe, *Sortir de la grande nuit*, 91; my translation.
28 Killingray, 413.

29 Comaroff and Comaroff, "Law and Disorder," 36.

30 Achebe takes the name of his District Officer from Thomas Winterbottom, a doctor who wrote an *Account of the Native Africans of Sierra Leone* at the end of the eighteenth century. Writing when Britain had just established its first colony in West Africa, the historical Winterbottom, an abolitionist, was remarkably less racist and less patronizing toward Africa and Africans than his twentieth-century fictional namesake is. Achebe's Winterbottom is much closer to Arthur Glyn Leonard, the colonial administrator who, as we have seen, wrote *The Lower Niger and Its Tribes* and was the model for the District Commissioner in *Things Fall Apart*. The fictional Winterbottom also speaks words taken directly from George Hazzledine's *The White Man in Nigeria*.

31 Britain and France might have gone to war in 1898 over the Fashoda incident, when the French, racing to extend their reach from west to east across Africa, were narrowly beaten by the British, who succeeded in extending their African empire south to north, more or less from Cape to Cairo.

32 Hobbes, *Leviathan*, 128.

33 Locke, *Two Treatises*, 13.

34 Ochiagha, *Achebe and Friends*.

35 Hobbes, 271.

36 In *Arrow of God* the white man on the bicycle whose killing sparked the Abame massacre is identified as Macdonald (108).

37 Harneit-Sievers, *Constructions of Belonging*, 57. R.F. Stevenson had first argued that Arochukwu represented an "emergent Ibo state" (qtd. in McIntosh, "Pathways to Complexity," 7). Northrup makes it clear that that the Aro never created a central authority.

38 Nwokeji, 53.

39 Like the nine villages of Umuofia, the six villages of Umuaro have always imagined that they are the descendants of a single ancestor, but kinship is no longer enough; a social contract is needed.

40 Osinubi, "Chinua Achebe and the Uptakes," 32.

41 Arendt, *On Revolution*, 169.

42 Ibid., 170.

43 Ibid., 170.

44 Ibid., 171.

45 Benton, *Law and Colonial Cultures*, 131.

46 Moore, 37.

47 Olaniyan, "Chinua Achebe and an Archeology," 24.

48 Warner, *The Letters of the Republic*, 76.

49 Achebe, "Foreword," viii.
50 Diagne, *Critique de la raison orale,* 213, my translation.
51 Tully, *Strange Multiplicity*, 115.
52 Moore, 33.
53 Fish, "Force," 522.

CHAPTER SEVEN

1 Coetzee, *Diary of a Bad Year*, 13. Coetzee puts some distance between himself and these opinions by making them the writings of one JC.
2 First edition, 235–9.
3 Ibid., 237.
4 Ibid., 239.
5 Mudimbe, *The Idea of Africa*, 192.
6 Beti, *Le roi miraculé*, 30, my translation.
7 Ibid., 31.
8 Tutuola, *Brave African Huntress,* 18.
9 Bourdieu, "Rethinking the State," 66.
10 "The Call" is lifted directly from "The call for men," a section in George Hazzledine's *The White Man in Nigeria* (1904).
11 The coin in question would have been issued between 1910, when George V acceded to the throne, and 1913, when British West African currency replaced English coins (Hopkins, "The Creation of a Colonial Monetary System," 128). Only the English coin identified itself as a florin; the West African coin that replaced it also bore the king's head but was labelled "two shillings." Sterling silver had almost completely disappeared from British West Africa by 1922 (ibid., 128), and the florin may have seemed appropriate for sacrifice to the gods because, as something from far away, out of the past, and rare, it had a significance beyond its denomination.
12 Walter Ofonagoro, writing about Nigeria, reports that "Africans accorded legal tender status only to coins bearing the image of the living monarch. A coin bearing the impression of a deceased monarch was never accepted as money, and was sometimes accepted with misgivings even for use as jewelry" ("From Traditional to British Currency," 645).
13 Pateman, *Sexual Contract*, 32.
14 Bivona, *British Imperial Literature,* 176. The classic statement of the distinction between European autonomy and African dependence is Octave Mannoni's *Prospero and Caliban*. In *Peau noire, masques blancs*, Frantz Fanon argued that "dependence" and "autonomy" were but psychological terms used to mask the force with which the colonial situation was imposed.

15 Freud, "The Ego and the Id," 34.
16 Kourouma, *En attendant le vote*, 205–6; my translation.
17 Mudimbe, 192.
18 Wren, *Achebe's World*, 124; George, "Achebe's *Arrow of God*," 356.
19 D.L. Miller, *Dreams of the Burning Child.*
20 Baucom, *Specters of the Atlantic*, 157.
21 Ekwefi in *Things Fall Apart* tells a similar story of a snake-lizard who kills his mother because he has given her "seven baskets of vegetables to cook and in the end there were only three" (83). He then cooks vegetables for himself and, when the same result is produced, commits suicide.
22 Mamdani, *Citizen and Subject.*
23 Jay, *Throughout Your Generations Forever*, 31.
24 Downes, *Democracy, Revolution, and Monarchism*, 178.
25 Coetzee, *Diary of a Bad Year*, 15.
26 Butler, *Psychic Life of Power*, 191.
27 Ibid., 191.
28 Ibid., 191–2.

CHAPTER EIGHT

1 In discussing *No Longer at Ease* after *Arrow of God*, that is, not in the order of their publication but in the order of the time when they are set, I am following the practice of Simon Gikandi in *Reading Chinua Achebe. Things Fall Apart* and *No Longer at Ease* were conceived as part of a trilogy, the second volume of which, the one dealing with Nwoye/Isaac Okonkwo, was never written. *Arrow of God* occupies the place in my book of the missing volume. The reordering allows me to contrast the depiction of war between village groups and the coming of British rule in Achebe's two village novels.
2 Lynch, *K.O. Mbadiwe*, 155.
3 Tignor, "Political Corruption," 175.
4 Ibid., 194.
5 Pierce, *State Formation*, 215.
6 Ibid., 12.
7 Ibid., 136.
8 Ibid., 18.
9 Nwakanma, *Christopher Okigbo*, 98.
10 Owen, "Positions of Security," 150.
11 Marie, "'Y a Pas l'Argent,'" 306, my translation.
12 Esposito, *Communitas*, 6.

13 Joseph, *Democracy and Prebendal Politics,* 67. Joseph is discussing the Second Republic and prebendalism along ethnic lines. What we have in *No Longer at Ease* involves groups much smaller than the ethnic group.
14 Owen, 150.
15 Esposito, 12.
16 Ibid., 13.
17 Godbout, *Ce cui circule,* chapter 1; my translation.
18 Sarthou-Lajus, qtd in Godbout, *Ce Qui Circule,* chapter 7; my translation.
19 Poovey, *Genres of the Credit Economy,* 400.
20 Sarthou-Lajus, *Éloge de la dette*, 7; my translation.
21 Simmel, *Philosophy of Money*, 297.
22 Beckett, "Legitimizing Democracy," 114.
23 Anderson, *Imagined Communities.*
24 Gregory, *Savage Money*, 166
25 Bersselaar, "Imagining Home," 62.
26 Nwokeji, *The Slave Trade and Culture,* 17.
27 Tilly, *Trust and Rule*, 13.
28 Gregory, 7–8.
29 Ibid., 166.
30 Pratten, "The Precariousness of Prebendalism," 252.
31 Gregory, 300.
32 Tilly, 8.
33 Bersselaar, 67.
34 Munonye, *Bridge to a Wedding,*132.
35 Ibid., 149.
36 Putnam, *Making Democracy Work,* 182–3.
37 Joseph, 68.
38 Ekeh, "Colonialism and the Two Publics," 100.
39 Olaniyan, "The Paddle," 52.
40 Locke, *Two Treatises,* 119.
41 Simmel, 299.
42 Hénaff, *The Price of Truth,* 153–4.
43 Sarthou-Lajus, 28, my translation.
44 Lazzarato, *The Making of the Indebted Man,* 77.
45 Nwakanma, 98.
46 In 1958 Nigerian federal employees earned on average £17.95 per month (Coleman, *Nigeria*, 95).
47 Guyer, *Marginal Gains*, 56.
48 Aluko, *One Man,* 40.

49 Rubenstein, *Public Works*, 59.
50 Caillé, *Anthropologie du don*, 30, my translation.
51 Tignor "Colonial Chiefs," 346.
52 Munonye, *Obi*, 84. Munonye has his numbers wrong: he likely means one hundred eighty ego (an ego is a group of six cowries). A "head" was two thousand cowries.
53 Ibid., 84–5.
54 Ibid., 85.
55 Guyer, "Representation," 54.
56 Robbins, *Upward Mobility*, 17.
57 Agamben, *The Kingdom and the Glory*, 66.
58 Herzfeld, *The Social Production of Indifference*.
59 Armah, *The Beautyful Ones*, 156.
60 Chabal, *Power in Africa*, 75.
61 Armah, 155.
62 Qtd. in Pierce, 200.
63 Darbon, ""Public Administration, State, and Society," 47.
64 Ibid., 48.
65 LeRoy, "Thirty Years of Legal Practice," 36.
66 Ekwensi, *Beautiful Feathers*, 78.
67 Achebe, *There Was a Country*, 43.
68 Ibid., 43.
69 Qtd. in Pierce, 201.
70 Pierce, 213.
71 Bivona, *British Imperial Literature*, 71.
72 Baxter, *Imagined States*, 31–2.
73 Bivona, 193.
74 Ibid., 198.
75 Bourdieu, "Rethinking the State," 72.
76 In Ekwensi's *Beautiful Feathers* an English civil servant is unfairly forced out by the policy of Nigerianization. His Nigerian lover laments, "I asked myself what is this stubborn, obstinate, implacable body of abstract creatures they call the government? I knew them as people, but when they come together it is a different thing. Whatever hath been written shall remain. They took a stand against him, and that was that. The God-men must be satisfied, so he had to go" (133).
77 Joseph, 78.

CHAPTER NINE

1 Leys, "What Is the Problem about Corruption?," 222n2.
2 Tignor, "Colonial Chiefs," 351.

3 Pierce, *State Formation*, 13.
4 Tignor, 352.
5 Harneit-Sievers, *Constructions of Belonging*, 166.
6 Munonye, *Bridge to a Wedding*, 125.
7 Scott, *Comparative Political Corruption*, 13.
8 Blundo and de Sardan, "The Popular Semiology of Corruption," 93.
9 Noonan, *Bribes*, 3.
10 Blundo, "Corruption in Africa," 34.
11 Caillé, *Anthropologie du don,* 84, my translation.
12 Simmel, *The Philosophy of Money*, 385.
13 Noonan, 697.
14 Laurent, "Sémantique populaire du détournement," 222.
15 Blundo, "La corruption," 16.
16 Laurent, 222.
17 Blundo, "La corruption," 16.
18 Buchan and Hill, *An Intellectual History of Political Corruption,* 10.
19 Ibid., 152.
20 Ibid., 151.
21 Pierce, 6.
22 Ibid., 163.
23 Chabal, *Power in Africa*, 95.
24 Tignor, 354.
25 Ibid., 351.
26 Noonan, xviii–xix.
27 The imagery of moral taint drawn from classical mythology derives from the "verbal pyrotechnics" that K.O. Mbadiwe (referred to in *No Longer at Ease* only as the Minister of Land) had introduced to Nigerian politics and that became an essential part of political rhetoric (Lynch, *Mbadiwe*, 4). Mbadiwe wrote in 1958, "It is necessary that we … clean the Augean stable of bad faith, false patriotism, mercenary politics, fascist tendencies, mass deception and enslaving patronage" (qtd. In ibid., 171).
28 Noonan, xvii.
29 Ibid., xvii.
30 Nietzsche, *Genealogy of Morals*, 78.
31 Derrida, "Force de loi," 993.
32 Ibid., 993.
33 Simmel, 388–9.
34 Munonye, *Bridge to a Wedding*, 130.
35 Ibid., 130.
36 Ibid., 136.

37 A highway robber in northern Chad tells Janet Roitman the same thing ("The Ethics of Illegality," 257).
38 Armah, *The Beautyful Ones*, 30–1.
39 Ibid., 56.
40 Chris's cavalier attitude toward authority and his libertine ways are surely based on the life of the poet Christopher Okigbo, who spent the years 1956 to 1958 in Lagos as a civil servant (see Nwakanma's biography). At the end of that period, bankrupt and dismissed from the civil service, Okigbo wrote the poem "Debtor's Lane."
41 Scott, 21.
42 Munonye, 81.
43 Ibid., 81–2.
44 Armah, 29–30.
45 Ibid., 108.
46 Ibid., 31–2.
47 Echewa, *The Land's Lord*, 130.
48 Ibid., 130.
49 Noonan, xxi.
50 Ndibe, *Foreign Gods*, 101.
51 Ibid., 101.
52 Tarot, "Repères pour une histoire," 96, my translation.
53 Tutuola, *The Palm-Wine Drinkard*, 67.
54 Ibid., 71.
55 Derrida, *Given Time: I*, 12.
56 Qtd. in Blumberg, *Victorian Sacrifice*, 180.
57 Hénaff, *The Price of Truth*, 144.
58 Abélès, *Anthropologie de l'État*, 38.
59 Caillé, 116–17, my translation.
60 Nietzsche, 76.
61 Noonan, xx.
62 Ibid., 79.
63 Caillé, 84.
64 Hobbes, *Leviathan*, 140.
65 Ibid., 153.
66 George, *Relocating Agency*, 179.
67 Munonye, *Obi*, 185–86.
68 Graeber, *Debt*, 69.
69 Kahn, *Sacred Violence*, 97.
70 Ibid., 98.
71 Sembène, *Bouts de bois*.

72 Simmel, 384–5.
73 Sarthou-Lajus, *Éloge de la dette*, 64; my translation.
74 Armah, 5.
75 Ibid., 162.

CHAPTER TEN

1 Olaniyan, "The Paddle."
2 Qtd. in Macpherson, *Harm's Way*, 16.
3 Northup, *Trade without Rulers*, 97–8.
4 Roitman, "The Ethics of Illegality," 258.
5 Tilly, "War Making," 171.
6 Armah, *The Beautyful Ones*, 4.
7 Ibid., 5.
8 Pierce, "Punishment," 197–8.
9 Ibid., 208–9.
10 Qtd. in Abélès, *Anthropologie de l'État,* 83; my translation.
11 D.A. Miller, *The Novel and the Police.*
12 Appiah, *The Honor Code,* 192.
13 Critchley, *Faith of the Faithless*, 37.
14 Scott, *Comparative Political Corruption*, 9.
15 Beckett, "Legitimizing Democracy."
16 Aluko, *One Man*, 194.
17 Derrida, "Force de loi," 993.
18 Ibid., 993.
19 Bartelsen, *Genealogy of Sovereignty*, 44.
20 Agamben, *State of Exception*, 15.
21 Smith, *Culture of Corruption*, 113.
22 Achebe, *There Was a Country*, 253.
23 Lynch, *Mbadiwe*, 157.
24 Ibid., 173.
25 Achebe, *Education,* 32.
26 Ibid., 32–3.
27 Mbembe, "On Politics," 312–13.
28 Qtd. in Joseph, *Democracy and Prebendal Politics,* 9.

CONCLUSION

1 Hunter, *Culture and Government*, 58.
2 Ibid., 137.

3 Ibid., 150.
4 Poovey, *Genres of the Credit Economy*, 166.
5 Azikiwe, *My Odyssey*, 73.
6 Gikandi, *Reading Chinua Achebe*, 99.
7 Achebe, "Chinua Achebe's Legacy."
8 The first coup in West Africa deposed President Olympio of Togo in 1963. In Congo-Kinshasa, Joseph Mobutu overthrew Patrice Lumumba in 1960 and then assumed sole authority in a second coup in November 1965. In the space of a few months in 1965 and 1966, no less than nine army takeovers took place: in Algeria, Benin, Burkina Faso, Burundi, the Central African Republic, Chad, Ghana, Nigeria, and Congo-Kinshasa.
9 Mahama, *My First Coup D'état*, 3.
10 Young, *Postcolonial State*, 129.
11 The 1946 Richards constitution, the 1951 MacPherson constitution, the 1954 constitution, and the 1959 independence constitution.
12 Quoted in Hyden, *African Politics*, 108.
13 Beckett and Young, "Introduction," 4.
14 Oyediran, "Transition without End," 175.
15 Appiah, *In My Father's House*, 150.
16 The earliest fictive African state invented by an African writer is Peter Abrahams' *A Wreath for Udomo*, published in 1956, but it was written by a South African about a state like the Gold Coast. In drama, the fictive state was inaugurated by Soyinka's 1965 play *Kongi's Harvest*, set in Isma. William Conton's *The African* (1960) is also set in a fictive country, but perhaps that can be explained by noting that Conton was a Sierra Leonean Creole.
17 There is, however, a Latin American equivalent of the fictive state, to be found in Alejo Carpentier's *Los pasos perdidos* and *El discurso del método* and in Gabriel Garcia Márquez's *Cien años de soledad* and *El otoño del patriarco*. And the same convention makes possible such Caribbean islands as George Lamming's San Cristobal, the Isabella of V.S. Naipaul's *The Mimic Men* and Nigel Thomas's *Spirits in the Dark*, and Harold Sonny Ladoo's Carib Island.
18 Martin, *African Political Thought*, 61–70.
19 Hansen and Stepputat, "Introduction: States of Imagination," 10.
20 Qtd. in Habermas, *Philosophical Discourse of Modernity*, 39.
21 Kahn, *Sacred Violence*, 154.
22 Miguel Angel Asturias wrote *El señor presidente*, Alejo Carpentier *El discurso del método*, Gabriel Garcia Márquez *El otoño del patriarco*,

Augusto Roa Bastos *Yo, el supremo*, Mario Vargas Llosa *La fiesta del chivo*.

23 Recent examples include the film *Ezra*, Nnedi Okorafor's *Lagoon*, Chinelo Okparanta's *Under the Udala Tree*, and Igoni Barrett's *Blackass*. Chekwube O. Danladi has a poem addressed to the hanged Okonkwo.

Bibliography

Abélès, Marc. *Anthropologie de l'État*. Paris: Armand Colin, 1990.

Abrams, Philip. "Notes on the Difficulty of Studying the State." *Journal of Historical Sociology* 1, no. 1 (1988): 58–89.

Achebe, Chinua. *Anthills of the Savannah*. London: Heinemann, 1988.

– *Arrow of God*. London: Heinemann, 1964.

– *Arrow of God*. 1974. Oxford: Heinemann, 1986.

– "Chinua Achebe's Legacy in His Own Words." *The Atlantic*, 22 March 2013.

– *The Education of a British-Protected Child*. New York: A.A. Knopf, 2009.

– "Foreword." In *A Selection of African Prose*, vol. 1: *Traditional Oral Texts*, edited by W.H. Whiteley, vii–x. Oxford: Oxford University Press, 1964.

– *No Longer at Ease*. 1960. London: Heinemann, 1963.

– *There Was a Country*. New York: Penguin, 2012.

– *Things Fall Apart*. 1958. New York: Random House, 2009.

– *The Trouble with Nigeria*. Exeter, UK: Heinemann, 1984.

– "Work and Play in Tutuola's *The Palm-Wine Drinkard*." In *Hopes and Impediments*, 68–76. New York: Doubleday, 1988.

Adéẹ̀kọ́, Adélékè. "Okonkwo, Textual Closure, Colonial Conquest." *Research in African Literatures* 42, no. 2 (2011): 72–86.

Adichie, Chimamanda Ngozi. *Purple Hibiscus*. New York: Random House, 2003.

Agamben, Giorgio.*The Kingdom and the Glory: For a Theological Genealogy of Economy and Government*, translated by Lorenzo Chiesa. Stanford, CA: Stanford University Press, 2011.

– *State of Exception*, translated by Kevin Attell. Chicago: University of Chicago Press, 2005.

Ajayi, Rotimi. "The Anti-Colonial Struggle in Nigeria." In *The Oxford Handbook of Nigerian Politics*, edited by Carl Levan and Patrick Ukata, 89–102. Oxford: Oxford University Press, 2018.

Aluko, T.M. *One Man, One Matchet*. London: Heinemann, 1965.
Amadi, Elechi. *Estrangement*. London: Heinemann, 1986.
– *The Great Ponds*. London: Heinemann, 1971.
– *The Slave*. London: Heinemann, 1978.
Amadiume, Ifi. *Male Daughters, Female Husbands: Gender and Sex in an African Society*. London: Zed, 1987.
Anderson, Benedict. *Imagined Communities*. London: Verso, 1991.
Andrade, Susan Z. *The Nation Writ Small: African Fictions and Feminisms 1958–1988*. Durham, NC: Duke University Press, 2011.
Anspach, Mark Rogin. À charge de revanche: Figures élémentaires de la réciprocité. Paris: Seuil, 2002.
Appiah, Kwame Anthony. "Cosmopolitan Patriots." In *For Love of Country: Debating the Limits of Patriotism*, edited by Joshua Cohen, 21–9. Boston: Beacon Press, 1996.
– *The Honor Code: How Moral Revolutions Happen*. New York: W.W. Norton, 2011.
– *In My Father's House: Africa in the Philosophy of Culture*. New York: Oxford University Press, 1992.
Arendt, Hannah. *The Origins of Totalitarianism*. New York: Houghton Mifflin Harcourt, 1973.
– *On Revolution*. London: Penguin, 1990.
Armah, Ayi Kwei. *The Beautyful Ones Are Not Yet Born*. London: Heinemann, 1968.
Armstrong, Nancy. *How Novels Think: The Limits of Individualism from 1719–1900*. New York: Columbia University Press, 2005.
Austin, Gareth. "Human Pawning in Asante, 1820–1950, Markets and Coercion, Gender and Cocoa." In *Pawnship, Slavery, and Colonialism in Africa*, edited by Paul Lovejoy and Toyin Falola, 187–224. Trenton, NJ: Africa World Press, 2003.
Azikiwe, Nnamdi. *Meditations: A Collection of Poems*. Nsukka: African Book Co., 1977.
– *My Odyssey: An Autobiography*. London: Hurst, 1970.
Baker, Jennifer J. *Securing the Commonwealth: Debt, Speculation, and Writing in the Making of Early America*. Baltimore, MD: Johns Hopkins University Press, 2005.
Bakhtin, M.M. "The *Bildungsroman* and Its Significance in the History of Realism (Toward a Historical Typology of the Novel)." In *Speech Genres and Other Late Essays*, translated by Vern W. McGee, edited by Caryl Emerson and Michael Holquist, 10–59. Austin, TX: University of Texas Press, 1986.

Balibar, Étienne. *Violence and Civility: On the Limits of Political Philosophy*, translated by G.M. Ghoshgarian. New York: Columbia University Press, 2015.

Balzac, Honoré de. *César Birotteau*. Éditions de la Bibliothèque Digitale, 2015.

Barber, Karin. "Money, Self-Realization, and the Person in Yorùbá Texts." In *Money Matters: Instability, Values, and Social Payments in the Modern History of West African Communities*, edited by Jane I. Guyer, 205–24. Portsmouth, NH: Heinemann, 1995.

Barkun, Michael. *Law without Sanctions: Order in Primitive Societies and the World Community*. New Haven: Yale University Press, 1968.

Bartelson, Jens. *A Genealogy of Sovereignty*. Cambridge: Cambridge University Press, 1995.

Bataille, Georges. *The Accursed Share: An Essay on General Economy*, vol. 1: *Consumption*, translated by Robert Hurley. New York: Zone, 1991.

Baucom, Ian. *Specters of the Atlantic: Finance Capital, Slavery, and the Philosophy of History*. Durham, NC: Duke University Press, 2005.

Baxter, Katherine Isobel. *Imagined States: Law and Literature in Nigeria, 1900–1966*. Edinburgh: Edinburgh University Press, 2019.

Bayart, Jean-François. *The State in Africa: The Politics of the Belly*, translated by Mary Harper, Christopher Harrison, and Elizabeth Harrison. London: Longman, 1993.

Beckett, Paul A. "Legitimizing Democracy: The Role of the Highly Educated Elite." In *Dilemmas of Democracy in Nigeria*, edited by Paul A. Beckett and Crawford Young, 111–34. Rochester, NY: University of Rochester Press, 1997.

Beckett, Paul, and Crawford Young. "Introduction: Beyond the Impasse of 'Permanent Transition' in Nigeria." In *Dilemmas of Democracy in Nigeria*, edited by Paul A. Beckett and Crawford Young, 1–12. Rochester, NY: University of Rochester Press, 1997.

Belasco, Bernard I. *The Entrepreneur as Culture-Hero*. New York: Praeger, 1980.

Benjamin, Walter. "Critique of Violence." In *Violence and its Alternatives: An Interdisciplinary Approach*, edited by Manfred B. Steger and Nancy S. Lind, 57–69. New York: St. Martin's, 1999.

Benton, Lauren. *Law and Colonial Cultures: Legal Regimes in World History, 1400–1900*. Cambridge: Cambridge University Press, 2002.

Bersselaar, Dmitri van den. "Imagining Home: Migration and the Igbo Village in Colonial Nigeria." *Journal of African History* 46, no. 1 (2005): 51–73.

Beti, Mongo. *Le roi miraculé*. Paris: Buchet/Chastel, 1958.

Bilakila, Anastase Nzeza. "The Kinshasa Bargain." In *Reinventing Order in the Congo: How People Respond to State Failure in Kinshasa*, edited by Theodore Trefon, 20–32. London: Zed, 2004.

Bivona, Daniel. *British Imperial Literature, 1870–1940*. Cambridge: Cambridge University Press, 1998.

Blumberg, Ilana M. *Victorian Sacrifice: Ethics and Economics in Mid-Century Novels*. Columbus, OH: Ohio State University Press, 2013.

Blundo, Giorgio. "La corruption entre scandales politiques et pratiques quotidiennes." In *Monnayer les pouvoirs: Espaces, mécanismes et représentations de la corruption*, edited by Giorgio Blundo, 11–19. Paris: Presses Universitaires de France, 2000.

– "Corruption in Africa and the Social Sciences: A Review of the Literature." In *Everyday Corruption and the State: Citizens and Public Officials in Africa*, edited by Giorgio Blundo, J.-P. Olivier de Sardan, N.B. Arifari, and M.T. Alou, 15–68. Claremont, South Africa: David Philip, 2006.

Blundo, Giorgio, and J.-P. Olivier de Sardan. "The Popular Semiology of Corruption." In *Everyday Corruption and the State: Citizens and Public Officials in Africa*, edited by Giorgio Blundo, J.-P. Olivier de Sardan, N.B. Arifari, and M.T. Alou, 110–34. Claremont, South Africa: David Philip, 2006.

Borman, David. "Playful Ethnography: Chinua Achebe's *Things Fall Apart* and Nigerian Education." ARIEL 46, no. 3 (2015): 91–112.

Bourdieu, Pierre. "Rethinking the State: Genesis and Structure of the Bureaucratic Field." In *State/Culture: State-Formation after the Cultural Turn*, edited by George Steinmetz, 53–75. Ithaca, NY: Cornell University Press, 1999.

Breckenridge, Keith. *The Biometric State: The Global Politics of Identification and Surveillance in South Africa, 1850 to the Present*. Cambridge: Cambridge University Press, 2014.

Brown, Nicholas. *Utopian Generations: The Political Horizon of Twentieth-Century Literature*. Princeton, NJ: Princeton University Press, 2006.

Bryce, Jane. "Evading Canonical Constraints: The 'Popular' as an Alternative Mode – The Case of Flora Nwapa." In *Emerging Perspectives on Flora Nwapa*, edited by Marie Umeh, 391–410. Trenton, NJ: Africa World Press, 1998.

Buchan, Bruce, and Lisa Hill. *An Intellectual History of Political Corruption*. Houndmills, UK: Palgrave Macmillan, 2014.

Butler, Judith. *The Psychic Life of Power: Theories of Subjection*. Stanford, CA: Stanford University Press, 1997.

Caillé, Alain. *Anthropologie du don: Le tiers paradigme*. Paris: Desclée de Brouwer, 2000.

Carroll, David. *Chinua Achebe*. Woodbridge, CT: Twayne, 1970.
Césaire, Aimé. *The Discourse of Colonialism*, translated by Joan Pinkham. New York: Monthly Review Press, 2000.
Chabal, Patrick. *Africa: The Politics of Suffering and Smiling*. London: Zed, 2009.
– *Power in Africa: An Essay in Political Interpretation*. New York: St. Martin's, 1994.
Chatterjee, Partha. *Lineages of Political Society: Studies in Postcolonial Democracy*. New York: Columbia University Press, 2011.
Coetzee, J.M. *Diary of a Bad Year*. London: Harvill Secker, 2007.
Coleman, James S. *Nigeria: Background to Nationalism*. Berkeley, CA: University of California Press, 1971.
Comaroff, John L., and Jean Comaroff. "Law and Disorder in the Postcolony: An Introduction." In *Law and Disorder in the Postcolony*, edited by Jean Comaroff and John L. Comaroff, 1–56. Chicago: University of Chicago Press, 2006.
Conrad, Joseph. *Heart of Darkness*. Harmondsworth: Penguin, 1973.
Cooper, Frederick. *Africa in the World: Capitalism, Empire, Nation-State*. Cambridge, MA: Harvard University Press, 2014.
– *Colonialism in Question: Theory, Knowledge, History*. Berkeley, CA: University of California Press, 2005.
Cott, Jonathan. "Chinua Achebe: At the Crossroads." In *Conversations with Chinua Achebe*, edited by Bernth Lindfors, 76–87. Jackson, MS: University Press of Mississippi, 1997.
Cover, Robert. *Narrative, Violence, and the Law: The Essays of Robert Cover*, edited by Martha Minow, Michael Ryan, and Austin Sarat. Ann Arbor, MI: University of Michigan Press, 1992.
Critchley, Simon. *The Faith of the Faithless: Experiments in Political Theology*. London: Verso, 2012.
Culler, Jonathan. "Anderson and the Novel." *Diacritics* 29, no. 4 (1999): 19–39.
Currey, James. *Africa Writes Back: The African Writers Series and the Launch of African Literature*. Oxford: James Currey, 2008.
Darbon, Dominique. "Public Administration, State, and Society." In *State and Society in Francophone Africa Since Independence*, edited by Anthony Kirk-Greene and Daniel Bach, 46–61. London: Macmillan, 1995.
Davis, David Brion. *Inhuman Bondage: The Rise and Fall of Slavery in the New World*. Oxford: Oxford University Press, 2006.
Derrida, Jacques. "Force de loi: Le 'Fondement mystique de l'autorité,'" translated by Mary Quaintance. *Cardozo Law Review* 11, nos. 5–6 (1990): 920–1046.

– *Given Time: I. Counterfeit Money*, translated by Peggy Kamuf. Chicago: University of Chicago Press, 1992.

Diagne, Mamoussé. *Critique de la raison orale: Les pratiques discursives en Afrique Noire*. Paris: Karthala, 2005.

Diamond, Jared. *The World until Yesterday: What Can We Learn from Traditional Societies?* New York: Penguin, 2012.

Downes, Paul. *Democracy, Revolution, and Monarchism in Early American Literature*. Cambridge: Cambridge University Press, 2002.

– *Hobbes, Sovereignty, and Early American Literature*. New York: Cambridge University Press, 2015.

Dunn, John. *Democracy: A History*. Toronto: Penguin, 2005.

Durkheim, Émile. *Suicide: A Study in Sociology* [1987], translated by John A. Spaulding and George Simpson. New York: Routledge, 2002.

Dyzenhaus, David. *Hard Cases in Wicked Legal Systems*. Oxford: Oxford University Press, 2010.

– "'The Organic Law' of *Ex Parte Milligan*." In *Sovereignty, Emergency, Legality*, edited by Austin Sarat, 16–57. Cambridge: Cambridge University Press, 2010.

Echewa, T. Obinkaram. *The Land's Lord*. London: Heinemann, 1976.

Ekechi, Felix. "Igbo Response to British Imperialism: The Episode of Dr Stewart and the Ahiara Expedition, 1905–1916." *Journal of African Studies* 1, no. 2 (1974): 145–57.

Ekeh, Peter P. "Colonialism and the Two Publics in Africa: A Theoretical Statement." *Comparative Studies in Society and History* 17, no. 1 (1975): 91–112.

– "The Concept of Second Liberation and the Prospects of Democracy in Africa: A Nigerian Context." In *Dilemmas of Democracy in Nigeria*, edited by Paul A. Beckett and Crawford Young, 83–110. Rochester, NY: University of Rochester Press, 1997.

Ekejiuba, Felicia. "Currency Instability and Social Payments among the Igbo of Eastern Nigeria, 1890–1990." In *Money Matters: Instability, Values, and Social Payments in the Modern History of West African Communities*, edited by Jane I. Guyer, 133–61. Portsmouth, NH: Heinemann, 1995.

Ekwensi, Cyprian. *Beautiful Feathers*. London: Heinemann, 1971.

– *Jagua Nana*. London: Heinemann, 1975.

Ellickson, Robert C. *Order without Law: How Neighbors Settle Disputes*. Cambridge, MA: Harvard University Press, 1991.

Equiano, Olaudah. *The Interesting Narrative and Other Writings*, edited by Vincent Carreta. New York: Penguin, 2003.

Ermarth, Elizabeth. *Realism and Consensus in the English Novel*. Princeton, NJ: Princeton University Press, 1983. 3–37.

Esposito, Roberto. *Communitas: The Origin and Destiny of Community*, translated by Timothy Campbell. Stanford, CA: Stanford University Press, 2010.

Ezenwa-Ohaeto. *Chinua Achebe: A Biography*. Oxford: James Currey, 1997.

Falola, Toyin. *Colonialism and Violence in Nigeria*. Bloomington, IN: Indiana University Press, 2009.

– "Money and Informal Credit Institutions in Colonial Western Nigeria." In *Money Matters: Instability, Values, and Social Payments in the Modern History of West African Communities*, edited by Jane I. Guyer, 162–87. Portsmouth, NH: Heinemann, 1995.

– "'My Friend the Shylock': Money-Lenders and Their Clients in South-Western Nigeria." *Journal of African History* 34, no. 3 (1993): 403–23.

Fanon, Frantz. *Black Skin, White Masks*, translated by Charles Lam Markmann. New York: Grove, 1952.

– *The Wretched of the Earth*, translated by Constance Farrington. Harmondsworth, UK: Penguin, 1967.

Fish, Stanley. "Force." In *Doing What Comes Naturally*, 503–24. Durham, NC: Duke University Press, 1989.

Flannery, Kent, and Joyce Marcus. *The Creation of Inequality: How our Prehistoric Ancestors Set the Stage for Monarchy, Slavery, and Empire*. Cambridge, MA: Harvard University Press, 2012.

Foucault, Michel. *Discipline and Punish: The Birth of the Prison*, translated by Alan Sheridan. New York: Random House, 1977.

– *"Society Must be Defended": Lectures at the Collège de France, 1975–76*, translated by David Macey. New York: Picador, 2003.

Fraenkel, Ernst. *The Dual State: A Contribution to the Theory of Dictatorship*, translated by E.A. Shils. New York: Octagon, 1969.

Franklin, Benjamin. *The Autobiography of Benjamin Franklin*. New York: Dover, 1996.

Freud, Sigmund. "The Ego and the Id." In *The Standard Edition of the Complete Psychological Works of Sigmund Freud*, vol. 19, edited by James Strachey, 3–66. London: Hogarth Press, 1961.

– *Totem and Taboo*. In *The Standard Edition of the Complete Psychological Works of Sigmund Freud*, vol. 13, edited by James Strachey. London: Hogarth Press, 1961.

Gallagher, Catherine. "The Rise of Fictionality." In *The Novel*, vol. 1, edited by Franco Moretti, 336–63. Princeton, NJ: Princeton University Press, 2006.

George, Olakunle. "Achebe's *Arrow of God*." *Comparative Literature Studies* 42, no. 4 (2005): 344–62.

– *Relocating Agency: Modernity and African Letters*. Albany, NY: SUNY Press, 2003.

Giddens, Anthony. *The Nation-State and Violence*. In *A Contemporary Critique of Historical Materialism*, vol. 2. Berkeley, CA: University of California Press, 1985.

Gikandi, Simon. "African Literature and Modernity." *Matatu* 35 (2007): 3–19.

– "Chinua Achebe and the Invention of African Culture." *Research in African Literatures* 32, no. 3 (2001): 3–8.

– *Reading Chinua Achebe*. London: James Currey, 1991.

Gillespie, Michael Allen. "On Debt." In *Debt: Ethics, the Environment, and the Economy*, edited by Peter Y. Paik and Merry Wiesner-Hanks, 56–71. Bloomington, IN: Indiana University Press, 2013.

Godbout, Jacques T. *Ce qui circule entre nous: Donner, recevoir, rendre*. Paris, Seuil, 2007.

– *The World of the Gift*, translated by Donald Winkler. Montreal and Kingston: McGill–Queen's University Press, 1998.

Graeber, David. *Debt: The First 5,000 Years*. New York: Melville House, 2011.

Gregory, C.A. *Gifts and Commodities*. London: Academic Press, 1982.

– *Savage Money: The Anthropology and Politics of Commodity Exchange*. Amsterdam: Harwood, 1997.

Guyer, Jane I. *Marginal Gains: Monetary Transactions in Atlantic Africa*. Chicago: University of Chicago Press, 2004.

– "Representation without Taxation." *African Studies Review* 35, no. 1 (1992): 41–80.

– "Wealth in People and Self-Realization in Equatorial Africa." *Man* 28, no. 2 (1993): 243–65.

Habermas, Jurgen. *The Philosophical Discourse of Modernity*, translated by Frederick Lawrence. Cambridge, MA: MIT Press, 1987.

Hansen, Thomas Blom, and Finn Stepputat. "Introduction: States of Imagination." In *States of Imagination: Ethnographic Explorations of the Postcolonial State*, edited by Thomas Blom Hansen and Finn Stepputat, 1–37. Durham, NC: Duke University Press, 2001.

Harlow, Barbara. "The Tortoise and the Birds; Strategies of Resistance in *Things Fall Apart*." In *Approaches to Teaching Things Fall Apart*, edited by Bernth Lindfors, 74–9. New York: MLA, 1991.

Harneit-Sievers, Axel. *Constructions of Belonging: Igbo Communities and the Nigerian State in the Twentieth Century*. Rochester, NY: University of Rochester Press, 2006.

Hart, Keith. "Heads or Tails? Two Sides of the Coin." *Man* 21, no. 4 (1986): 637–56.

Hazzledine, George Douglas. *The White Man in Nigeria*, London: Edward Arnold, 1904.

Hénaff, Marcel. *The Price of Truth: Gift, Money, and Philosophy*, translated by Jean-Louis Morhange. Stanford, CA: Stanford University Press, 2010.
Herbst, Jeffrey. *States and Power in Africa: Comparative Lessons in Authority and Control*. Princeton, NJ: Princeton University Press, 2000.
Herzfeld, Michael. *The Social Production of Indifference: Exploring the Symbolic Roots of Western Bureaucracy*. Chicago: University of Chicago Press, 1993.
Hobbes, Thomas. *Leviathan* [1651]. New York: Penguin, 2017.
Hogendorn, Jan, and Marion Johnson. *The Shell Money of the Slave Trade*. Cambridge: Cambridge University Press, 1986.
Hopkins, A.G. "The Creation of a Colonial Monetary System: The Origins of the West African Currency Board." *African Historical Studies* 3, no. 1 (1970): 101–32.
Horton, Robin. "Stateless Societies in the History of West Africa." In *History of West Africa*, vol. 1, edited by J.F. Ade Ajjayi and Michael Crowder, 78–119. London: Longman, 1971.
Huggan, Graham. *The Postcolonial Exotic: Marketing the Margins*. New York: Routledge, 2001.
Hunter, Ian. *Culture and Government: The Emergence of Literary Education*. London: Macmillan, 1988.
Hussain, Nasser. *The Jurisprudence of Emergency: Colonialism and the Rule of Law*. Ann Arbor, MI: University of Michigan Press, 2003.
Hyde, Lewis. *Trickster Makes This World*. New York: Farrar, Straus and Giroux, 1998.
Hyden, Goran. *African Politics in Comparative Perspective*. New York: Cambridge University Press, 2013.
Isichei, Elizabeth. *A History of the Igbo People*. New York: St. Martin's, 1976.
Isin, Engin F. "Theorizing Acts of Citizenship." In *Acts of Citizenship*, edited by Engin F. Isin and Greg M. Nielsen, 15–43. London: Zed, 2008.
Jameson, Fredric. "Third-World Literature in the Era of Multinational Capitalism." *Social Text* 15 (1986): 65–88.
Jay, Nancy. *Throughout Your Generations Forever: Sacrifice, Religion, Paternity*. Chicago: University of Chicago Press, 1992.
Johnson, Rev. Samuel. *The History of the Yorubas*. Lagos: CMS, 1921.
Joseph, Richard A. *Democracy and Prebendal Politics in Nigeria: The Rise and Fall of the Second Republic*. Cambridge: Cambridge University Press, 1987.
Julien, Eileen. *African Novels and the Question of Orality*. Bloomington, IN: Indiana University Press, 1992.
Kahn, Paul W. *Sacred Violence: Torture, Terror, and Sovereignty*. Ann Arbor, MI: University of Michigan Press, 2008.

Kelly, John D., and Martha Kaplan. "Nation and Decolonization: Towards a New Anthropology of Nationalism." *Anthropological Theory* 1, no. 4 (2001): 419–37.

Killingray, David. "The Maintenance of Law and Order in British Colonial Africa." *African Affairs* 85 (1986): 411–37.

Kirk-Greene, Anthony. "'Le roi est mort! Vive le roi!': The Comparative Legacy of Chiefs after the Transfer of Power in British and French West Africa." In *State and Society in Francophone Africa Since Independence*, edited by Anthony Kirk-Greene and Daniel Bach, 16–33. London: Macmillan, 1995.

Klein, Martin A. "The Slave Trade and Decentralized Societies." *Journal of African History* 42, no. 1 (2001): 49–65.

Korang, Kwaku Larbi. "Making a Post-Eurocentric Humanity: Tragedy, Realism, and *Things Fall Apart*." *Research in African Literatures* 42, no. 2 (2011): 1–29.

Kourouma, Ahmadou. *En attendant le vote des bêtes sauvages*. Paris: Seuil, 1998.

Laurent, Pierre-Joseph. "Sémantique populaire du détournement dans les associations de développement en Pays Mossi (Burkina Faso)." In *Monnayer les pouvoirs: Espaces, mécanismes et représentations de la corruption*, edited by Giorgio Blundo, 221–48. Paris: Presses Universitaires de France, 2000.

Lazzarato, Maurizio. *The Making of the Indebted Man*, translated by Joshua David Jordan. Amsterdam: Semiotexte, 2011.

Lefort, Claude. *The Political Forms of Modern Society*. Cambridge, MA: MIT Press, 1986.

Leonard, Major Arthur Glyn. *The Lower Niger and Its Tribes*. London: Macmillan, 1906.

LeRoy, Etienne. "Thirty Years of Legal Practice in the Shadow of the State: The Taming of Leviathan." In *State and Society in Francophone Africa since Independence*, edited by Anthony Kirk-Greene and Daniel Bach, 34–45. London: Macmillan, 1995.

Lévi-Strauss, Claude. *The Elementary Structures of Kinship*, translated by James Harle Bell, John Richard von Sturmer, and Rodney Needham, edited by Rodney Needham. Boston: Beacon, 1969.

Lewinnek, Elaine. "'I Consider It Un-American Not to Have a Mortgage': Immigrant Home Ownership in Chicago." In *Debt: Ethics, the Environment, and the Economy*, edited by Peter Y. Paik and Merry Wiesner-Hanks, 26–38. Bloomington, IN: Indiana University Press, 2013.

Leys, Colin. "What Is the Problem about Corruption?" *Journal of Modern African Studies* 3, no. 2 (1965): 215–30.

Li, Yiyun. *Dear Friend, from My Life I Write to You in Your Life*. New York: Random House, 2017.

Locke, John. *Two Treatises of Government* [1689]. London: Dent, 1993.
Lonsdale, John. "States and Social Processes in Africa: A Historiographical Survey." *African Studies Review* 24, nos. 2–3 (1981): 139–225.
Lukács, Georg. *Studies in European Realism*. New York: Grosset and Dunlop, 1964.
Lynch, Hollis R. *K.O. Mbadiwe: A Nigerian Political Biography, 1915–1990*. New York: Palgrave Macmillan, 2012.
Lynn, Thomas Jay. *Chinua Achebe and the Politics of Narration*. New York: Palgrave Macmillan, 2017.
Macpherson, Sandra. *Harm's Way: Tragic Responsibility and the Novel Form*. Baltimore, MD: Johns Hopkins University Press, 2010.
Mahama, John Dramani. *My First Coup D'état and Other True Stories from the Lost Decades of Africa*. New York: Bloomsbury, 2012.
Mair, Lucy. *New Nations*. London: Weidenfeld and Nicolson, 1963.
Mamdani, Mahmood. *Citizen and Subject: Contemporary Africa and the Legacy of Late Colonialism*. Princeton, NJ: Princeton University Press, 1996.
– *Define and Rule*. Cambridge, MA: Harvard University Press, 2012.
Manning, Patrick. *Slavery and African Life: Occidental, Oriental, and African Slave Trades*. Cambridge: Cambridge University Press, 1990.
Mannoni, O. *Prospero and Caliban: The Psychology of Colonization*, translated by Pamela Powesland. Ann Arbor, MI: University of Michigan Press, 1990.
Marie, Alain. "'Y a pas l'argent': L'endetté insolvable et le créancier floué, deux figures complémentaires de la pauvreté Abidjanaise." *Tiers Monde* 36, no. 142 (1995): 303–24.
Martin, Guy. *African Political Thought*. New York: Palgrave Macmillan, 2012.
Mauss, Marcel. *The Gift*, translated by W.D. Halls. New York: W.W. Norton, 1990.
Mbembe, Achille. "On Politics as a Form of Expenditure." In *Law and Disorder in the Postcolony*, edited by Jean Comaroff and John L. Comaroff, 299–333. Chicago: University of Chicago Press, 2006.
– *On the Postcolony*. Berkeley, CA: University of California Press, 2001.
– *Sortir de la grande nuit: Essai sur l'Afrique décolonisée*. Paris: La Découverte, 2010.
McCaskie, T.C. "Wealth and Belief in Asante History, II: The Twentieth Century." *Africa* 56, no. 1 (1986): 3–23.
McIntosh, Susan Keech. "Pathways to Complexity: An African Perspective." In *Beyond Chiefdoms: Pathways to Complexity in Africa*, edited by Susan Keech McIntosh, 1–30. Cambridge: Cambridge University Press, 1999.
Meek, C.K. *Law and Authority in a Nigerian Tribe: A Study in Indirect Rule*. Oxford: Oxford University Press, 1937.

Meierhenrich, Jens. *The Legacies of Law: Long-Run Consequences of Legal Development in South Africa, 1652–2000*. Cambridge: Cambridge University Press, 2008.

Meillassoux, Claude. *Maidens, Meal, and Money: Capitalism and the Domestic Economy*. Cambridge: Cambridge University Press, 1981.

Melville, Herman. *The Confidence-Man: His Masquerade*. New York: Dix, Edwards, 1857.

Miller, D.A. *The Novel and the Police*. Berkeley, CA: University of California Press, 1988.

Miller, David Lee. *Dreams of the Burning Child: Sacrificial Sons and the Father's Witness*. Ithaca, NY: Cornell University Press, 2003.

Moodie, Susannah. *Roughing It in the Bush*. A Public Domain Book.

Moore, Sally Falk. "Treating Law as Knowledge: Telling Colonial Officers What to Say to Africans about Running 'Their Own' Native Courts." *Law and Society Review* 26, no. 1 (1992): 11–46.

Morrison, Jago. *Chinua Achebe*. Manchester: Manchester University Press, 2014.

Mudimbe, V.Y. *The Idea of Africa*. Bloomington, IN: Indiana University Press, 1994.

Munonye, John. *Bridge to a Wedding*. London: Heinemann, 1978.

– *Obi*. London: Heinemann, 1969.

Naanen, Ben. "Economy within an Economy: The Manilla Currency, Exchange Rate Instability, and Social Conditions in South-Eastern Nigeria, 1900–48." *Journal of African History* 34 (1993): 425–46.

Ndibe, Okey. *Foreign Gods Inc*. New York: Soho, 2014.

Newell, Stephanie. *Literary Culture in Colonial Ghana: "How to Play the Game of Life."* Manchester: Manchester University Press, 2002.

– *The Power to Name: A History of Anonymity in Colonial West Africa*. Athens, OH: Ohio University Press, 2013.

– *West African Literatures*. Oxford: Oxford University Press, 2006.

Nietzsche, Friedrich. *On the Genealogy of Morals*, translated by Michael A. Scarpitti. London: Penguin, 2013.

Nnolim, Charles E. "The Form and Function of the Folk Tradition in Achebe's Novels." *ARIEL* 14, no. 1 (1983): 35–47.

Noonan, John T. Jr. *Bribes*. New York: Macmillan. 1984.

Northrup, David. *Trade without Rulers: Pre-Colonial Economic Development in South-Eastern Nigeria*. Oxford: Clarendon, 1978.

Nunn, Nathan, and Leonard Wantchekon. "The Slave Trade and the Origins of Mistrust in Africa." *American Economic Review* 101, no. 7 (2011): 3221–52.

Nwakanma, Obi. *Christopher Okigbo. 1930–67: Thirsting for Sunlight*. Rochester, NY: James Currey, 2010.

– "Metonymic Eruptions: Igbo Novelists, the Narrative of the Nation, and New Developments in the Contemporary Nigerian Novel." *Research in African Literatures* 39, no. 2 (2008): 1–14.

Nwana, Pita. *Omenuko*, translated by Ernest Emenyonu. New Rochelle, NY: African Heritage Press, 2014.

Nwankwo, Nkem. *Danda*. London: Deutsch, 1964.

Nwapa, Flora. *Efuru*. London: Heinemann, 1966.

– "Priestesses and Power among the Riverine Igbo." In *Queens, Queen Mothers, Priestesses, and Power: Case Studies in African Gender*, edited by Flora Edouwaye S. Kaplan, 415–24. New York: New York Academy of Sciences, 1997.

Nwokeji, G. Ogo. *The Slave Trade and Culture in the Bight of Biafra: An African Society in the Atlantic World*. Cambridge: Cambridge University Press, 2010.

Nwokolo, Chuma, Jr. *Diaries of a Dead African*. Nigeria: County Books, 2013.

Nzegwu, Nkiru Uwechia. *Family Matters: Feminist Concepts in African Philosophy of Culture*. Albany, NY: SUNY Press, 2006.

Obeng, R.E. *Eighteenpence*. Legon: Sub-Saharan, 1998.

Ochiagha, Terri. *Achebe and Friends at Umuahia: The Making of a Literary Elite*. Woodbridge, CT: James Currey, 2015.

– *A Short History of Chinua Achebe's Things Fall Apart*. Athens, OH: Ohio University Press, 2018.

Ofeimun, Odia. "Taking Nigeria Seriously (II)" ZNet. https://zcomm.org/znetarticle/taking-nigeria-seriously-ii-by-odia-ofeimun. Posted 25 October 2003. Consulted 2 June 2020.

Ofonagoro, Walter I. "From Traditional to British Currency in Southern Nigeria: Analysis of a Currency Revolution, 1880–1948." *Journal of Economic History* 39, no. 3 (1979): 623–54.

Ohadike, Don. "The Decline of Slavery among the Igbo People." In *The End of Slavery in Africa*, edited by Suzanne Miers and Richard Roberts, 437–61. Madison, WI: University of Wisconsin Press, 1988.

Okereafọezeke, Nọnso. *Law and Justice in Post-British Nigeria: Conflicts and Interactions between Native and Foreign Systems of Social Control in Igbo*. Westport, CT: Greenwood, 2002.

Okleme, S.K. "R.E. Obeng's *Eighteenpence*: A Critical Study." In *Goatskin Bags and Wisdom: New Critical Perspectives on African Literature*, edited by Ernest Emenyonu, 105–26. Trenton, NJ: Africa World Press, 2000.

Okri, Ben. *The Famished Road*. London: Vintage, 1991.

Olaniyan, Tejumola. "Chinua Achebe and an Archaeology of the Postcolonial African State." *Research in African Literatures* 32, no. 3 (2001): 22–9.

– "The Paddle That Speaks English: Africa, NGOs, and the Archaeology of an Unease." *Research in African Literatures* 42, no. 2 (2011): 46–59.

Onwueme, Osonye Tess. "Shifting Paradigms of Profit and Loss: Men in Flora Nwapa's Fiction." In *Emerging Perspectives on Flora Nwapa*, edited by Marie Umeh, 291–333. Trenton, NJ: Africa World Press, 1998.

Oppenheimer, Franz. *The State*, translated by John M. Gitterman. Montreal: Black Rose, 2007.

Orwell, George. "The Lion and the Unicorn." In *Why I Write*, 11–94. London: Penguin, 2004.

Osinubi, Taiwo Adetunji. "Chinua Achebe and the Uptakes of African Slaveries." *Research in African Literatures* 40, no. 4 (2009): 25–46.

Owen, Olly. "Positions of Security and the Security of Position: Bureaucratic Prebendalism inside the State." In *Democracy and Prebendalism in Nigeria*, edited by Wale Adebanwi et al., 147–73. New York: Palgrave Macmillan, 2013.

Owomoyela, Oyekan. *The Columbia Guide to West African Literature in English Since 1945*. New York: Columbia University Press, 2008.

Oyediran, Oyeleye. "Transition without End: From Hope to Despair – Reflections of a Participant-Observer." In *Dilemmas of Democracy in Nigeria*, edited by Paul A. Beckett and Crawford Young, 175–92. Rochester, NY: University of Rochester Press, 1997.

Parry, Jonathan. "The Gift, the Indian Gift and the 'Indian Gift.'" *Man* 21, no. 3 (1986): 453–73.

Pateman, Carole. *The Sexual Contract*. Cambridge: Polity, 1988.

Patterson, Orlando. *Slavery and Social Death: A Comparative Study*. Cambridge, MA: Harvard University Press, 1982.

Phillips, Anne. *The Enigma of Colonialism: British Policy in West Africa*. London: James Currey, 1989.

Pierce, Steven. "Punishment and the Political Body: Flogging and Colonialism in Northern Nigeria." In *Discipline and the Other Body: Correction, Corporeality, Colonialism*, edited by Anupama Rao and Steven Pierce, 186–214. Durham, NC: Duke University Press, 2006.

– *State Formation and Political Culture in Nigeria*. Durham, NC: Duke University Press, 2016.

Pinker, Steven. *The Better Angels of Our Nature*. New York: Viking, 2012.

Piot, Charles. "Of Persons and Things: Some Reflections on African Spheres of Exchange." *Man* 26, no. 3 (1991): 405–24.

Poovey, Mary. "Demonizing Debt, Naturalizing Finance." In *Debt: Ethics, the Environment, and the Economy*, edited by Peter Y. Paik and Merry Wiesner-Hanks, 39–55. Bloomington, IN: Indiana University Press, 2013.

– *Genres of the Credit Economy: Mediating Value in Eighteenth- and Nineteenth-Century Britain*. Chicago: University of Chicago Press, 2008.

Pratten, David. "The Precariousness of Prebendalism." In *Democracy and Prebendalism in Nigeria*, edited by Wale Adebanwi et al., 243–58. New York: Palgrave Macmillan, 2013.

Premchand. *The Gift of a Cow*, translated by Gordon C Roadarmel. Bloomington, IN: Indiana University Press, 2002.

Priebe, Richard K. "Teaching *Things Fall Apart* in a Criticism Course." In *Approaches to Teaching Things Fall Apart*, edited by Bernth Lindfors, 123–8. New York: MLA, 1991.

Putnam, Robert D. *Making Democracy Work: Civic Traditions in Modern Italy*. Princeton, NJ: Princeton University Press, 1993.

Quayson, Ato. "Realism, Criticism, and the Disguises of Both: A Reading of Chinua Achebe's *Things Fall Apart* with an Evaluation of the Criticism Relating to It." *Research in African Literatures* 25, no. 4 (1994): 117–36.

Robbins, Bruce. *Upward Mobility and the Common Good: Toward a Literary History of the Welfare State*. Princeton, NJ: Princeton University Press, 2007.

Rodney, Walter. *How Europe Underdeveloped Africa*. London: Bogle-L'Ouverture, 1972.

Rogers, Philip. "*No Longer at Ease*: Achebe's Heart of Whiteness." *Research in African Literatures* 14, no. 2 (1983): 165–83.

Roitman, Janet. "The Ethics of Illegality in the Chad Basin." In *Law and Disorder in the Postcolony*, edited by Jean and John L. Comaroff, 247–72. Chicago: University of Chicago Press, 2006.

– "Unsanctioned Wealth; or, The Productivity of Debt in Northern Cameroon." *Public Culture* 15, no. 2 (2003): 211–37.

Rospabé, Philippe. *La dette de vie: Aux origines de la monnaie sauvage*. Paris: La Découverte, 1995.

Rousseau, Jean-Jacques. *The Social Contract and Other Later Political Writings*. Cambridge: Cambridge University Press, 2003.

Rowell, Charles H. "An Interview with Chinua Achebe." In *Conversations with Chinua Achebe*, edited by Bernth Lindfors, 76–7. Jackson, MS: University Press of Mississippi, 1997.

Rubenstein, Michael. *Public Works: Infrastructure, Irish Modernism, and the Postcolonial*. Notre Dame, IN: University of Notre Dame Press, 2010.

Rubin, Gayle. "The Traffic in Women: Notes on the 'Political Economy' of Sex." In *Toward an Anthropology of Women*, edited by Rayna Reiter, 157–210. New York: Monthly Review Press, 1975.

Ryan, Alan. *On Politics*. New York: Liveright, 2012.

Sahlins, Marshall. *Stone Age Economics*. London: Routledge, 2017.

Santner, Eric L. *The Royal Remains: The People's Two Bodies and the Endgames of Sovereignty*. Chicago: University of Chicago Press, 2011.

Sarthou-Lajus, Nathalie. *Éloge de la dette*. Paris: Presses Universitaires de France, 2012.

Schreiner, Olive. *The Story of an African Farm*. London: Penguin, 2005.

Scott, James C. *Comparative Political Corruption*. Englewood Cliffs: Prentice-Hall, 1972.

Selvon, Sam. *The Lonely Londoners*. Toronto, TSAR, 1991.

Sembène, Ousmane. *Les bouts de bois de dieu*. Paris: Le Livre contemporain, 1960.

Siegert, Bernhard. *Relays: Literature as an Epoch of the Postal System*, translated by Kevin Repp. Stanford, CA: Stanford University Press, 1999.

Sifton, John. *Violence All Around*. Cambridge, MA: Harvard University Press, 2015.

Simmel, Georg. *The Philosophy of Money*. London: Routledge, 1978.

Sitze, Adam. *The Impossible Machine: A Genealogy of South Africa's Truth and Reconciliation Commission*. Ann Arbor, MI: University of Michigan Press, 2013.

Smith, Daniel Jordan. *A Culture of Corruption: Everyday Deception and Popular Discontent in Nigeria*. Princeton, NJ: Princeton University Press, 2007.

Soyinka, Wole. *Death and the King's Horseman*. London: Eyre Methuen, 1975.

Stratton, Florence. *Contemporary African Literature and the Politics of Gender*. London: Routledge, 1994.

Tarot, Camille. "Repères pour une histoire de la naissance de la grâce." *Revue du MAUSS* 1 (1993): 90–114.

Thompson, E.P. *Whigs and Hunters: The Origin of the Black Act*. New York: Pantheon, 1975.

Thornton, John. *Africa and Africans in the Making of the Atlantic World 1400–1800*. Cambridge: Cambridge University Press, 1998.

Tignor, Robert L. "Colonial Chiefs in Chiefless Societies." *Journal of Modern African Studies* 9, no. 3 (1971): 339–59.

– "Political Corruption in Nigeria before Independence." *Journal of Modern African Studies* 31, no. 2 (1993): 175–202.

Tilly, Charles. *Coercion, Capital, and European States,* AD *990–1992*. Cambridge: Blackwell, 1992.
– *Trust and Rule*. Cambridge: Cambridge University Press, 2005.
– "War Making and State Making as Organized Crime." In *Bringing the State Back In*, edited by Peter B. Evans, Dietrich Rueschemeyer, and Theda Skocpol, 169–91. Cambridge: Cambridge University Press, 1985.
Tully, James. *Strange Multiplicity: Constitutionalism in an Age of Diversity*. Cambridge: Cambridge University Press, 1995.
Tutuola, Amos. *The Brave African Huntress* [1958]. New York: Grove, 1970.
– *The Palm-Wine Drinkard*. London: Faber, 1961.
– *The Witch-Herbalist of the Remote Town*. London: Faber, 1981.
Verdier, Raymond. "Le système vindicatoire." In *La vengeance: Études d'ethnologie, d'histoire et de philosophie*, vol. 1, edited by Raymond Verdier, 11–42. Paris: Cujas, 1980.
Warner, Michael. *The Letters of the Republic: Publication and the Public Sphere in Eighteenth-Century America*. Cambridge, MA: Harvard University Press, 1990.
Weber, Eugen. *Peasants into Frenchmen: The Modernization of Rural France, 1870–1914*. Stanford, CA: Stanford University Press, 1976.
Weber, Max. *The Protestant Ethic and the Spirit of Capitalism* [1905]. New York: Penguin, 2002.
Wehrs, Donald R. *Pre-Colonial Africa in Colonial African Narratives: From* Ethiopia Unbound *to* Things Fall Apart, *1911 to 1958*. Aldershot: Ashgate, 2008.
Wilder, Gary. *Freedom Time: Negritude, Decolonization, and the Future of the World*. Durham, NC: Duke University Press, 2015.
Winterbottom, Thomas. *An Account of the Native Africans in the Neighbourhood of Sierra Leone* [1803]. 2 vols. London: Cass, 1969.
Wise, Christopher. "Excavating the New Republic: Post-Colonial Subjectivity in Achebe's *Things Fall Apart*." *Callaloo* 22, no. 4 (1999): 1054–70.
Wren, Robert M. *Achebe's World: The Historical and Cultural Context of the Novels of Chinua Achebe*. Washington: Three Continents Press, 1980.
Young, Crawford. "Permanent Transition and Changing Conjuncture: Dilemmas of Democracy in Nigeria in Comparative Perspective." In *Dilemmas of Democracy in Nigeria*, edited by Paul A. Beckett and Crawford Young, 65–82. Rochester, NY: University of Rochester Press, 1997.
– *The Postcolonial State in Africa: Fifty Years of Independence, 1960–2010*. Madison, WI: University of Wisconsin Press, 2012.
Žižek, Slavoj. *Enjoy Your Symptom!: Jacques Lacan in Hollywood and Out*. New York: Routledge, 2001.

Index